THE BRITISH POLITICAL TRADITION
EDITED BY ALAN BULLOCK AND F. W. DEAKIN

BOOK THREE

BRITAIN AND EUROPE
1793–1940

BRITAIN AND EUROPE

PITT TO CHURCHILL
1793–1940

EDITED BY

JAMES JOLL
FELLOW OF ST. ANTONY'S COLLEGE, OXFORD

ADAM & CHARLES BLACK
LONDON

FIRST PUBLISHED 1950
REPRINTED, WITH MINOR CHANGES, 1961

© 1961 A. AND C. BLACK LIMITED
4, 5 AND 6 SOHO SQUARE LONDON W.1

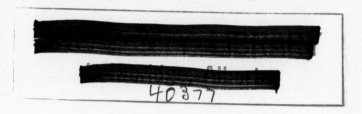

PRINTED IN GREAT BRITAIN
BY UNWIN BROTHERS LIMITED WOKING AND LONDON

GENERAL PREFACE

ONE of the unique contributions the English people
have made to civilisation has been the discussion of
political issues which has been going on in Britain con-
tinuously since the sixteenth century. It is a discussion
which has ranged over the whole field of political
thought and experience. It began with the relation of
the State to the individual in religious matters; for the
last half century it has been increasingly preoccupied
with the relation of the State to the individual in
economic matters. The strength of tradition, the right
of rebellion; the demand for equality, the rights of
property; the place of justice and morality in foreign
policy, the relations between Britain and her overseas
territories; the claims of minorities, the value of civil
and religious freedom; the rule of law, the Rule of the
Saints; the rights of the individual, the claims of the
State—all these have been the subject of passionate
and incessant argument among Englishmen since the
time of the Reformation.

This debate has never been of an academic character.
There are, it is true, masterpieces of political philosophy
in the English language: Hobbes' *Leviathan* is an
obvious example. But the true character of this debate
has been empirical: the discussion of particular and
practical issues, in the course of which a clash of principle and attitude is brought out, but in which the element
of abstract thought is always kept in relation to an

immediate and actual situation. The riches of British political thought are to be found less in the philosophers' discussions of terms like 'The State', 'freedom' and 'obligation'—important though these are—than in the writings and speeches on contemporary political issues of men like Lilburne, Locke, Bolingbroke, Burke, Tom Paine, Fox, the Mills, Cobden, Disraeli, Gladstone, and the Fabians. No other literature in the world is so rich in political pamphlets as English, and the pages of *Hansard* are a mine not only for the historian of political events but also for the historian of political ideas. It is in the discussions provoked by the major crises in British history—the Civil War, the Revolt of the American Colonies, the Reform Bills of the nineteenth century—that our political ideas have been hammered out.

One unfortunate result of this is that much of the material which anyone interested in English political ideas needs to read is inaccessible. Pamphlets and speeches are often only to be found in contemporary publications hidden away on the more obscure shelves of the big libraries. Even when the reader has secured a volume of seventeenth-century pamphlets or of Gladstone's speeches, he may well be deterred by the large amount of now irrelevant detail or polemic through which he has to make his way before striking the characteristic ideas and assumptions of the writer or speaker. It is to meet the need of the reader who is interested in English political ideas but has neither the time, the patience, nor perhaps the opportunity, to read through a library of books to find the material he is looking for that this present series of books is designed. Its aim is to present from sources of the most varied kind, books, pamphlets, speeches, letters, newspapers, a selection of original material illustrating the different facets of Englishmen's discussion of politics. Each volume will include an introductory essay by the editor together with sufficient explanation of the circumstances to make each extract intelligible. In some cases it has seemed best to make a particular crisis the focus of the discussion: this has been done with Mr. Beloff's volume, 'The Debate on the American Revolution', and with Dr. Cobban's 'The Debate on the French Revolution'. In other cases the development of a particular view has been traced over a long period of years: this is the case for instance with the volumes on the Conservative, the Liberal, and the Radical Traditions. In a third case, that of the volume on 'Britain and Europe', our idea has been to single out a recurrent problem in English politics and trace its discussion from Pitt's day to our own.

To begin with, we have concentrated our attention on the period between the Revolt of the American Colonies and the Great War of 1914. When that has been covered we hope to treat the earlier period in the same way, notably the political discussions of the seventeenth century.

We do not believe that any one of these facets can be singled out and labelled as in some particular way more characteristic than others of the British Political Tradition: the rebels have as great a part in our political tradition as those who have argued the case for the claims of prescription and established authority. The wealth of that tradition is that it includes Lilburne, Tom Paine, Richard Cobden and the Early English Socialists as well as Locke, Burke and Disraeli.

We have tried to hold the balance even. In no sense do we wish to act as propagandists or advocates. While each editor has been given complete freedom to present his material as he wishes, we have been concerned as general editors to see that equal representation is given to different views in the series as whole. Only in this way, we believe, is it possible to display the British Political Tradition in its unequalled richness, as built up out of a variety of political opinions and out of the clash between them, as the great and continuous debate of the nation to which, in its very nature, there can be no end.

ALAN BULLOCK

F. W. DEAKIN

Oxford

ACKNOWLEDGEMENT

The help is gratefully acknowledged of all those who have allowed copyright material to be used in this book, in particular

The Marquess of Salisbury

The Marquess of Lansdowne

The Earl Lloyd George of Dwyfor

Viscount Cecil of Chelwood

Lord Henderson

Lady Keynes

Lady Clema Crowe

Mrs. Carnegie

Mrs. Neville Chamberlain

Mrs. Terence Maxwell

The Right Hon. Sir Winston Churchill

Her Majesty's Stationery Office

Roval Institute of International Affairs

Cassell & Company Limited

The Daily Telegraph

Victor Gollancz Limited

The Guardian

McClelland & Stewart Limited

Odhams Press Limited

The Times Publishing Company Limited

TABLE OF CONTENTS

xi

Part III. *CANNING AND THE PRINCIPLES OF THE BRITISH POLICY*, 1822–30

Part IV. *THE PALMERSTONIAN PERIOD*, 1830–65

xiii

INTRODUCTION

I

A CENTURY and a half is a short time over which to trace a tradition; and much in the beliefs of those who shaped British policy towards Europe in the period between 1790 and 1940 derives from an earlier period, just as many ideas have been carried over into the new era that started after the Second World War. The insular position and the maritime economy provide the inevitable framework of British policy at all periods, while recollection of past crises survived is evoked as a source of strength in new dangers. Echoes of the struggles with Philip of Spain and Louis XIV are consciously aroused to give encouragement against Napoleon or Hitler. Nor is it only the memory of foreign wars that helps to shape subsequent policy; the internal development of Britain provides a standard for judging the conduct of other countries and Lord John Russell, for instance, sees the Italian struggle for unity in terms of the Revolution of 1688.

However, there is some justification for treating the period between the French Revolution and the Second World War as one in which the position of Britain was unique, and the question of her relations with Europe of peculiar importance. Until at least 1870 England's industrial development was far ahead of that of any other European country; her exports of manufactured goods were bought in increasing quantities all over the

B   I

world; her capital financed the growing industries of the continental countries and developed new markets and sources of supply in hitherto unexploited regions. Even after the economic crisis of the seventies and the growing challenge of German and American industrial expansion, Britain's relative decline was slow. The boast " England is the workshop of the world," and the taunt " The English are a nation of shopkeepers " are each reflections of this unique position, and it is only in the last few years that we have come to realize its uniqueness, instead of accepting it as part of the natural order established by Providence.

While the Industrial Révolution marks the beginning of a period of British economic predominance, the French Revolution inaugurates a period of British political predominance—or rather, political pre-eminence. While France develops a tradition of change by revolution—an oscillation between revolt and reaction— England is developing and enlarging a tradition of peaceful change that makes her the model and the envy of democrats all over Europe. Even the war with France in 1793, a cause denounced by Fox and his followers as aligning Britain with the tyrants, turns into a liberal cause when national feeling in the occupied countries unites much of Europe against Napoleon. At least from the time of the war in Spain in 1808, there is always a section of opinion abroad that regards England, not only as the natural ally of constitutional governments, but also as the friend of oppressed nationalities—and there are always sentiments among some English people that justify that opinion. It is this clash, often disregarded or even treated as a harmony, between the predominance of England's economic position as the leading industrial power of Europe and the pre-eminence of her political position as the leading liberal power of Europe that makes her policy confusing to Europeans and produces the divergent traditions in foreign policy that this volume aims to illustrate.

But if the Industrial Revolution and the war with France mark the beginning of a period in the history of British relations with Europe, 1940 equally marks an end. Although once again England can claim in the Second World War to have saved herself by her exertions and Europe by her example, the end of that war left her in a position that had in fact been imperceptibly weakening since 1919. The economic predominance that was once England's has passed to America, and with it much of her political pre-eminence; it is American capital that has restored the economic life of Europe; it is the American way of life that is the new political pattern for much of the world. But it is not only the English position that America has taken over; she has also inherited much of the English political tradition.

II

Looking over the story of British policy towards Europe in the last 150 years, one is tempted to wonder whether the tradition to which reference is constantly made is not a myth, and whether it may not be best described in the words Lord Salisbury once used in a mood of exasperation (although it applies perfectly to much of his own practice): " English policy is to float lazily downstream, occasionally putting out a diplomatic boat-hook to avoid collisions."[1] However,

[1] Lady Gwendolen Cecil, *Life of the Marquis of Salisbury*, Vol. II, p. 130.

behind the specific acts of British policy, it is possible to trace a tradition of beliefs about that policy, beliefs about the ends which it is to serve and the grounds for its adoption. It is with these traditional beliefs about British policy towards Europe and not with that policy itself that this volume is mainly concerned. The selection of extracts aims at showing the similarity of these beliefs at different moments in the history of the period, and the way in which the beliefs are expressed in similar language, so that gradually a series of axioms is built up, a collection of *clichés* about foreign policy that can be used on suitable occasions in the future. Some of them are beliefs based on genuine British economic and strategic interests; some of them are based on political principles; others are those platitudes that are the resource of every politician.

Behind these beliefs about Britain's relations with Europe lie certain psychological attitudes towards Europe and its problems which must be mentioned before discussing the beliefs themselves. The first is, of course, a natural insularity of temperament formed by geographical, religious and political separation from the main developments on the Continent. This leads to a popular distrust of foreigners that is reflected by certain ministers—by Lord Derby for instance who said " One can trust none of these governments,"[1] or by Stanley Baldwin of whom Churchill has written " He knew little of Europe, and disliked what he knew."[2] It is this temperamental reaction that gives emotional force to the recurrent appeal of isolationism, but it is at its strongest when, as in the crisis of 1875–8, the English feel confident enough to face intervention in Continental affairs—but an intervention in which they

[1] Lord Newton: *Life of Lord Lyons*, p. 349.
[2] *The Gathering Storm*, p. 173.

4

will not be bothered with Continental allies, from whom they have taken care to dissociate themselves in advance.

However, insularity and lack of understanding for European problems and modes of thought not only find expression in an isolationist policy; they also lie behind the over-eager interventionist policy that is sometimes advocated. Since the British are the only nation (in Europe—for the virtues of their British origins are reluctantly conceded to the Americans) that have successfully solved their political problems, surely, the argument runs, their political system can be applied universally in the solution of the difficulties of every other nation. It was this sense of superiority that led Lord William Bentinck to try and teach the Sicilians how to govern themselves in 1813, by imposing a constitution on the British model, and the disillusion that inevitably followed was characteristic of many such interventions elsewhere. " The British power," he wrote, " had been interposed to ameliorate the condition of the people and to bring forward the resources of the state; but it was never intended to permit the introduction of a wild democracy or to allow the Crown to be endangered and the island to be reduced to still greater weakness by a misguided parliament."[1] It is this same spirit that leads to the interest in the establishment of democracy in Spain in the nineteen-thirties and forties, as it had to the interest in the establishment of a constitutional monarchy in the eighteen-thirties and forties, often without any understanding of the peculiar features of Spanish economic and political life. Even the preservation of the Ottoman Empire could be turned into a liberal cause by this means, for the Sultan was always

[1] See C. K. Webster, *The Foreign Policy of Castlereagh*, Vol. I, p. 253 *sqq.*

ready with promises of constitutional reform; and even after Gladstone's campaign of the seventies and Salisbury's acceptance in 1896 that, in the Crimean War, England "had put her money on the wrong horse," there was still a last revival of this belief after the Young Turk revolution in 1908. Liberal support for the Ottoman Empire is surely one of the most curious examples of optimistic insularity.

Yet it would be misleading to think of this insularity —whether it results in isolationism or the insistence on the universal application of British institutions—as the only psychological factor in British relations with Europe. There is also a deep romanticism that leads the English again and again enthusiastically to adopt a foreign cause: sometimes this is done directly—by Byron in Greece in 1823-4, by the volunteers who joined Garibaldi in 1860 or the Spanish Republicans in 1936, or by those who volunteered to serve causes not their own in the Balkans in the Second World War. More often the cause is adopted vicariously: money is collected, speeches are made in Parliament or outside, the leaders of the current movement—a Kossuth, a Garibaldi, a Paderewski—are given a warm popular welcome when they visit England. Sometimes such movements are powerful enough to affect policy— Gladstone's agitation of the seventies for example, or the movement for Southern Slav unity and Czech independence at the end of the First World War. It is, however, more usual for the devoted adherents to be able to do little more than keep their cause before the public; and there is always the danger which Peel pointed out[1], of arousing false hopes of English assistance. Such causes are adopted uncritically, and it was

[1] See No. 20.

6

regarded as heretical to point out that, for instance, the Hungarian constitution was not so much a liberal system of government as a means of maintaining the domination of the Magyar landowners over their Slav and Roumanian peasants. The voice of the dispassionate student of the subject is unheeded, and it is in vain, for instance, for Richard Cobden to write of " Poland, upon which has been lavished more false sentiment, deluded sympathy, and amiable ignorance, than on any other subject of the present age " and add that " the declaimers and writers upon the subject invariably appeal to us in behalf of the oppressed and enslaved *Polish Nation*; carefully obscuring amidst the cloud of epithets about 'ancient freedom,' 'national independence,' ' glorious republic,' and such like, the fact that . . . the term *nation* implied only the nobles— that, down to the partition of their territory, about nineteen out of every twenty of the inhabitants were slaves, possessing no rights, civil or political. . . ."[1]

In the selection of extracts printed there is not enough space to include examples of all the movements in Europe that arouse generous enthusiasm in Britain: Greece at all times in the period, Poland and Spain at most, Hungary at least until the early years of the twentieth century, when the work of Professor Seton-Watson and others spread knowledge of the rival Slav cause, these are the commonest objects of this kind of political belief, but one could add to them. This is an aspect of British belief about Europe that cannot be ignored, for it provides one of the rival traditions to isolationism and to the assertion that Britain is right and all other countries wrong in dealing with political

[1] *Russia* (1836). *The Political Writings of Richard Cobden* (London 1878), pp. 92-3.

problems. It is also one of the reasons why England is regarded on the Continent during this period as the natural friend of small nations, a belief that the policy of some English statesmen, notably Gladstone and Lloyd George, did much to justify.

III

These emotional reactions to European affairs, on the part of public and politicians alike, are only the background to their beliefs about specific policies in particular situations. In the shaping of these beliefs there are other, more rational, factors which must now be considered. These are, first, the traditional beliefs about what are essential British interests and, second, beliefs about the nature of the political relationship that it is desired to establish between Britain and the European powers whether treated singly or regarded as a " Concert of Europe." It is natural that the clearest expression of these attitudes will be found on the occasions when England becomes most critically involved in Europe, that is to say on the occasions when England actually embarks on a European war. The crises of 1793, 1854, 1914 and 1939 all produce definite statements of the interests which, it is alleged, are involved to such an extent as to warrant England going to war. Similarly, the declarations of war aims during the war and the discussion of the settlement at the end of the war give an opportunity for the expression of general views about the kind of political organization it is desirable to see in Europe (though this aspect naturally is less evident in the Crimean War—a partial and not a general European war). The most fundamental beliefs about British interests are those

8

arising out of Britain's position as a maritime and
commercial power: the areas in which we are most
interested are those that command the sea routes to the
Empire or the trade routes to the Continent—the Low
Countries and the Scheldt, Portugal and the Straits of
Gibraltar, Turkey and the Mediterranean route to
India. Fear for the fate of the Low Countries finally
precipitates war in 1793 and 1914. Portugal and Spain
are the constant object of British political interest and
diplomatic or even naval interference, while it is interest in Turkey that drives us to war in 1854 and to the
brink of war in 1877–8.

Nevertheless, the declaration of vital strategic and
economic interests has not normally been thought in
itself sufficient to persuade the British public of the necessity of war. Some further threat has to be added, some
nobler pretext adduced. The threat—and it is a real
one for a nation dependent on exports for prosperity and
imports for existence—is that of the establishment of a
single power in control of Europe. It is a threat emphasized in 1793 and 1914, brought forward to give
respectability to an unnecessary war in 1854, and
quoted in 1938 and 1939 by Mr. Chamberlain as the
one reason that would justify war. At the same time,
this threat is represented as being a threat, not only to
England, but also to the whole system of international
law in Europe. It is defiance of treaties, contempt for
" scraps of paper " and gentlemen's agreements that
finally make the arguments of the peace party invalid;
it takes the violation of Belgian neutrality to silence the
opposition of a large section of liberal opinion inside
and outside the Government in 1914; it takes the violation of the Munich agreement to turn a policy of
appeasement into one of resistance in 1939.

9

One of the elements in the tradition of British policy towards Europe is, then, a belief in the desirability of applying the " rule of law " to international affairs. The least that this involves is a belief in the sanctity of treaties, a rejection of the Bismarckian doctrine that if treaties stand in the way then they must be broken. But it is often a feeling stronger than belief in the validity of single treaties; it is something that at different periods leads British policy to base itself on faith in " a system of public law in Europe," the Concert of Europe, the League of Nations or the United Nations Organization. In the Napoleonic and the two German Wars plans for the establishment of such organizations are made in the midst of the struggle. It is a healthy desire, so far as it goes, that so regularly leads a section of English opinion to ask " What are we fighting for ? " and to demand a statement of war aims—though it must be admitted that the people who ask usually allow themselves to be fobbed off with a statement of principles which the final conditions of peace make quite unrealizable. Again, just as the Opposition have to be convinced that the enemy really cannot be persuaded to negotiate fairly any longer over the issues that provoke the outbreak of war, so they will lose no opportunity of suggesting a peace by negotiation during the war—Fox and Whitbread in the Napoleonic Wars are echoed by Lord Lansdowne in 1917. If this movement was less noticeable in the Second World War and was confined to a few cranks and sympathisers with Fascism, it is because that was more clearly a life-and-death struggle in which England was in imminent physical danger: yet even here the controversy about "unconditional surrender " recalls similar controversies in previous wars.

For there is a deep strain of pacifism in the British political tradition. There is no need to suspect Grey of hypocrisy when he exclaimed to Sir Arthur Nicolson on August 3rd 1914, " I hate war, I hate war", any more than to question Mr. Chamberlain's sincerity when he asserted " I myself am a man of peace to the depths of my soul. Armed conflict between nations is a nightmare to me." Even in moments of popular nationalist enthusiasm such as the eve of the Crimean War or the crisis of 1877 there are always responsible voices to be heard opposing a war policy and affirming a traditional English belief in peace.

It would be foolish, however, to think of this mistrust of war as based only on emotional or ethical conviction. To a people living by trade it is the wastefulness of war that is most shocking; and it did not need the catastrophic consequences to the British economy of the two world wars to teach the dangers of war to Fox or Cobden. Indeed, Cobden's faith in the ability of internationally minded business-men to prevent war is shared in our own day by many of the business-men themselves: it has survived in the " interlopers in diplomacy," (to steal a phrase from Professor Namier), Sir Ernest Cassel in 1914 and Mr. Dahlerus' English friends in 1939, who made a last attempt before each war to save the peace on which the prosperity of the business world hangs. Even Palmerston himself, the most vigorous champion of the need for giving English merchants armed assistance in the prosecution of their calling, usually maintained a discretion very different from the mood of his most quoted pronouncements, when the peace of Europe as a whole looked like being in danger.

Anxiety about strategic interests and respect for international law, ethical pacifism and economic necessity are all bewilderingly connected in the British tradition of political behaviour in its crises on the eve of the European wars in which Britain is involved in this period. This confusion of interests and motives leads to the familiar continental reproach of perfidy and hypocrisy. Yet the traditions revealed in time of war become even more complicated in times of peace, and it is these that we must now consider.

IV

For many years there has existed a belief in the "continuity of British Foreign Policy." This perhaps has meant little more than that this policy has been an empirical one based on few *a priori* principles, and rather dealing with each situation on a practical basis as it arises. The continuity of type that has existed through successive generations of permanent officials in the Foreign Office and Diplomatic Service has given support to belief in a continuity of policy. "In the course of a long career of diplomacy he had become imbued with that negative, methodical, conservative spirit, called ' governmental,' which is common to all governments, and, under every government, particularly inspires its Foreign Office. He had imbibed, during that career, an aversion, a dread, a contempt for the methods of procedure, more or less revolutionary and in any event quite incorrect, which are those of an opposition."[1] The words describe an imaginary French diplomat, but they could be applied to many real English ones. The " governmental

[1] Marcel Proust, *Within a Budding Grove*, Vol. I, pp. 7-8. cf. also R. M. MacIver *The Modern State* pp. 208-9.

spirit " is based on an accumulation of precedents and specific actions in particular cases rather than on general principles, and it is this that gives continuity to British policy, in the face of " the methods of procedure which are those of an opposition."

The difficulty in distinguishing specific trends in the British tradition in policy towards Europe lies in the fact that these " governmental " and " opposition" attitudes are not to be found solely in any one political party. " What attracts men one to another is not a common point of view but a consanguinity of spirit."[1] One of the constantly recurring debates in English foreign policy is that between the supporters of " intervention " and of " non-intervention." But this is a debate that can take many forms and in which the sides do not by any means correspond to the political parties. Castlereagh, regarded by many as the arch-Conservative, commits England to a policy of joint action with the Continental powers and is denounced (e.g., by Cobbett and Mackintosh)[2] as an interventionist. Palmerston is alternately urged to more vigorous support of liberal causes abroad (as, for instance, the Hungarian Revolution of 1848)[3] and denounced for a policy of " meddle and muddle."

In the Eastern crisis of the seventies, Disraeli and the Queen are for isolated intervention in the Russo-Turkish war on the Turkish side, while Gladstone's agitation implies, even if it does not explicitly demand, intervention on the Russian side to protect the Christians of Eastern Europe. In Grey's time it is the Radical Liberals who are suspicious of involving Britain with the European powers, and Conservatives who ask for more specific

[1] Ibid.
[2] See Nos. 7 and 8.
[3] See No. 19.

statements of our commitments. After 1918 it is the Left who are calling for vigorous intervention in the Abyssinian dispute or in Spain, but it is the Conservatives who join the dictators in re-drawing the map of Europe at Munich, and then in committing England to a guarantee of central European frontiers.

These generalized and over-simplified examples suggest that the traditional division between " intervention " and " non-intervention " is not a particularly useful one as a clue to what gives British policy its continuity, and that the truth lies in Talleyrand's famous *mot* " Non-intervention is a word signifying much the same as intervention." In this matter, perhaps, the true British tradition lies just in this avoidance of extremes and in the desire to judge each question on its merits. This is not only because, as British statesmen constantly have to explain to foreign diplomats, the English constitutional system precludes the giving of any general guarantee of a future course of action in circumstances that have not yet arisen. It is also because the English Foreign Office has a natural preference in favour of the middle course. Canning said " I was—I still am—an enthusiast for national independence; but I cannot—I hope I never shall be—an enthusiast in favour of revolution," while Palmerston echoed the sentiment: " Though friends of free institutions we are not promoters of revolution." This reluctance to interfere practically in the internal affairs of other countries is paralelled by the reluctance with which a British Government embarks on any policy involving commitments the extent of which cannot be exactly foreseen: it leads Austen Chamberlain to prefer the precision of the Locarno Agreement to the uncertainties of the Geneva Protocol, and

also, one might add, leads the Labour Party to
hesitate about undertaking any of the more vigorous
steps advocated by supporters of a European Union.[1]
It is this caution that is characteristic of the " government spokesmen " whenever they talk of foreign policy
and which even Palmerston himself, the most trucu-
lent of English Foreign Ministers, was prepared to
observe when the diplomatic situation was really
critical. Perhaps there is another reason for this
restraint; British statesmen tend to apply to their

[1] It is worth quoting, as an example of the continuity of Foreign Office
habits of thinking even under a Labour government, an extract from the memorandum drawn up inside the Foreign Office on M. Briand's proposals for a
European Union in 1930.

" It is submitted that the attitude of His Majesty's Government towards
M. Briand's proposals should be one of caution, though cordial caution.
Neither the real meaning of the proposals nor the real nature of M. Briand's
intentions can be elucidated without much further information than has yet
arrived from Paris and other European centres. The proposals in the first
place concern Continental Europe more directly and fully than they do this
country. It therefore appears right and proper and politically advisable that
His Majesty's Government should not commit themselves to any definite
view of the proposals till the countries primarily concerned have spoken their
minds. But at the same time it is urged that His Majesty's Government,
while non-committal as to acceptance of the proposals themselves, should
show themselves entirely sympathetic towards the principle invoked and
stressed by M. Briand of the importance of the friendly co-operation of
European States to promote their common interests. An expression of
sympathy in very general terms would particularly seem called for (1)
because M. Briand is an old and valued friend of this country and one of the
few good ' Europeans ' in France, and anything which could be considered
by other countries as a snub to him on the part of His Majesty's Government
would undermine not only his own position but the whole cause of European
co-operation. (2) If the proposals are impracticable, as in part they appear
to be, there is surely no reason why His Majesty's Government should take
upon themselves the onus of turning down something which Germany and
Italy, who are far more directly concerned, will do themselves. (3) If,
however, the proposals are capable of being used to make a new start on
practical lines in the improved economic (and perhaps subsequently also
political) co-operation, opposition on the part of His Majesty's Government
might at this stage do real harm. On this hypothesis what would seem necessary would be careful study of the course of events coupled with a discriminat-
ing sympathy for all such reorganization of Europe as is not in unjustified
contravention of British rights and interests, of the peculiar and indissoluble
connexion of the British Isles with the world-wide territories of the British
Empire and of the prestige and efficiency of the League of Nations which is
the sheet anchor of British policy. . . .

diplomacy the values of their own private lives. By Grey, nations are expected to respect in their relations to one another the high standards of gentlemanly conduct he observed in his own relations to other people; for Joseph and Neville Chamberlain, diplomacy is something that can be carried on in the style of a business deal.

Obviously there are exceptions: Canning's doctrine " A menace not designed to be executed is an engine that Britain should never condescend to employ " is not always observed—by Palmerston in dealing with Denmark and Prussia in 1864 or by Lloyd George in the Greco-Turkish affair in 1921. Sometimes also an extreme view prevails within the Cabinet itself as in the crisis of 1877–8 when the Queen and Beaconsfield finally force the resignation of Derby, a typical representative of a cautious, conservative and deeply pacific policy. But it is Derby who is more characteristic of governmental beliefs about foreign policy than Disraeli. A firm conviction that, in Austen Chamberlain's words, " the true line of progress is to proceed from the particular to the general " dominates official British policy. This is as true of Canning and Palmerston as of Salisbury. It lies behind Grey's interpretation of the *Entente* with France. It can even be traced in Neville Chamberlain's stubborn and ignorant pursuit

---

" If these principles are accepted, it is suggested that His Majesty's Government, if they reply before or on July 15, should confine themselves to an expression of warm sympathy with the high ideals of European co-operation and to the assurance that they will give these and all future proposals from the French Government the fullest consideration both on their own part and in consultation with His Majesty's Governments in the Dominions. . . ."

From *Documents on British Foreign Policy 1919–39*, edited by E.L.Woodward and Rohan Butler, Second Series, Vol. I, pp. 330–1.

of an understanding with Hitler and Mussolini: for the basis of Chamberlain's policy was a belief that if a direct attempt were made to discuss particular problems with the dictators, it would be possible to reach a settlement impossible through the more general and ideological methods he associated with the League of Nations and Geneva.

If empiricism marks this particular "governmental" approach to foreign policy, romanticism and idealism mark the "opposition" attitude in whatever political party it is to be found. It is an idealism that takes several forms often directly opposed to one another. There is an idealism of the Right expressed in the jingoism of the eighteen-fifties or eighteen-seventies, the exuberant confidence inspired by prosperity at home and naval superiority abroad, and infecting not only some conservatives but also many Radicals. There is the imperialism of the nineties, a movement in this case inspired perhaps by doubt—a doubt about England's position in Europe and her economic supremacy—that could only be stilled by asserting energetically that Britain's greatness lies in her overseas empire. This, too, is a movement that influences Conservatives, Liberals, and even Fabians like Sidney Webb. Throughout the period it is the idealists of the Right who are clamouring for the protection of British interests and British subjects regardless of the circumstances and consequences, believing with Canning that "England is strong enough to brave consequences." At the same time, it is they who believe increasingly that Britain's imperial position is a ground for cutting loose from European affairs and conflicts.

Even stronger than these "idealisms of the Right"

is what may be called " idealism of the Left ". Part
of this—the romantic adoption of foreign causes—has
already been discussed, but there is another aspect of it
to be considered. This is the idealism of an internationalist kind that repeatedly recurs in the period,
in the form of demands for statements of war aims, in
demands for support of international organizations, or,
more generally, in criticism of " realism " in foreign
policy and in the assertion of faith in a set of ethical
beliefs. Pitt included the establishment of a " system
of public law " in Europe as one of the aims of the
peace treaty, and Castlereagh succeeded in carrying
over a war-time alliance into a post-war congress.
The experiment was not directly successful; the objectives of the European powers were too much at variance with those of England, and liberal opinion saw
in the Congress system only a method of enforcing
tyrannical régimes on reluctant peoples. Yet the idea
survived of a Concert of Europe, of conferences of the
Great Powers to regulate the problems of international
relations in a peaceable fashion. Indeed, later it was
to become one of the staple doctrines of Liberal
foreign policy. Gladstone, for instance, in 1870 insists
on the summoning of a conference to deal with the
situation created by Russian denunciation of certain
clauses of the Treaty of Paris, and his main criticism of
Disraeli's policy later is based, not so much on disapproval of intervention as such, but on disapproval of
unilateral interference in a problem only rightly to be
solved by the powers of Europe acting in concert. This
is accompanied in Gladstone's case, as in that of many
of his successors, by the belief in " open covenants
openly arrived at ", as Woodrow Wilson was to phrase
it. Thus, when a general European settlement of the

Eastern Question was eventually achieved at the Congress of Berlin in 1878, Gladstone still criticized the Government for making secret agreements beforehand and simply using the Congress as a means of confirming them.

This belief in " open diplomacy," in the settlement of international disputes by public discussion within the framework of an international organization, is at its strongest in the years after 1918 when the League of Nations is flourishing. The controversies over British policy towards the League are partly based on the argument already mentioned about limited and unlimited commitments in Europe, and partly on a discussion of the merits of the " old " or " new " methods of diplomacy. The belief in open diplomacy, in negotiation by public discussion is, of course, an aspect of the belief mentioned earlier in the inherent superiority of English institutions. It is believed that English government is " government by discussion " and that international assemblies can be made to resemble the British Parliament. The fact that this is a wrong interpretation of the British system—where Acts of Parliament are not the products of discussion between the parties, but measures initiated and carried by the party with a majority in the House, and where any real discussion likely to affect the outcome is carried on in the secrecy of the Cabinet room—does not rob the idea of its emotional force.

The argument about the extent to which England should be involved in Europe is only one aspect of the fundamental cleavage between isolationism and internationalism. But there have, in fact, been very few complete isolationists who thought that Britain could avoid playing any part whatever in European affairs.

It is far more usual to maintain that there are only a few traditional reasons and a few traditional areas for which Britain need become involved in Europe—the Low Countries, the Mediterranean, the Straits, etc. Even here, the argument runs, it is impossible to state in advance just how Britain may become involved. The internationalist, however, believes that Britain is irrevocably part of Europe and that she has a duty to act in conjunction with the other states of Europe in maintaining certain political principles in whatever area these may be at stake. This particular debate can be heard at the time of Castlereagh, and again, with the roles of the parties reversed, between Gladstone and Disraeli. But it is after 1918 that it achieves its most explicit form. Membership of the League of Nations ostensibly committed Britain to the maintenance of an international order extending far beyond Europe, and supporters of the League emphasized that any limited agreements such as the Locarno pacts might weaken the more general undertakings involved in the Covenant. The debate was to have disastrous consequences; when the time for action under the general commitments involved in membership of the League arrived, the occasions were to be outside Europe in Manchuria or Abyssinia. The remoteness of the scene and the complexity of the local circumstances were such that it was difficult for the British public to believe that it was committed to international action, and action by force if necessary; and the confusion caused to the whole of international relations in Europe by these events in turn prevented the efficient operation in 1936 of the very specific and limited undertakings to which Britain and France had subscribed at Locarno—a confusion that led Mr. Attlee to say " The real League position does not . . . say that this country is more interested in the frontiers of Holland and Belgium, because of the historic position, than in the frontiers of Czechoslovakia or the frontiers of Poland."[1] Yet the failure to make effective the policy of limited liability adopted at Locarno was, during the following years, to involve interest in the frontiers of Czechoslovakia and Poland on a scale scarcely envisaged even by the most ardent internationalist, but with the possibility of effective and organized international action greatly diminished.

Lloyd George wrote " War has always been fatal to Liberalism. ' Peace, Retrenchment and Reform ' have no meaning in war,"[2] and here he touches on an important element in the internationalist position, which he also describes thus: " The real political sectary in his heart argued thus: ' War is a hideous thing. You must show your aversion by waging it half-heartedly. Wield the sword with your left hand, and let your right nurse its strength until the blessed day arrives when it will be needed once more for swinging the sword of the Lord and of Gideon in the eternal fight for the principles to which we are attached.' "[3] What is true of the Liberal attitude in war is, of course, even truer in peace, and one of the most notable features of the Liberal opposition throughout the period is its combination of a belief in retrenchment and disarmament with advocacy of intervention on behalf of liberal causes abroad, and in support of joint international action for regulating international disputes. This duality dates from the Palmerstonian period. Liberals of all shades were

[1] See No. 59.
[2] *War Memoirs*, Popular Edition, Vol. I, p. 448.
[3] *Ibid.*, pp. 444–6.

convinced of the virtues of British political ideas and of Free Trade; British industrial supremacy led to a demand for British merchants to be free to trade where they liked and to be guaranteed British armed force for their protection and assistance; equally, foreign Liberals had a right to expect help in the establishment of liberal institutions. This was the simple view accepted by most of Palmerston's Radical supporters and in part by Palmerston himself. But there was, on the other hand, an alternative Liberal view held by the original exponents of Free Trade doctrine, the members of the Manchester School; and many of their beliefs appealed to Radicals of all types.

The most complete statement of these beliefs is to be found in the writings and speeches of Richard Cobden. He believed in Free Trade not merely as an economic doctrine but also as a basis for international political organization. Wars are organized by aristocrats, he believed—aristocrats controlling large armies or aristocrats working in sinister secrecy in embassies and chancelleries. Peace, on the other hand, is the work of the commercial middle classes. If they are allowed to circulate and communicate freely throughout Europe, they will ensure that peace, their own greatest interest, will be preserved. If they are free to win the highest administrative posts they will work to abolish expenditure on armaments, they will undo the influence of warlike aristocrats, and wars will be banished from Europe. The flaw in the argument is that it presupposes an inevitable community of interests between the middle classes of all European states (the later idea of a Socialist International was to suffer from a similar weakness). Even in Cobden's own day the German economist, Friedrich List, was arguing that this was not necessarily so and pointing out how convenient to English ambitions the doctrine of Free Trade was in preventing a challenge to British industrial supremacy. " It is a rule of common prudence on reaching the summit of greatness to push down the ladder by means of which we have reached it in order to take away from others the means of climbing up after us."[1]

A fear of expenditure on armaments links Cobden's followers both with the extreme Whigs of Fox's day and with the Radicals of Lloyd George's day, who saw in expenditure on armaments a threat to expenditure on social improvement. Behind the Radical dilemma of wishing to give active support to European causes while reducing armaments at home, lies the instinctive pacifism that has already been noted. Liberal internationalists are rarely prepared to abandon their pacifism sufficiently to recognize the role of power in international politics: yet it is only a few with the deepest moral convictions—a John Bright or a George Lansbury—who can carry their pacifism through to a logical, and absolute, conclusion

The most usual form in which liberal suspicion of an aristocratic control of foreign policy expresses itself, is in attacks on the doctrine of the Balance of Power. This is one of those constantly recurring phrases throughout the whole period from 1815 to which it is hard to assign any precise meaning. It appears to be a product of the axiom mentioned earlier that no single Continental power must be able to dominate the whole of Europe. This, it is argued, is best prevented by

[1] *National System of Political Economy*, quoted by E. Halévy, *Histoire du Socialisme Européen*, p. 307.

using British power to hold the balance between two equally matched groups of powers in Europe who will thus each be prevented from winning supremacy. Criticism of this policy is combined with the attacks on the " old diplomacy " and cynical secret international bargains that have already been mentioned. It is argued that a policy of maintaining the balance of power divides the natural unity of Europe, and splits the powers into two hostile groups. In Cobden's day, a community of interest between the mercantile classes of all nations was recommended as an alternative; after 1918 it was hoped that universal arbitration and " collective security " within the League of Nations would replace the traditional balance of power. Yet the vagueness of the whole concept is shown by the ease with which a doctrine of maintaining the balance of power can be transformed—as by Austen Chamberlain and Anthony Eden—into a doctrine of England's mission as a mediator between rival powers, while the conception of " collective security " when expressed in the form of the organization of " peace-loving powers " against " potential aggressors " does not seem unlike the old conception of the balance of power.

V

A British political tradition in foreign policy, therefore, is hard to discover, if what is sought is a continuity of specific policy advocated by each political party. What there has been is a recognition of certain economic and strategic interests in certain areas of

Europe, and a diplomatic tradition—a tradition inside the Government of how to handle specific questions as they arise. But around these purely empirical aims of policy there has been a constant discussion between groups divided as much by temperament as political conviction. This debate between " isolationists " and " internationalists," " idealists " and " realists," about " intervention " and " non-intervention," "collective security " or the " balance of power " and so on, has sometimes influenced the actual policy pursued, and always influenced beliefs about the grounds and aims of that policy. Something must therefore be said of the manner in which the debate has been conducted and where we can look for evidence of it.

The most important place in which discussion of policy towards Europe has been carried on is, of course, Parliament; and extracts from Parliamentary debates form a large part of this volume. Throughout the period it is particularly noticeable with regard to foreign policy how adequately every view-point has been represented in Parliament even if only by a limited group of members. It is perhaps because the number of measures affecting foreign policy actually required to be passed as Acts in the House of Commons has remained small, that free debate and criticism have survived in the sphere of foreign policy, when large majorities and ready-made legislative programmes have reduced the importance of Parliament in home affairs. Throughout the period, too, Parliament has formed a channel by which the secret negotiations conducted by the Foreign Office become known to the public since it is before Parliament that Government Blue Books and White Papers are laid, and from Parliament that the first comments come.

In the time of Pitt and Castlereagh there was, indeed, little public discussion of foreign policy outside Parliament since the circulation of pamphlets and periodicals was not large, in spite of Cobbett's efforts at extending the range of critical comment. Canning, however, won considerable popular support for his policies by speeches appealing directly to audiences outside Parliament—although they were audiences limited in number when compared with those which later Gladstone, Joseph Chamberlain or Lloyd George were to address. Palmerston, too, was to rely on public support outside Parliament, and it was he who first realized the potentialities of the newspaper Press as a means of influencing public opinion in matters of foreign policy. It was, however, Gladstone who carried the direct appeal to mass audiences outside Parliament to its height in his agitation in 1876–7 and in his election campaign in Midlothian in 1880, where his speeches to popular audiences are especially remarkable for their discussion of the ethical principles behind his beliefs about foreign policy. In the twentieth century the direct personal appeal was to be widened still more by the development of broadcasting, a technique which Baldwin was the first English minister to study, and of which Winston Churchill was to prove himself a master.

Even more important than the widening of the audience to which direct appeals on matters of foreign policy could be addressed is the steady growth of the means by which opinion was being formed and influenced, and of the media in which foreign policy was being discussed. The pamphlets and review articles in which for example Cobden, Dilke, Gladstone and Salisbury spread their views to an increasing degree in the eighteen-fifties, sixties and seventies were all succeeded, though not wholly replaced, by the growing popular Press. Meanwhile the pace of diplomacy itself quickens, as telegraph, telephone and radio, typewriters and duplicators, railways and aeroplanes increase the methods of communication. As each diplomatic move is made it is caught up, magnified and often distorted by the sounding board that the Press provides for it; and the nature of foreign policy as well as the audience by which it is discussed changes accordingly.

In this volume some examples are given of the various media in which foreign policy is discussed. But it is obviously impossible in a short selection to deal adequately with the effects of modern Press and publicity methods on attitudes towards European affairs. In the later extracts, therefore, examples of the basic views and beliefs have been given as they were expressed by responsible leaders of opinion; the aim has been to show the similarity of these basic views and beliefs to those held at earlier dates, but it must be remembered that it is possible to find reflections and distortions of them many times over in the Press discussions to which they give rise. But in these respects the Press, with a few exceptions,[1] is imitative rather than inventive.

The ultimate execution of British policy, and therefore the embodiment of the political tradition in one

---

[1] With regard to the best known exception it is worth quoting the views of Lord Clarendon writing on 18 June 1848: " I don't care a straw what any other thinks or says. They are all regarded on the Continent as representing persons or cliques, but *The Times* is considered to be the exponent of what English public opinion is or will be, and as it is thought that whatever public opinion determines with us, the Government ultimately does, an extraordinary and universal importance attaches to the views of *The Times*." See *The History of* The Times, Vol. II, p. 73.

of its aspects, rests with the Foreign Office. For that reason a certain number of documents drawn up inside the Foreign Office have been included in this selection where they have influenced subsequent policy, like Castlereagh's great State Paper of May 1820,[1] or when they provide a summing up of a whole epoch of British policy like Salisbury's memorandum on isolation in 1901.[2] They also illustrate not only the way in which a powerful minister—a Canning or a Palmerston—will stamp a type of policy with his personality, but also the growing influence—particularly as improved communications reduce the freedom of action of individual representatives abroad—of the Foreign Office official who remains anonymous to the outside public. Sir Eyre Crowe's Memorandum of January 1st 1907[3] is no less part of a political tradition, which it both appraises and shapes, for being intended for a limited circulation.

VI

In making the selection for this volume no attempt has been made to discover extracts about British policy which are not already well known. A tradition is formed by what is considered traditional; and it would defeat the purpose of this series if the traditional passages were not quoted. There are, naturally, many omissions and it would be possible to compile an alternative selection of completely different passages that would illustrate the generalizations that have been attempted in this introduction as well or better. (It would also doubtless be possible to produce a selec-

[1] No. 9.
[2] No. 40.
[3] No. 42.

tion that would refute them). Moreover any selection limited to British policy towards Europe must be a one-sided one, for it ignores the whole of those wide areas outside Europe in which Britain has vital economic and strategic interests and which in turn influence Britain's European policy. The period with which this selection deals is not only that in which Britain is the strongest power in Europe; it is also a period that sees a consolidation and expansion of British overseas power and the emergence of a new conception of Empire that is to be an increasingly important factor in determining British policy.

Professor Seton-Watson ends his great record *Britain in Europe* in 1914, and Professors Temperley and Penson stop their invaluable *Foundations of British Foreign Policy* in 1901. The debt that this selection owes to their ideas is so obvious as hardly to need recording. In a sense they were wise to accept the end of an epoch in British policy towards Europe before 1914. Although many of the traditional solutions and attitudes survive the First and even the Second World War, and can be traced in British views about the Peace in 1919 and in the attempts to make the League of Nations work or to come to a settlement with Germany, Britain's position has been steadily changing in the twentieth century. Some of the changes are explained in the paper by Sir Austen Chamberlain from which extracts are printed as No. 56. It is not only that Britain's economic position has fundamentally altered; the scale of international affairs has become enlarged. The liberal principles of self-determination and nationalism are quoted as effectively by the peoples of Asia now as they were by the Balkan peoples half a century ago.

More important still, the world is faced with the hitherto unparalleled spectacle of two non-European great powers aligned against one another in a way that makes the old catchwords about the Balance of Power even more meaningless than before. But, as has already been suggested, America has inherited much of the British political tradition in foreign policy. Wilson came to Paris in 1919 full of ideas inherited from Cobden and Gladstone. Isolation versus intervention, realism versus idealism, universal economic interests and a confident belief in the universal applicability of a way of life—all these discussions repeat much in British experience. It is, therefore, not entirely illogical that a selection of the kind contained in this volume should end with Mr. Churchill looking for a time " when the New World with all its power and might, steps forth to the rescue and liberation of the old."

PART I

ENGLAND AND THE WAR WITH FRANCE
1793–1812

THE international repercussions of the French
Revolution gathered strength throughout 1792. Austria declared war on France in April, and Prussia
followed in July.

France was declared a Republic in September and
on November 19th the French Convention passed a
decree promising "*fraternité et secours*" to any people
wishing to regain its freedom; on December 15th it
was decreed that the French commanders were to introduce revolutionary social and economic changes in
the countries they occupied. On November 27th,
Savoy was declared an integral part of the French
Republic.

These decrees, and the situation in the Low Countries, made French relations with England increasingly
strained during the following weeks, although diplomatic relations were still maintained.

Louis XVI was executed on January 21st 1793.
The French declared war on England and Holland on
February 1st. On the same day, the House of Commons voted an address approving the King's proposal
for augmenting the armed forces. [For Pitt's speech
on this occasion, and for other aspects of the discussions on the Revolutionary War see the volume in this
series *The Debate on the French Revolution.*]

The speech which follows was made in the House of Commons on the transmission of the following message from the King:

" His Majesty thinks proper to acquaint the House of Commons, that the assembly now exercising the powers of government in France have, without previous notice, directed acts of hostility to be committed against the persons and property of His Majesty's subjects, in breach of the law of nat.ons and of the most positive stipulations of treaty; and have since, on the most groundless pretences, actually declared war against His Majesty and the United Provinces. Under the circumstances of this wanton and unprovoked aggression, His Majesty has taken the necessary steps to maintain the honour of his crown and to vindicate the rights of his people; and His Majesty relies with confidence on the firm and effectual support of the House of Commons and on the zealous exertions of a brave and loyal people, in prosecuting a just and necessary war, and in endeavouring, under the blessing of Providence, to oppose an effectual barrier to the further progress of a system which strikes at the security and peace of all independent nations, and is pursued in open defiance of every principle of moderation, good faith, humanity, and justice.

" In a cause of such general concern, His Majesty has every reason to hope for the cordial co-operation of those Powers who are united with His Majesty by the ties of alliance, or who feel an interest in preventing the extension of anarchy and confusion, and in contributing to the security and tranquillity of Europe."

1 : WILLIAM PITT. Speech on French Declaration of War

12 February 1793

Mr. PITT rose and observed, that in proposing to the House an address in answer to His Majesty's message he did not conceive that there could be any necessity, in the present instance, at least in view of the subject, for troubling them much at large. Whatever difference of opinion might formerly have existed with respect to subjects on which, however, the great majority both of that House and the nation had coincided in sentiment, whatever doubts might have been entertained as to the interest which this country had in the recent transactions on the Continent, whatever question might be made of the satisfaction to which this country was entitled, or whatever question might be made of the mode of conduct which had been pursued by Government, which lately had not been carried so far as to produce even a division: yet when the situation in which we now stood was considered, when those circumstances which had occurred to produce an alteration in the state of affairs since the last address, were taken into the account, he could not doubt but that there would be one unanimous sentiment and voice expressed on the present occasion. The question now was not what degree of danger and insult we should find it necessary to repel, from a regard to our safety, or from a sense of honour; it was not whether we should adopt in our measures a system of promptitude and vigour, or of tameness and procrastination; whether we should sacrifice every other consideration to the continuance of an uncertain and insecure peace. When war was declared and the event no longer in our option, it remained only to be considered, whether we should prepare to meet it with a firm determination, and support His Majesty's Government with zeal and courage against every attack. War now was not only declared, but carried on at our very doors; a war which aimed at an object no less destructive than the total ruin of the freedom and independence of this country. In this situation of affairs, he would not do so much injustice to the members of that House, whatever differences of opinion might formerly have existed, as to suppose there could be any but one decision, one fixed resolution, in this so urgent necessity, in this imminent and common danger, by the ardour and firmness of their support, to testify their loyalty to their sovereign, their attachment to the constitution, and their sense of those inestimable blessings which they had so long enjoyed under its influence. Confident, however, as he was, that such would be their unanimous decision, that such would be their determined and unalterable resolution, he should not consider it as altogether useless to take a view of the situation of the country at the time of His Majesty's last message, of the circumstances which had preceded and accompanied it, and of the situation in which we now stood, in consequence of what had occurred during that interval. When His Majesty, by his message, had informed them, that in the present situation of affairs he conceived it indispensably necessary to make a further

augmentation of his forces, they had cheerfully con-
curred in that object, and returned in answer, what
then was the feeling of the House, the expression of
their affection and zeal, their readiness to support His
Majesty in those purposes, for which he had stated an
augmentation of force to be necessary. They saw the
justice of the alarm which was then entertained, and
the propriety of affording that support which was
required. He should shortly state the grounds upon
which they had given their concurrence. They considered that whatever temptations might have existed
to this country from ancient enmity and rivalship—
paltry motives indeed!—or whatever opportunity
might have been afforded by the tumultuous and distracted state of France, or whatever sentiments might
be excited by the transactions which had taken place
in that nation, His Majesty had uniformly abstained
from all interference in its internal government, and
had maintained, with respect to it, on every occasion
the strictest and most inviolable neutrality.

Such being his conduct towards France, he had a
right to expect on their part a suitable return; more
especially, as this return had been expressly condi-
tioned for by a compact, into which they entered, and
by which they engaged to respect the rights of His
Majesty and his allies, not to interfere in the government of any neutral country, and not to pursue any
system of aggrandizement, or make any addition to
their dominions, but to confine themselves, at the conclusion of the war, within their own territories. These
conditions they had all grossly violated, and had
adopted a system of ambitious and destructive policy,
fatal to the peace and security of every government,
and which in its consequences had shaken Europe

itself to its foundation. Their decree of November 19, which had been so much talked of, offering fraternity and affiance [*sic*] to all people who wish to recover their liberty, was a decree not levelled against particular nations, but against every country where there was any form of government established; a decree not hostile to individuals, but to the human race; which was calculated everywhere to sow the seeds of rebellions and civil contention, and to spread war from one end of Europe to the other, from one end of the globe to the other. While they were bound to this country by the engagements which he had mentioned, they had showed no intention to exempt it from the consequences of this decree. Nay, a directly contrary opinion might be formed, and it might be supposed that this country was more particularly aimed at by this very decree, if we were to judge from the exultation with which they had received from different societies in England, every address expressive of sedition and disloyalty, and from the eager desire which they had testified to encourage and cherish the growth of such sentiments. Not only had they showed no inclination to fulfil their engagements, but had even put it out of their own power, by taking the first opportunity to make additions to their territory in contradiction to their own express stipulations. By express resolutions for the destruction of the existing government of all invaded countries, by the means of Jacobin societies, by orders given to their generals, by the whole system adopted in this respect by the National Assembly, and by the actual connexion of the whole country of Savoy, they had marked their determination to add to the dominions of France, and to provide means, through the medium of every new conquest, to carry their principles over Europe. Their conduct was such as in every instance had militated against the dearest and most valuable interests of this country. . . .

He had already given it as his opinion, that if there was no other alternative than either to make war or to depart from our principles, rather than recede from our principles a war was preferable to a peace; because a peace, purchased upon such terms, must be uncertain, precarious, and liable to be continually interrupted by the repetition of fresh injuries and insults. War was preferable to such a peace, because it was a shorter and surer way to that end which the House had undoubtedly in view as its ultimate object—a secure and lasting peace. What sort of peace must that be in which there was no security? Peace he regarded as desirable only so far as it was secure. If, said Mr. Pitt, you entertain a sense of the many blessings which you enjoy, if you value the continuance and safety of that commerce which is a source of so much opulence, if you wish to preserve and render permanent that high state of prosperity by which this country has for some years past been so eminently distinguished, you hazard all these advantages more, and are more likely to forfeit them, by submitting to a precarious and disgraceful peace, than by a timely and vigorous interposition of your arms. By tameness and delay you suffer that evil which might now be checked to gain ground, and which, when it becomes indispensable to oppose, may perhaps be found irresistible.

It had on former debates been alleged that by going to war we expose our commerce. Is there, he would ask, any man so blind and irrational, who does not know that the inevitable consequence of every war

37

must be much interruption and injury to commerce ?
But, because our commerce was exposed to suffer, was
that a reason why we should never go to war ? Was
there no combination of circumstances, was there no
situation in the affairs of Europe, such as to render it
expedient to hazard for a time a part of our commercial interests ? Was there no evil greater, and which a
war might be necessary to avoid, than the partial inconvenience to which our commerce was subject,
during the continuance of hostile operations ? But he
begged pardon of the House for the digression into
which he had been led—while he talked as if they were
debating about the expediency of a war, war was
actually declared: we were at this moment engaged in
a war. . . .

[After dealing with the actual charges made by
the French Government], he now came to his
conclusion. We, said Mr. Pitt, have, in every instance,
observed the strictest neutrality with respect to the
French: we have pushed, to its utmost extent, the
system of temperance and moderation; we have held
out the means of accommodation: we have waited till
the last moment for satisfactory explanation. These
means of accommodation have been slighted and
abused, and all along there has appeared no disposition
to give any satisfactory explanation. They have now,
at last, come to an actual aggression, by seizing our
vessels in their very ports, without any provocation
given on our part. Without any preparations having
been adopted but those of necessary precaution, they
have declared, and are now waging, war. Such is the
conduct which they have pursued; such is the situation
in which we stand. It now remains to be seen whether,
under Providence, the efforts of a free, brave, loyal,

and happy people, aided by their allies, will not be successful in checking the progress of a system, the principles of which, if not opposed, threaten the most fatal consequences to the tranquillity of this country, the security of its allies, the good order of every European Government, and the happiness of the whole human race!

The War Speeches of William Pitt the Younger, selected by R. Coupland (Oxford 1915), pp. 53–77.

2: CHARLES JAMES FOX. Speech moving Resolutions against the War with France

House of Commons, 18 February 1793

THE necessity of the war might be defended on two principles: first, that *malus animus*, or general bad disposition of the French towards this country; the crimes they have committed among themselves; the systems they have endeavoured to establish, if systems they might be called; in short, the internal government of their country. On this principle, there were few indeed that would venture to defend it: and this being disavowed as the cause of war by His Majesty's ministers, it was unnecessary for him to dwell upon it. Secondly, that various things have been done by the French, manifestly extending beyond their own country, and affecting the interests of us and our allies; for which unless satisfaction was given, we must enforce satisfaction by arms. This he considered as the only principle on which the necessity of the war could be truly defended, and in this he was sure the great majority of the House and of the country were of the same opinion. . . . In examining the alleged causes of provocation, he had maintained that they were all objects of negotiation, and such as, till satisfaction was explicitly demanded and refused, did not justify resorting to the last extremity. He had perhaps also said, that ministers did not appear to have pursued the course which was naturally to be expected from their professions. He did not mean to charge them with adopting one principle for debate and another for action; but he thought they had suffered themselves to be imposed upon, and misled by those who wished to go to war with France on account of her internal government, and therefore took all occasions of representing the French as utterly and irreconcilably hostile to this country. It was always fair to compare the conduct of men in any particular instance with their conduct on other occasions. If the rights of neutral nations are now loudly held forth; if the danger to be apprehended from the aggrandizement of any power was magnified as the just cause of the present war; and if, on looking to another quarter, we saw the rights of Poland,[1] of a neutral and independent nation, openly trampled upon, its territory invaded, and all this for the manifest aggrandizement of other powers, and no war declared or menaced, not even a remonstrance interposed—for if any had been interposed it was yet a secret—could we be blamed for suspecting that the pretended was not the real object of the present war—that what we were not told, was in fact the object, and what we were told, only the colour and pretext ?

The war, however, be the real cause what it might, would be much less calamitous to this country, if, in the prosecution of it, we could do without allying ourselves with those who had made war on France, for the avowed purpose of interfering in her internal

[1] Poland had adopted a new constitution in May 1791, but a year later the Empress Catherine of Russia occupied Poland " to restore the liberty and laws of the Republic." At this Prussia also intervened, and in August 1792 proposals for a partition of the country were accepted by Russia and Prussia. In spite of protests from Austria, this second partition of Poland was finally signed on 23 January 1793.

government; if we could avoid entering into engagements that might fetter us in our negotiations for peace, since negotiation must be the issue of every war that was not a war of absolute conquest; if we should shun the disgrace of becoming parties with those who, in first attempting to invade France, and some of them in since invading Poland, had violated all the rights of nations. . . .

Our causes of complaint against France were, first, the attempt to open the navigation of the Scheldt: second, the decree of the 19th of November, supposed to be directed against the peace of the nations: third, the extension of their territory by conquest. The first of these was obviously and confessedly an object of negotiation. The second was also to be accomplished by negotiation; because an explanation that they did not mean what we understood by it, and a stipulation that it should not be acted upon in the sense in which we understood it, was all that could be obtained even by war. The third was somewhat more difficult, for it involved in it the evacuation of the countries conquered, and security that they should in no sense be annexed to France; and no such security could, perhaps, at present be devised. But if we were averse to this; if we saw that during the war the French are engaged in with other powers, they had no such security to offer; if we knew that we were asking what could not be given, the whole of our pretended negotiation, such as it had been, was a farce and a delusion; not an honest endeavour to preserve the blessings of peace, but a fraudulent expedient to throw dust in the eyes of the people of this country in order that they might be hurried blindly into war. . . . We told them they must keep within their own territory; but how were they to do this when attacked by two armies, that retired out of their territory only to repair the losses of their first miscarriage and prepare for a fresh irruption ? When to this studied concealment of terms were added the haughty language of all our communications, and the difficulties thrown in the way of all negotiations, we must surely admit, that it was not easy for the French to know with what we would be satisfied, nor to discover on what terms our amity . . . could be cultivated. When to all these he added the language held in that house by ministers . . . and last of all, the paper transmitted by Lord Auckland at the Hague to the States General—a paper which for the contempt and ridicule it expressed of the French, stood unparalleled in diplomatic history—a paper in which the whole of them, without distinction, who had been in the exercise of power since the commencement of the Revolution, were styled " a set of wretches investing themselves with the title of philosophers, and presuming in the dream of their vanity to think themselves capable of establishing a new mode of society, etc."—how could we hope the French, who were thus wantonly insulted, to expect that anything would be considered as satisfactory, or any pledge a sufficient security . . . ? Thus, while, as they pretended, they were courting peace, they were using every manœuvre to provoke war. For those reasons, he should move that ministers had not employed proper means of preserving peace, without sacrificing the honour or the safety of this country. . . .

Having dwelt very copiously on the impolicy of viewing, without emotion, the dismemberment of Poland, by three mighty powers, and considering the balance of power engaged only when France had gained the advantage, Mr. Fox deprecated, of all things, anything so infamous as our being supposed to be a party to this abominable confederacy of kings. . . . He therefore lamented openly that England could be supposed to be in the least involved in that detested league.

He could wish, that if we had quarrels, we should fight them by ourselves: or if we were to have allies, that we should keep our cause of quarrel completely separated from theirs, or without meddling with the internal concerns of the French Republic, nor burden ourselves with any stipulations which should prevent us at any time from making a separate peace, without the concurrency or approbation of those sovereigns.

Mr. Fox concluded with moving the following resolutions:

1. That it is not for the honour or interest of Great Britain to make war upon France on account of the internal circumstances of that country, for the purpose either of suppressing or punishing any opinions and principles, however pernicious is their tendency, which may prevail there, or of establishing among the French people any particular form of government.

2. That the particular complaints which have been stated against the conduct of the French Government are not of a nature to justify war in the first instance, without having attempted to obtain redress by negotiation.

3. That it appears to this House, that in the late negotiation between His Majesty's ministers and the agents of the French Government, the said ministers did not take such measures as were likely to procure redress, without a rupture, for the grievances of which they complained: and particularly that they never

stated distinctly to the French Government any terms and conditions, the accession to which, on the part of France, would induce His Majesty to persevere in a system of neutrality.

4. That it does not appear that the security of Europe, and the rights of independent nations, which have been stated as grounds of war against France, have been attended to by His Majesty's ministers in the case of Poland, in the invasion of which unhappy country, both in the last year, and more recently, the most open contempt of the law of nations, and the most unjustifiable spirit of aggrandizement has been manifested, without having produced, as far as appears to this House, any remonstrance from His Majesty's ministers.

5. That it is the duty of His Majesty's ministers, in the present crisis, to advise His Majesty against entering into engagements which may prevent Great Britain from making a separate peace, whenever the interests of His Majesty and his people may render such a measure advisable, or which may countenance the opinion in Europe, that His Majesty is acting in concert with other powers for the unjustifiable purpose of compelling the people of France to submit to a form of government not approved by that nation.

The Speeches of the Right Honourable Charles James Fox in the House of Commons, Vol. V, (*London 1815*). p. 394, *et sqq.*

3: CHARLES JAMES FOX. Address on the Preliminaries of Peace with the French Republic

25 March 1801

Pitt's administration fell in February 1801, and in March the Addington government entered into negotiations with France that culminated in the Peace of Amiens on October 1st.

Fox and the small group of Whigs who followed him had consistently advocated a negotiated peace.

IF I am asked what my opinion is of the future, my reply is, that, to put us in complete enjoyment of the blessings of peace, small establishments alone are necessary. It is by commercial pursuits and resources that we must attempt to compensate for the aggrandizement of our ancient rival: to cope with him in large establishments, in expensive navies and armies, will be the surest way to unnerve our efforts and diminish our means. Sir, I am not sanguine enough, though I think and hope the peace will be lasting, to calculate on a seventy years' peace. But still I am sanguine to a certain degree in my expectations, that the new state of France will turn the disposition of her people to a less hostile mind towards this country. I do think that Bonaparte's government is less likely to be adverse to Great Britain than the House of Bourbon was. . . .

Sir, for my own part, I cannot help thinking that the arts and sciences, the increasing patronage in France of agriculture and of commerce, will make the minds of the people more pacific. . . . Many persons are afraid that our commerce will suffer from the competition of France. I have no such fears. As far as our trade can be attacked by the rivalship of France, I think that rivalship will do us good.

Ibid., Vol. VI, p.463 *et sqq.*

4: WILLIAM PITT. Official Communication made to the Russian Ambassador at London, explanatory of the views which His Majesty and the Emperor of Russia formed for the deliverance and security of Europe

19 January 1805

In October 1804 the Czar sent Novosiltzov to London with proposals for an alliance. The discussions dealt with the main problems of the war and final peace settlement. The document from which extracts are printed is a draft prepared, almost certainly by Pitt personally, for the Russian Ambassador, Voronzov, and represents Pitt's final views both on the detailed European settlement and on general questions of international relations. Part of this document was laid before Parliament by Castlereagh in May, 1815 to justify his own policy towards the Peace Settlement.

His MAJESTY is . . . happy to perceive that the views and sentiments of the Emperor respecting the means of effecting the deliverance of Europe, and providing for the future tranquillity and safety correspond so entirely with his own. He is therefore desirous of entering into the most explicit and unreserved explanations on every point connected with this great object, and of forming the closest Union of Councils and Concert of Measures with His Imperial Majesty, in order, by their joint influence and exertions, to insure the co-operation and assistance of other Powers of the Continent, on a Scale adequate to the Magnitude and importance of an Undertaking, on the success of which the future Safety of Europe must depend.

For this purpose the first Step must be, to fix as precisely as possible, the distinct objects to which such a Concert is to be directed.

These, according to the explanation given of the Sentiments of the Emperor, in which His Majesty entirely concurs, appear to be three:

1st. To rescue from the Dominion of France those Countries which it has subjugated since the beginning of the Revolution, and to reduce France within its former limits, as they stood before that time.—

2ndly. To make such an arrangement with respect to the territories recovered from France, as may provide for their Security and Happiness, and may at the same time constitute a more effectual barrier in future against Encroachments on the part of France.—

3rdly. To form, at the Restoration of Peace, a general Agreement and Guarantee for the mutual protection and Security of different Powers, and for re-establishing a general System of Public Law in Europe.— . . .

Supposing the Efforts of the Allies to have been completely successful, His Majesty would nevertheless consider this Salutary Work as still imperfect, if the Restoration of Peace were not accompanied by the most effectual measures for giving Solidity and Permanence to the System which shall thus have been established. Much will undoubtedly be effected for the future Repose of Europe by these Territorial Arrangements, which will furnish a more effectual Barrier than has before existed against the Ambition of France. But in order to render this Security as complete as possible, it

E

seems necessary, at the period of a general Pacification, to form a Treaty to which all the principal Powers of Europe should be Parties, by which their respective Rights and Possessions, as they then have been established, shall be fixed and recognized, and they should all bind themselves mutually to protect and support each other, against any attempt to infringe them—It should re-establish a general and comprehensive system of Public Law in Europe, and provide, as far as possible, for repressing future attempts to disturb the general Tranquillity, and above all, for restraining any projects of Aggrandizement and Ambition similar to those which have produced all the Calamities inflicted on Europe since the disastrous era of the French Revolution. This Treaty should be put under the Special Guarantee of Great Britain and Russia, and the Two Powers should, by a separate engagement, bind themselves to each other jointly to take an active Part in preventing its being infringed. . . .

Printed in *British Diplomacy 1813–15. Select Documents Dealing with the Reconstruction of Europe*, edited by C. K. Webster (London 1921), Appendix I.

5: DEBATE IN HOUSE OF COMMONS

5 January 1807

The war broke out again in May 1803 in spite of the protests of Fox and his followers, Whitbread among them. Pitt died in January 1806 and the " Ministry of All the Talents," composed of a coalition of the followers of Grenville, Addington and Fox, was formed with Fox as Secretary of State for Foreign Affairs until his death in September. By January 1807 the negotiations which Fox had begun had broken down: Napoleon started the blockade of Britain by his Decree of 21 November 1806 and the British retaliated by the Order in Council of 7 January 1807. In March the Grenville administration fell, and Canning became Foreign Secretary in a Government formed by the Duke of Portland.

MR. WHITBREAD. . . . This rooted and rancorous hatred and animosity, which may be created even in one country towards another, can never afford just ground for war; but it may prevent, and I fear during the last few melancholy years, has materially contributed to prevent, the restoration of the blessings of peace.—

Such, sir, are my sentiments. . . . Sir, we are told in the declaration of His Majesty, that he looks forward with confidence to the issue of the contest, the continuance of which he laments. The address holds out no hope of peace, it includes not even the word. . . . Good God! if peace be not the issue of the contest, whither are we hurrying ? Contemplate, Sir, if you can with composure, these two mighty empires exerting their utmost efforts each for the destruction of the other; and think upon it, if you can without horror, that before the contest be ended one or the other must be destroyed. Sir, this is a catastrophe I cannot bring my mind to anticipate, without sensations of the deepest anguish; it is a prospect which I do not think, with the blessing of God, it is necessary, even in the present disastrous state of the world to look forward to. If it be, how trifling are the woes and calamities already suffered by mankind to those which are yet to come!! Sir, I for one will cherish the hope that even in the days of some now living, peace may be achieved, and I will not contribute to increase the difficulties in its way by saying or allowing that it is impossible. . . .

Cobbett's Parliamentary Debates, Vol. VIII, pp. 371–2.

MR. CANNING. . . . There is an end, I hope for ever, of the doctrine of being " agreeable to the enemy." France is no respector of persons. The single rule for the conduct of a British statesman is, attachment to the interests of Great Britain.

. . . The course that is now before us cannot be mistaken; and I trust we shall manfully pursue it. The country has the means, and I am confident it has the spirit and determination, to persevere with firmness in a struggle, from which there is no escape or retreat; and which cannot be concluded, with safety to Great Britain, but in proportion as with that object is united the liberty and tranquillity of Europe. . . .

Ibid., pp. 407–8.

PART II

ENGLAND AND THE PEACE SETTLEMENT
1812-22

LORD CASTLEREAGH became Foreign Secretary in Spencer Perceval's Government in February 1812 and retained his office under Lord Liverpool, who became Prime Minister in May. Castlereagh remained Foreign Secretary until his death in 1822.

The following document is a despatch to the British Ambassador to Russia and enclosed a draft treaty of alliance. This began the negotiations leading to the Treaty of Chaumont in March 1814—a treaty in which Austria, Britain, Prussia and Russia allied themselves for the continuance of the war, undertook to protect the peace settlement once it was established and reserved " to themselves to concert together on the conclusion of a peace with France, as to the means best adopted to guarantee to Europe, and to themselves reciprocally, the continuance of the peace."

6: ROBERT STEWART VISCOUNT CASTLEREAGH. Dispatch to Cathcart the British Ambassador to Russia

18 September 1813

HOSTILITIES having recommenced, and the Emperor of Austria having joined his arms to those of the Allies, it has become necessary to reconsider the foreign relations of the country with a view of seeing whether a greater degree of union and consistency may not be given to the Confederacy against France than results from the several treaties which have been successively signed between the respective powers.

The present Confederacy may be considered as the union of nearly the whole of Europe against the unbounded and faithless ambition of an individual. It comprehends not only all the great monarchies, but a great proportion of the secondary Powers. It is not more distinguished from former Confederacies against France by the number and magnitude of the Powers engaged than by the national character which the war has assumed throughout the respective states. On former occasions it was a contest of sovereigns, in some instances perhaps, against the prevailing sentiment of their subjects; it is now a struggle dictated by the feeling of the people of all ranks as well as by the necessity of the case. The sovereigns of the [sic] Europe have at last confederated together for their common safety, having in vain sought that safety in detached and insulated compromises with the enemy. They have

54

successively found that no extent of submission could procure for them either safety or repose, and that they no sooner ceased to be objects of hostility themselves, than they were compelled to become instruments in the hands of France for effectuating the conquest of other unoffending states. The present Confederacy may therefore be pronounced to originate in higher motives and to rest upon more solid principles than any of those that have preceded it, and the several powers to be bound together for the first time by one paramount consideration of an imminent and common danger.

It is this common danger which ought always to be kept in view as the true basis of the alliance, and which ought to preclude deflection from the common cause. It must be represented to the allies that having determined to deliver themselves from the vengeance of the conqueror by their collective strength, if collectively they fail, they are separately lost. He never will again trust any one of them with the means of self-defence—their only rational policy then is inseparable union—to make the contest that of their respective nations, to persevere under every disaster, and to be satisfied that to end the contest safely the enemy must be compelled to treat with them collectively, whilst the best chance of an early peace is at once to satisfy the enemy that a separate negotiation is unattainable.

As opposed to France, a peace concluded in concert, though less advantageous in its terms, would be preferable to the largest concessions received from the enemy as the price of disunion. The great object of the Allies, whether in war or negotiation, should be to keep together, and to drive back and confine the armies of France within the circle of their own immediate resources. This alone can bring down the military force of the enemy to its natural level, and save Europe from being progressively conquered with its own spoils.

To suppose that the Powers on the side of Germany might be induced to sign a peace, leaving Great Britain and the nations of the Peninsula to carry on the war, or that the enemy being expelled from the Peninsula, Spain[1] might sheathe the sword, leaving the Continental Powers to sustain the undivided shock of French power, is to impute to them all a total blindness to their common safety. Were either of these interests to attempt to shelter themselves in a separate peace, it must leave France master of the fate of the other, and ultimately of both. It is by the war in Spain that Russia has been preserved, and that Germany may be delivered; it is by the war in Germany that Spain may look to escape the subjugation that otherwise ultimately await [sic] her. So long as both manfully contend in the field against France, neither can be absolutely overwhelmed, and both, upon every sound principle of military calculation, must by perseverance triumph. To determine to stand or fall together is their only safety, and to effect this the confederates must be brought to agree to certain fixed principles of common interest. . . .

[1] Spanish resistance to Napoleon from 1808 onwards had aroused great enthusiasm in England. The *Morning Chronicle* wrote on 15 June 1808, " At this moment the English people would cordially acquiesce in any effort, however expensive, that could assist the cause of that brave and noble nation, so truly intimately do they sympathize in the struggle of a people for liberty." (See Michael Roberts, *The Whig Party 1807–12* [London 1939].)

Printed in C. K. Webster, *British Diplomacy 1813–15*. pp. 19-21.

7: WILLIAM COBBETT. Letter to Lord Castlereagh

1 April 1815

William Cobbett kept up a steady attack on Castlereagh's policy in his *Political Register* from which the next extract is taken. The popular attacks on Castlereagh whether on isolationist grounds or on the grounds that he was the associate and accomplice of tyrants continued till his death. Byron's lines after Castlereagh's suicide are a typical example.

> " So Castlereagh has cut his throat!—The worst
> Of this is—that his own was not the first."

and

> " So HE has cut his throat at last!—He! Who ?
> The man who cut his country's long ago."

. . . In truth, my Lord, military achievements have turned our heads. We have gone on from step to step, till, at last, we really seem to conceit ourselves as a greater *military* than we are a *naval* power. Too many amongst us seem to look with sorrow on any thing which shall deprive us of all excuse for keeping up a great army. Never was there seen so much reluctance to lay aside the gorget and the sash. We have fallen into a set of notions quite foreign from all our former notions. We are military-mad; and, in the midst of the rage, we seem almost to forget the *fleet*, the defence which reason and nature so clearly point out to us.

Continental connexions, against which our forefathers were so anxious to guard, are now really sought after with eagerness; and, indeed, full of the notion that it was *we*, who reduced France, we seem to think it necessary, that we should become almost an integral part of the continent. To defend the Kingdom of Hanover, we must first defend the King of the Netherlands. To defend the Kingdom of the Netherlands we must *constantly* keep a large army on foot in the Netherlands, and more troops ready to go to the assistance of that army. That country must always be filled with troops in our pay, in peace or in war. And, is this nation in a state to support such an expense ?

Shall I be told that no peace can be *safe* which leaves Belgium in the hands of France ? *You*, my Lord, will hardly tell me so, who defended the *peace of Amiens*, which left *Belgium in the hands of France*; nor will the Earl of Liverpool, who *made* that treaty and who contended in its defence, that the *extension of territory* which France *had gained had not rendered her more formidable to us*. Come back, then, to your former doctrines; disclaim all connection with a continent where we never can have power without the ruin of this island; and then we shall have peace; the fund-holders will be paid; our fleet will be our bulwark; we shall prosper and shall be as great as France.

But, if war is again to be our lot; if we are to send out armies to fight amidst the fortresses of Belgium; if millions are to be expended in the Kingdoms of the Netherlands and of Hanover; if a war without prospect of termination and almost without a clearly defined object is to be our lot, where are the means to come ? What new sufferings are in store for us ? It is well known to your Lordship, that the rejoicing of the people at the late peace arose chiefly from the hope of their being relieved from the long-endured burdens of the war. It is well known to you, that, even in *peace*, our resources without the war taxes are insufficient. It is well known to you, that *loans* are in contemplation to supply, in part, in *peace*, the absence of the Prosperity Tax. What, then, is to be the fate of the fund-holder if a new war is to be our lot?

Cobbett's Political Register, Vol. XXVII, pp. 402–4.

8: SIR JAMES MACKINTOSH. Extracts from a Speech

House of Commons, 27 April 1815

Sir James Mackintosh (1765–1832) was one of the leading Whig speakers on foreign policy, and the author of *Vindiciae Gallicae* published in 1791.

(The occasion of the speech which follows was a motion condemning the policy of the Government as revealed by papers concerning Genoa laid before the House of Commons on April 7th. Genoa had been incorporated in Piedmont by a decision of the Congress of Vienna in December 1814 which was embodied in an enactment attached to the Final Act of the Congress signed on 9 June 1815.)

FROM the earliest periods of Parliament, and during the most glorious reigns in our history, the counsel of the House of Commons has been proffered and accepted on the highest questions of peace and war. The interposition was necessarily even more frequent and more rough in these early times—when the boundaries of authority were undefined, when the principal occupation of Parliament was a struggle to assert and fortify their rights, and when it was sometimes as important to establish the legality of a power by exercise, as to exercise it well—than in these more fortunate periods of defined and acknowledged right, when a mild and indirect intimation of the opinion of Parliament ought to preclude the necessity of resorting

60

to those awful powers, with which they are wisely armed. But though these interpositions of Parliament were more frequent in ancient times, partly from the necessity of asserting contested right, and more rare in recent periods, partly from the more submissive character of the House, they are wanting at no time in number enough to establish the grand principle of the constitution, that Parliament is the first counsel of the King, in war as well as in peace. This great principle has been acted on by Parliament in the best times; it has been reverenced by the Crown in the worst. A short time before the Revolution, it marked a struggle for the establishment of liberty—a short time after the Revolution, it proved the secure enjoyment of liberty. The House of Commons did not suffer Charles II to betray his honour and his country, without constitutional warning to choose a better course. Their first aid to William III, was counsel relating to war; when, under the influence of other counsels, the House rather thwarted than aided their great deliverer; even the party hostile to liberty, carried the Rights of Parliament, as a political counsel, to their utmost constitutional limit when they censured the Treaty of Partition, as " passed under the Great Seal of England during the meeting of Parliament, and without the advice of the same." During the War of the Succession, both Houses repeatedly counselled the Crown on the conduct of war, on negotiation with allies, and even on the terms of peace with the enemy. But what needs any further enumeration ? Did not the vote of this House put an end to the American war ?

Even if the right of Parliament to advise had not been as clearly established, as the prerogative of the Crown to make war or peace—if it had not been thus

61

constantly exercised—if the wisest and best men had not been the first to call it forth into action; we might reasonably have been more forward than our ancestors to exercise this great right, because we contemplate a system of political negotiation, such as our ancestors never saw. All former Congresses were assemblies of the ministers of belligerent Powers to terminate their differences by treaty, to define the rights and decide on the pretensions which had given rise to war, or to make compensation for the injuries which had been suffered in the course of it. The firm and secure system of Europe admitted no rapid, and few great changes of power and possession. A few fortresses in Flanders, a province on the frontiers of France and Germany, were generally the utmost cessions earned by the most victorious wars, and secured by the most important treaties. Those who have lately compared the transactions at Vienna with the Treaty of Westphalia—which formed the code of the Empire and an era in diplomatic history, which terminated civil wars of religion not only in Germany, but throughout Christendom, and which removed all that danger with which, for more than a century, the power of the House of Austria had threatened the liberties of Europe—will perhaps feel some surprise when they are reminded, that except secularizing a few ecclesiastical principalities, that renowned and memorable Treaty ceded only Alsace to France, and part of Pomerania to Sweden; that its stipulations did not change the political condition of half a million of men; that it affected no pretension to dispose of any territory but that of those who were parties to it, and that not an acre of land was ceded without the express and formal consent of its legal sovereign. Far other were the

pretensions, and indeed the performances of the ministers assembled at Vienna. They met under the modest
pretence of carrying into effect the thirty-second article
of the Treaty of Paris. But under colour of this humble
language, they arrogated the power of doing that in
comparison with which the whole Treaty of Paris was
a trivial Convention, and which made the Treaty of
Westphalia appear no more than an adjustment of
parish boundaries. They claimed the absolute disposal of every territory which had been occupied by
France and her vassals, from Flanders to Livonia, and
from the Baltic to the Po. Over these—the finest
countries in the world, inhabited by twelve millions
of mankind whom they had taken up arms under pretence of delivering from a conqueror—they arrogated
to themselves the harshest rights of conquest. It is
true, that in this vast territory they restored, or rather
granted, a great part to its ancient sovereigns. But
these sovereigns were always reminded by some new
title, or by the disposal of some similarly circumstanced
neighbouring territory, that they owed their restoration to the generosity, or at most to the prudence of the
Congress, and that they were not entitled to require it
from its justice. They came in by a new tenure. They
were the feudatories of the new corporation of kings
erected at Vienna, exercising joint power in effect over
all Europe, consisting in form of eight or ten princes,
but in substance of three great military powers—the
spoilers of Poland, the original invaders of the European constitution, sanctioned by the support of
England; checked, however feebly, by France alone. On
these three Powers, whose reverence for national independence and title to public confidence were so firmly
established by the partition of Poland, the dictatorship

of Europe had fallen. Every restored state was restored as their vassal. They agree that Germany shall have a federal constitution; that Switzerland shall govern herself; that unhappy Italy shall, as they say, be composed of sovereign states. But it is all by grant from these lords paramount. Their will is the sole title to dominion; the universal tenure of sovereignty. A single acre granted on such a principle is, in truth, the signal of a monstrous revolution in the system of Europe. Were the House of Commons to remain silent when it was applied in practice to a large part of the Continent, and proclaimed in right over the whole? Were they to remain silent, when they heard the king of Sardinia, at the moment when he received possession of Genoa from a British garrison, and when the British commander stated himself to have made the transfer in consequence of the decision at Vienna, proclaim to the Genoese that he took possession of their territory " in concurrence with the wishes of the principal Powers of Europe ? "

It is to this particular act of the Congress, that I now desire to call the attention of the House, not only on account of its own atrocity, but because it seems to represent in miniature the whole system of that body, to be a perfect specimen of their new public law, and to exemplify every principle of that code of partition which they are about to establish on the ruins of that ancient system of national independence and balanced power which gradually raised the nations of Europe to the first rank of the human race. I contend, that all the parties to this violent transfer, and more especially the British Government, have been guilty of perfidy, have been guilty of injustice; and I shall also contend, that the danger of these violations of faith and justice is much increased when they are considered as examples of those principles by which the Congress of Vienna arrogate to themselves the right of regulating a considerable portion of Europe. . . .

It is not the principle of the balance of power, but one precisely opposite. The system of preserving some equilibrium of power; of preventing any state from becoming too great for her neighbours, is a system purely defensive, and directed towards the object of universal preservation. It is a system which provides for the security of all states, by balancing the force and opposing the interests of great states. The independence of nations is the end, the balance of power is only the means. To destroy independent nations in order to strengthen the balance of power, is the most extravagant sacrifice of the end to the means. This inversion of all the principles of the ancient and beautiful system of Europe, is the fundamental maxim of what the noble lord, enriching our language with foreign phrases as well as doctrines, calls " a repartition of power." In the new system small states are annihilated by a combination of great. In the old, small states were secured by the mutual jealousy of the great. The noble lord very consistently treats the re-establishment of small states as an absurdity. This single feature betrays the school where he has studied. Undoubtedly, small communities are an absurdity, or rather their permanent existence is an impossibility on his new system. They could have no existence in the continual conquests of Asia. They were soon destroyed amidst the turbulence of the Grecian confederacy. They must be sacrificed on the system of rapine established at Vienna. Nations powerful enough to defend themselves, may subsist securely in most tolerable

F   65

conditions of society. But states too small to be safe by their own strength can exist only where they are guarded by the equilibrium of force, and the vigilance which watches over its preservation. When the noble lord represents small states as incapable of existence, he, in truth, avows that he is returned in triumph from the destruction of that system of the balance of power of which indeed great empires were the guardians, but of which the perfect action was indicated by the security of feebler commonwealths. Under this system, no great violation of national independence had occurred, from the first civilization of the European states, till the partition of Poland. The safety of the feeblest states, under the authority of justice, was so great, that there seemed little exaggeration in calling such a society the commonwealth of Europe. Principles, which stood in the stead of laws and magistrates, provided for the security of defenceless communities, as the safety of the humblest individual is maintained in a well-ordered commonwealth. Europe can no longer be called a commonwealth, when her members have no safety but in strength.

In truth, the Balancing System is itself only a secondary guard of national independence. The paramount principle, the moving power, without which all such machinery would be perfectly inert, is national spirit. The love of country, the attachment to laws and government, and even to soil and scenery; the feelings of national glory in arms and arts, the remembrances of common triumph and common suffering, with the mitigated, but not obliterated recollection of common enmities, and the jealousy of dangerous neighbours, instruments employed (also by nature) to draw more closely the bands of affection to our country and to each other—this is the only principle by which sovereigns could in the hour of danger rouse the minds of their subjects. Without this principle, the policy of the Balancing System would be impotent. To sacrifice a people actuated by this spirit, to over-rule that repugnance to the yoke of a neighbour, which is one of the chief bulwarks of nations, is in the effect, and much more in the example, to erect a pretended balance of power by the destruction of that spirit, and of those sentiments, which alone render that balance effectual for its only useful purpose—the protection of independence.

The Congress of Vienna seems, indeed, to have adopted every part of the French system, except that they have transferred the dictatorship of Europe from an individual to a triumvirate. One of the grand and patent errors of the French Revolution, was the fatal opinion, that it was possible for human skill to make a government. . . .

But though we no longer dream of making govern-ments, the Confederacy of Kings seems to feel no doubt of their own power to make nations. Yet the only reason why it is impossible to make a government is, because it is impossible to make a nation. A nation cannot be made, because its whole spirit and principles arise from the character of the nation. There would be no difficulty in framing a government, if the habits of a people could be changed by a lawgiver; if he could obliterate their recollections, transfer their attach-ment and reverence, extinguish their animosities, and correct those sentiments which, being at variance with his own, he calls prejudices. Now this is precisely the power which our statesmen at Vienna have arrogated to themselves. They not only form nations, but they compose them of elements apparently the most irreconcilable. They make one nation of Norway and Sweden; they tried to make another of Prussia and Saxony. They have in the present case forced together Piedmont and Genoa to form a nation, which is to guard the avenues of Italy, and to be one of the main securities of Europe against universal monarchy. . . .

The object of the new system is to crush the weak by the combination of the strong—to subject Europe in the first place to an oligarchy of sovereigns, and ultimately to swallow it up in the gulf of universal monarchy; where civilization has always perished, with freedom of thought, with controlled power, with national character and spirit, with patriotism and emulation, in a word, with all its characteristic attributes and all its guardian principles.

I am content, Sir, that these observations should be thought wholly unreasonable by those new masters of civil wisdom, who tell us that the whole policy of Europe consists in strengthening the right flank of Prussia and the left flank of Austria; who see in that wise and venerable system, long the boast and safeguard of Europe, only the millions of souls to be given to one power, or the thousands of square miles to be given to another; who consider the frontier of a river is a better protection for a country, than the love of its inhabitants; and who provide for the safety of their states by wounding the pride and mortifying the patriotic affection of a people, in order to fortify a line of military posts. . . .

9: LORD CASTLEREAGH. State Paper

5 May 1820

The unity established by the Treaty of Vienna between England and the Continental powers began to weaken as Russia and Austria, at the Congress at Aix-la-Chapelle in 1818, and subsequently, revealed that they wished to use the Alliance to suppress revolution wherever it might break out in Europe.

In January 1820 a military revolt broke out in Spain and purported to restore constitutional government: Russia, France, and Prussia urged various forms of active intervention. Accordingly, Castereagh was asked by the Cabinet to state his views on British policy towards intervention in Spain. The result was the State Paper from which extracts are printed below. Parts of this document were published by Canning in 1823.

. . . The British Cabinet, upon this, as upon all other occasions, is ever ready to deliberate with those of the Allies, and will unreservedly explain itself upon this great question of common interest; but as to the form in which it may be prudent to conduct these deliberations, They conceive, They cannot too early recommend that course of deliberation which will excite the least attention or alarm, or which can least provoke jealousy in the mind of the Spanish Nation or Gov(ernmen)t. In this view it appears to them advisable studiously to avoid any reunion of the Sovereigns —to abstain, at least in the present Stage of the Question, from charging any ostensible Conference with Commission to deliberate on the affairs of Spain—

69

They conceive it preferable that their Intercourse should be limited to those confidential Communications between the Cabinets which are in themselves best adapted to approximate ideas, and to lead, as far as may be, to the adoption of common principles, rather than to hazard a discussion in a Ministerial Conference, which, from the necessarily limited Powers of the Individuals composing it, must ever be better fitted to execute a purpose already decided upon than to frame a course of policy under delicate and difficult circumstances.

There seems the less motive for precipitating any Step of this nature in the case immediately under consideration, as, from all information which reaches us, there exists in Spain no order of things upon which to deliberate, nor as yet any governing Authority with which Foreign Powers can communicate. . . . This important Subject having been referred to, and considered by, the Duke of Wellington—His Grace does not hesitate, upon his intimate experience of Spanish Affairs, to pronounce that the Spanish Nation is of all the European People that which will the least brook any interference from abroad—He states the many instances in which, during the last War, this distinguishing Trait of national Character rendered them obstinately blind to the most pressing Considerations of publick Safety—He states the imminent danger in which the Suspicion of foreign interference, and more especially of interference on the part of France, is likely to involve the King; and he further describes the difficulties which would oppose themselves to any military operations in Spain, undertaken for the purpose of reducing by force the Nation to submit themselves to an order of things to be either suggested or prescribed to them from without. . . .

At all events therefore until Some Central Authority shall establish itself in Spain, all Notion of operating upon Her Councils seems utterly impracticable, and calculated to lead to no other possible result than that of compromising either the King or the Allies, or probably both. . . .

It remains to be considered what Course can best be pursued by the Allies in the present Critical State of Europe, in order to preserve in the utmost Cordiality and vigour, the Bonds which at this Day so happily unite the great European Powers together, and to draw from their Alliance, should the moment of Danger and Contest arrive, the fullest extent of Benefit, of which it is in its nature susceptible——

In this Alliance as in all other human Arrangements, nothing is more likely to impair or even to destroy its real utility, than any attempt to push its duties and obligations beyond the Sphere which its original Conception and understood Principles will warrant— It was an union for the Reconquest and liberation of a great proportion of the Continent of Europe from the Military Dominion of France, and having subdued the Conqueror it took the State of Possession as established by the Peace under the Protection of the Alliance—It never was intended as an Union for the Government of the World, or for the Superintendence of the Internal Affairs of other States—

It provided specifically against an infraction on the part of France of the State of Possession then created: It provided against the Return of the Usurper or of any of his family to the Throne: It further designated the Revolutionary Power which had convulsed France and desolated Europe, as an object of it's constant solicitude; but it was the Revolutionary Power more particularly in it's Military Character actual and existent within France against which it intended to take Precautions, rather than against the Democratic Principles, then as now, but too generally spread throughout Europe.

In thus attempting to limit the objects of the Alliance within their legitimate Boundary, it is not meant to discourage the utmost Frankness of Communication between the Allied Cabinets—their Confidential Intercourse upon all Matters, however foreign to the purposes of the Alliance, is in itself a valuable Expedient for keeping the current of Sentiment in Europe as equable and as uniform as may be: It is not meant that in particular and definite Cases, the Alliance may not (and especially when invited to do so by the Parties interested) advantageously interpose, with due Caution, in matters lying beyond the Boundaries of their immediate and particular Connection; but what is intended to be combated as forming any part of their Duty as Allies, is the Notion, but too perceptibly prevalent, that whenever any great Political Event shall occur, as in Spain, pregnant perhaps with future Danger, it is to be regarded almost as a matter of course, that it belongs to the Allies to charge themselves collectively with the Responsibility of exercising some Jurisdiction concerning such possible eventual Danger——

One objection to this view of our duties, if there was no other is, that unless We are prepared to support our interference with force, our judgement or advice is likely to be but rarely listened to, and would by frequent Repetition soon fall into complete contempt. So long as We keep to the great and simple conservative principles of the Alliance, when the dangers therein contemplated shall be visibly realized, there is little risk of difference or of disunion amongst the Allies: All will have a common interest: But it is far otherwise when We attempt with the Alliance to embrace subordinate, remote, and speculative cases of danger—all the Powers may indeed have an interest in averting the assumed danger, but all have not by any means a common faculty of combating it, in it's more speculative Shapes, nor can they all without embarrassing seriously the internal administration of their own affairs be prepared to show themselves in jealous observation of transactions, which, before they have assumed a practical character, publick opinion would not go along with them in counteracting.—

This principle is perfectly clear and intelligible in the case of Spain: We may all agree that nothing can be more lamentable, or of more dangerous example, than the late revolt of the Spanish Army: We may all agree, that nothing can be more unlike a monarchical Government, or less suited to the wants and true interests of the Spanish Nation, than the Constitution of the year 1812; We may also agree, with shades of difference, that the consequence of this state of things in Spain may eventually bring danger home to all our own doors, but it does not follow, that We have therefore equal means of acting upon this opinion: For instance the Emperor of Russia, from the nature of his authority, can have nothing to weigh, but the physical or moral difficulties external from his own Gov(ernmen)t or Dominions, which are in the way of giving effect to his Designs—If H(is) I(imperial) M(ajesty)'s Mind is settled upon these points, His Action is free and His Means are in His own hands. The King of Great Britain, from the nature of our Constitution, has

on the contrary all His means to acquire through
Parliament, and He must well know that if embarked
in a War, which the Voice of the Country does not
support, the Efforts of the strongest Administration
which ever served the Crown would soon be unequal
to the prosecution of the Contest. In Russia there is
but little publick Sentiment with regard to Spain,
which can embarrass the decision of the Sovereign;
In Great Britain there is a great deal, and the Current
of that Sentiment runs strongly against the late policy
of the King of Spain. Besides, the People of this
Country would probably not recognize (unless Portugal was attacked) that our Safety could be so far
menaced by any State of things in Spain, as to warrant
their Government in sending an Army to that Country
to meddle in it's internal affairs; We cannot conceal
from ourselves how generally the Acts of the King of
Spain since His restoration have rendered His Government unpopular and how impossible it would be to
reconcile the People of England to the use of force, if
such a Proceeding could for a moment be thought of
by the British Cabinet for the purpose of replacing
power in His hands, however He might engage to
qualify it. . . . The interposition of our good offices,
whether singly, or in concert with the Allied Gov(ernmen)ts, if uncalled for by any authority within Spain,
even by the King Himself, is by no means free from a
like inconvenience as far as regards the Position of the
British Government at Home; This species of intervention especially when coming from Five Great
Powers, has more or less the air of dictation and menace, and the possibility of it's being intended to be
ultimately pushed to a forcible intervention is always
assumed or imputed by an adverse party. The grounds

of the intervention thus become unpopular, the intention of the parties is misunderstood, the publick Mind is agitated and perverted, and the General Political Situation of the Government is thereby essentially embarrassed.—

This Statement is only meant to prove, that We ought to see somewhat clearly to what purpose of real Utility our Effort tends, before We embark in proceedings which can never be indifferent in their bearings upon the Government taking part in them.—In this country at all times, but especially at the present conjuncture, when the whole Energy of the State is required to unite reasonable men in defence of our existing Institutions, and to put down the spirit of Treason and Disaffection which in certain of the Manufacturing Districts in particular, pervades the lower orders, it is of the greatest moment, that the publick Sentiment should not be distracted or divided, by any unnecessary Interference of the Government in events passing abroad, over which they can have none or at best but very imperfect means of controul.—Nothing could be more injurious to the Continental Powers than to have their affairs made matter of daily discussion in our Parliament, which nevertheless must be the consequence of Their precipitately mixing themselves in the affairs of other States, if We should consent to proceed *pari passu* with them in such interferences. It is not merely the temporary inconvenience produced to the British Government by being so committed, that is to be apprehended, but it is the exposing ourselves to have the publick mind soured by the effects of a meddling policy, when it can tend to nothing really effectual, and pledged perhaps beforehand against any exertion whatever in Continental Affairs—the fatal effects of such a false step might be irreparable when the moment at which we might be indispensably called upon by Duty and Interest to take a part should ar(r)ive.

These Considerations will suggest a doubt whether that extreme degree of unanimity and supposed concurrence upon all political subjects w(oul)d be either a practicable or a desirable principle of action among the Allied States, upon matters not essentially connected with the main purposes of the Alliance. If this Identity is to be sought for, it can only be attained by a proportionate degree of inaction in all the States. . . . The fact is that we do not, and cannot feel alike upon all Subjects—Our Position, our Institutions, the Habits of thinking, and the prejudices of our People, render us essentially different—We cannot in all matters reason or feel alike; We should lose the Confidence of our respective Nations if we did, and the very affectation of such an Impossibility would soon render the Alliance an Object of Odium, and Distrust, whereas, if we keep it within its *common Sense* limits, the Representative Governments, and those which are more purely Monarchical, may well find each a common Interest, and a common facility in discharging their Duties under the Alliance, without creating an Impression that they have made a surrender of the first principles upon which their respective Gov(ernment)s are founded.—Each Government will then retain it's due faculty of independent Action, always recollecting, that they have all a common Refuge in the Alliance, as well as a common Duty to perform, whenever such a Danger shall really exist, as that against which the Alliance was specially intended to provide.

76

There is at present very naturally a widespread apprehension of the fatal Consequences to the publick Tranquillity of Europe, that may be expected to flow from the dangerous Principles of the present Day, at work more or less in every European State, Consequences which no human foresight can presume to estimate.

In all Dangers the first Calculation of Prudence is to consider what we should avoid and on what we should endeavour to rely—In considering Continental Europe as divided into two great Masses, the Western, consisting of France and Spain, the Eastern of all the other Continental States still subsisting with some limited exceptions, under the form of their ancient Institutions, the great Question is, what System of General and defensive Policy (subject of course to special Exceptions arising out of the Circumstance of the particular Case) ought the latter States to adopt with a view of securing themselves against those dangers, which may directly or indirectly assail them from the former.—By the late Proceedings at Vienna, which for all purposes of internal tranquillity, bind up the various States of Germany into a single and undivided Power, a great degree of additional simplicity as well as Strength has been given to this Portion of Europe. By this Expedient there is established on that side of Europe, instead of a multitude of dispersed States, two great Bodies, Russia and Germany, of the latter of which, Austria and Prussia may for purposes of internal tranquillity be regarded as component parts. In addition to these there remain but few Pieces on the board to complicate the Game of Publick Safety.

In considering then how the game can best be

played, the first thing that occurs for our Consideration is, what good can these States hope to effect in
France or Spain by their mere Councils? Perhaps it
would not be far from the truth to say, None whatever—When the chances of Error, jealousy and
National Sentiment are considered, the Probability of
Mischief would be more truly assigned to the System
of constant European Interference upon these Vol-
canick Masses. . . .

What could The Allied Powers look to effect by
their Arms, if the supposition of an armed interference
in the internal affairs of another State could be admitted? Perhaps as little; Because in supposing them
finally triumphant, We have the problem still to solve,
how the country in which such Interference had been
successful was to provide for its Self-Government after
the Allied Armies shall have been withdrawn, without
soon becoming an equal Source of danger to the
tranquillity of neighbouring States; but when we consider how much danger may arise to the internal Safety
of the rest of Europe, by the absence of those Armies
which must be withdrawn to overrun the Country in
which the supposed Interference was to take place—
what may be the danger of these Armies being con-
taminated—what may be the incumbrances to be
added by such renewed exertions to the already overwhelming Weight of the debts of the different States—
what the local irritation which must be occasioned by
pouring forth such immense armies pressing severely
as they must do upon the resources of Countries
already agitated and inflamed—no rational Statesman
surely w(oul)d found his prospects of Security on such
a calculation: He would rather be of opinion, that the
only necessity which could in wisdom justify such an

attempt is, that which, temperately considered, appears to leave to Europe no other option, than that of either going to meet that danger which they cannot avoid, or having it poured in the full tide of military invasion upon their own States.—The actual Existence of such a danger may indeed be inferred from many circumstances short of the visible preparations for attacks, but it is submitted that on this basis the conclusion should always be examined.

If this position is correctly laid down, it may be asserted that the case supposed, not only does not at present exist, but the chances of such a danger have latterly rather declined in proportion as both France and Spain are almost exclusively and deeply occupied by their own internal embarrassments: The military Power in France at this day is circumscribed within those limits which are not more than competent to the necessary duties of the Interior; That of Spain is upon even a more reduced Scale, whilst the military Establishments of all the other European States, and especially that of Russia, were never perhaps at any period of their history upon a footing of more formidable efficiency both in point of Discipline and Numbers; Surely then, if these States can preserve harmony among themselves, and exercise a proper degree of vigilance with respect to their interior Police, there is nothing in this state of things which should prevent them from abiding with patience and with firmness the result of the great Political process to which circumstances have given existence in the States to the Westward of their Frontiers. They may surely permit these Nations to work out by their own means, and by the lights of their own Councils, that result which no doubt materially bears upon the general Interests of the World, but which is more especially to decide their own particular destinies, without being led to interfere with them, at least so long as their own immediate Security is not directly menaced, or until some Crisis shall arise which may call for some specifick, intelligible and practicable interposition on their part.

The principle of one State interfering by force in the internal affairs of another, in order to enforce obedience to the governing authority, is always a question of the greatest possible moral as well as political delicacy, and it is not meant here to examine it.—It is only important on the present occasion to observe that to generalize such a principle and to think of reducing it to a System, or to impose it as an obligation, is a Scheme utterly impracticable and objectionable. There is not only the physical impossibility of giving execution to such a System, but there is the moral impracticability arising from the inaptitude of particular States to recognize, or to act upon it.—No Country having a Representative System of Gov(ern-men)t could act upon it—and the sooner such doctrine shall be distinctly abjured as forming in any Degree the Basis of our Alliance, the better—in order that States, in calculating the means of their own Security may not suffer Disappointment by expecting from the Allied Powers, a support which, under the special Circumstances of their National Institutions they cannot give—Great Britain has perhaps equal Power with any other State to oppose Herself to a practical and intelligible Danger, capable of being brought home to the National Feeling—When the Territorial Balance of Europe is disturbed, she can interfere with effect, but She is the last Gov(ernmen)t in Europe, which can be expected, or can venture to commit Herself on any question of an abstract Character.

These observations are made to point attention to what is practicable and what is not.—If the dreaded Moral Contagion should unfortunately extend itself into Germany, and if the flame of Military Revolt should for example, burst forth in any of the German States, it is in vain for that State, however anxiously and sincerely we deprecate such a Calamity, to turn it's Eyes to this Country for the means of effectually suppressing such a Danger—If External Means are indispensable for it's Suppression, such State must not reckon for assistance upon Gov(ernmen)ts constituted as that of Great Britain, but it is not therefore without it's Resource.

The internal Peace of each German State is by Law placed under the protection of the Army of the Empire—The Duty which is imposed by the Laws of the Confederacy upon all German States, to suppress, by the Military Power of the whole mass, Insurrection within the Territories of Each and Every of the Co-Estates, is an immense Resource in itself, and ought to give to the Centre of Europe a sense of Security which previous to the Reunion of Vienna was wholly wanting —The Importance of preventing the Low Countries, the Military Barrier of Europe, from being lost, by being melted down into the general Mass of French Power, whether by Insurrection or by Conquest, might enable the British Gov(ernmen)t to act more promptly upon this, than perhaps upon any other Case of an internal Character that can be stated—But upon all such Cases we must admit ourselves to be, and our Allies should in fairness understand that we are, a Power that must take our Principle of action, and our

Scale of acting, nor merely from the Expediency of the Case, but from those Maxims, which a System of Government strongly popular, and national in it's character has irresistibly imposed upon us. We shall be found in our place when actual danger menaces the System of Europe, but this Country cannot, and will not, act upon abstract and speculative Principles of Precaution—The Alliance which exists had no such purpose in view in its original formation—It was never so explained to Parliament; if it had, most assuredly the sanction of Parliament would never have been given to it, and it would now be a breach of Faith were the Ministers of the Crown to acquiesce in a Construction being put upon it, or were they to suffer themselves to be betrayed into a Course of Measures, inconsistent with those Principles which they avowed at the time, and which they have since uniformly maintained both at Home and Abroad. . . .

Printed in Temperley and Penson, *Foundations of British Foreign Policy* (London 1938), pp. 49–50, 50–1, 53–63.

10: LORD CASTLEREAGH states his attitude on the Greek question, in a Dispatch to Bagot, the British Ambassador to Russia

28 October, 1821

. . . It will naturally occur to every virtuous and generous mind, and to none more probably than to the Emperor of Russia's own—indeed it is the first impression which presents itself to every reflecting observer when he contemplates the internal state of European Turkey—viz.: Is it fit that such a state of things should continue to exist ? Ought the Turkish yoke to be for ever rivetted upon the necks of their suffering and Christian subjects; and shall the descendants of those, in admiration of whom we have been educated, be doomed in this fine country to drag out, for all time to come, the miserable existence to which circumstances have reduced them ?

It is impossible not to feel the appeal; and if a statesman were permitted to regulate his conduct by the counsels of his heart instead of the dictates of his understanding, I really see no limits to the impulse, which might be given to his conduct, upon a case so stated. But we must always recollect that his is the grave task of providing for the peace and security of those interests immediately committed to his care; that he must not endanger the fate of the present generation in a speculative endeavour to improve the lot of

83

that which is to come. I cannot, therefore, reconcile it to my sense of duty to embark in a scheme for new modelling the position of the Greek population in those countries at the hazard of all the destructive confusion and disunion which such an attempt may lead to, not only within Turkey but in Europe. I am by no means persuaded, were the Turks even miraculously to be withdrawn (what it would cost of blood and suffering forcibly to expel them I now dismiss from my calculations) that the Greek population, as it now subsists or is likely to subsist for a course of years, could frame from their own materials a system of government less defective either in its external or internal character, and especially as the question regards Russia, than that which at present unfortunately exists. I cannot, therefore, be tempted, nor even called upon in moral duty under loose notions of humanity and amendment, to forget the obligations of existing Treaties, to endanger the frame of long established relations, and to aid the insurrectionary efforts now in progress in Greece, upon the chance that it may, through war, mould itself into some scheme of government, but at the certainty that it must in the meantime, open a field for every ardent adventurer and political fanatic in Europe to hazard not only his own fortune, but what is our province more anxiously to watch over, the fortune and destiny of that system to the conservation of which our latest solemn transactions with our Allies have bound us. . . .

Printed in C. K. Webster, *The Foreign Policy of Castlereagh 1815–22* (London 1934), pp. 376–7.

PART III

CANNING AND THE PRINCIPLES OF BRITISH POLICY, 1822–30

CANNING became Foreign Secretary on Castle-reagh's death in 1822. He had to deal with situations in which the policies of England and the Continental allies became increasingly divergent. The next four extracts show him stating the principles of his policy in connection with the situation created in Spain by the French intervention in 1823 to overturn the so-called constitutional régime established by the revolution of 1820.

11 : GEORGE CANNING. From Speech on Spain

House of Commons, 14 April 1823

THE object which the King's Government had constantly in view, was the preservation of the peace of the world; the principle by which they had been guided in the pursuit of that object had been clearly stated. . . . He meant, respect for the faith of treaties —respect for the independence of nations—respect for that established line and policy known by the name of " The balance of power" in Europe—and last, but not least, respect for the honour and interests of this country. . . . England was bound to protect Portugal, if Portugal were attacked, but not if Portugal attacked others. He thought it right to make this statement because England had never yet made any arrangement, or entered any treaty, which she had not, when called upon, fulfilled to the very letter, however arduous was the struggle into which she entered, and however great the sacrifice which she was compelled to make to procure its fulfilment; and it was on account of that rare scrupulousness in fulfilling her engagements that it became the more necessary for her to understand precisely what the nature of those engagements was. . . .

R. Therry, *The Speeches of the Right Honourable George Canning*, Vol. V (London 1828). pp. 4-5, 26.

12: GEORGE CANNING. From Speech against
     repeal of Foreign Enlistment Bill

House of Commons, 16 April 1823

GENTLEMEN say, that we must be drawn into a
war, sooner or later. Why, then, I answer, let it be
later. I say, if we are to be drawn into a war, let us be
drawn into it on grounds clearly British. I do not say
—God forbid I should—that it is no part of the duty
of Great Britain to protect what is termed the balance
of power, and to aid the weak against the insults of the
strong. I say, on the contrary, that to do so is her
bounden duty; but I affirm also, that we must take
care to do our duty to ourselves. The first condition of
engaging in any war—the *sine qua non* of every such
undertaking—is, that the war must be just; the
second, that being just in itself, we can also with justice
engage in it; and the third, that being just in its nature,
and it being possible for us justly to embark in it, we
can so interfere without sentiment or prejudice to ourselves. I contend that he is a visionary politician who
leaves this last condition out of the question; and I say
further, that though the glorious abandonment of it
may sound well in the generous speech of an irrespon-
sible orator—with the safety of a nation on his lips, and
none of the responsibility upon his shoulders—it is
matter deeply to be considered. . . .

Ibid., Vol. V, p. 47.

87

13: GEORGE CANNING: From Speech at Plymouth

23 October 1823

GENTLEMEN, I hope that my heart beats as high for the general interest of humanity—I hope that I have as friendly a disposition towards other nations of the earth, as anyone who vaunts his philanthropy most highly; but I am compelled to confess, that in the conduct of political affairs, the grand object of my contemplation is the interest of England.

Not, Gentlemen, that the interest of England is an interest which stands isolated and alone. The situation which she holds forbids an exclusive selfishness; her prosperity must contribute to the prosperity of other nations, and her stability to the safety of the world. But, intimately connected as we are with the system of Europe, it does not follow that we are therefore called upon to mix ourselves on every occasion, with a restless and meddling activity, in the concerns of the nations which surround us. It is upon a just balance of conflicting duties, and of rival, but sometimes incompatible, advantages, that a government must judge when to put forth its strength, and when to husband it for occasions yet to come.

Our ultimate object must be the peace of the world. That object may sometimes be best attained by prompt exertions—sometimes by abstinence from interposition in contests that we cannot prevent. It is upon these

88

principles that, as has been most truly observed by my worthy friend, it did not appear to the government of this country to be necessary that Great Britain should mingle in the recent contest between France and Spain.

Your worthy Recorder has accurately classed the persons who would have driven us into that contest. There were undoubtedly among them those who desired to plunge this country into the difficulties of war, partly from the hope that those difficulties would overwhelm the Administration; but it would be most unjust not to admit that there were others who were actuated by nobler principles and more generous feelings, who would have rushed forward at once from the sense of indignation at aggression, and who deemed that no act of injustice could be perpetrated from one end of the universe to the other, but that the sword of Great Britain should leap from its scabbard to avenge it. But as it is the province of law to control the excess even of laudable passions and propensities in individuals, so it is the duty of Government to restrain within due bounds the ebullition of national sentiment, and to regulate the course and direction of impulses which it cannot blame. Is there anyone among the latter class of persons described by my honourable friend (for to the former I have nothing to say), who continues to doubt whether the Government did wisely in declining to obey the precipitate enthusiasm which prevailed at the commencement of the contest in Spain? Is there anybody who does not now think, that it was the office of Government to examine more closely all the various bearings of so complicated a question, to consider whether they were called upon to assist a united nation, or to plunge themselves into the internal feuds by which that nation was divided—to aid in repelling a foreign invader, or, to take part in a civil war. . . . Is there anyone who does not acknowledge that, under such circumstances the enterprise would have been one to be characterized only by a term we borrowed from that part of the Spanish literature with which we are most familiar—Quixotic; an enterprise, romantic in its origin, and thankless in the end ?

But while we thus control even our feelings by our duty, let it not be said that we cultivate peace, either because we fear, or because we are unprepared for war; on the contrary, if eight months ago the Government did not hesitate to proclaim that the country was prepared for war, if war should be unfortunately necessary, every month of peace that has since passed, has but made us so much the more capable of exertion. The resources created by peace are means of war. In cherishing those resources, we but accumulate those means. Our present repose is no more a proof of inability to act, than the state of inertness and inactivity in which I have seen those mighty masses that float in the waters above your town, is a proof that they are devoid of strength and incapable of being fitted out for action. You will know, gentlemen, how soon one of those stupendous masses, now reposing on their shadows in perfect stillness—how soon, upon any call of patriotism, or of necessity, it would resume the likeness of an animated thing, instinct with life and motion —how soon it would unfurl, as it were, its swelling plumage—how quickly it would put forth all its beauty and its bravery, collect its scattered elements of strength, and awaken its dormant thunder. Such as is one of those magnificent machines when springing from inaction into a display of its might—such is

England herself, while apparently passive and motion-
less she silently concentrates the power to be put forth
on an adequate occasion. But God forbid that that
occasion should arise. After a war sustained for nearly
a quarter of a century—sometimes single handed, and
with all Europe arrayed at times against her or at her
side, England needs a period of tranquillity, and may
enjoy it without fear of misconstruction. Long may we
be enabled, gentlemen, to improve the blessings of our
present situation, to cultivate the arts of peace, to give
to commerce, now reviving, greater extension and new
spheres of employment, and to confirm the prosperity
now generally diffused throughout this island.

Ibid., Vol. VI, p. 421. sqq.

14: GEORGE CANNING. Dispatch to A'Court, the British Minister to Spain.

18 September 1823

THE British Government will not, in any case, undertake any guaranty whatever, whether of territory or internal Institutions.

The scrupulousness with which England is in the habit of fulfilling her obligations makes it the more necessary for her not to contract them lightly. A guaranty is one of the most onerous obligations which one State can contract towards another. A defensive Alliance binds the Government contracting it, to come to the aid if its Ally, in case of an unprovoked attack upon his Dominions: and to make in his behalf, every reasonable and practicable exertion—practicable in extent, and reasonable in duration. But it does not bind the assisting Government to the alternative of either a successful result, or an indefinite prolongation of the War. A guaranty, strictly construed, knows no limits either of time, or of degree. It would be, unless distincly restricted in that respect, claimable in a War commenced by the Power to whom the guaranty is given, as well as in a War of unjust aggression against that Power; and the integrity of the territory of that Power must be maintained, at whatever cost the effort to maintain it is prolonged: nay, though the guaranteed Power itself should contribute almost nothing to the maintaining it. If . . . the engagement is to be restricted in these particulars, it would constitute an unilateral defensive Alliance, but it would cease to be a guarantee. Objectionable as a territorial guaranty is shown to be, the objections to a guaranty of internal institutions are infinitely stronger. It is difficult to say whether these objections apply with greater force to the party giving, or to that which receives such a guaranty.

The very principle on which the British Government so earnestly deprecated the War against Spain, was, that of the right of any Nation to change, or to modify, its internal Institutions.

Is that War to end in His Majesty's consenting to assume to Himself the province of defending, against all Challengers, from within, as well as from without, the Institutions, whatever they might be, which the War may leave standing in Spain?

Is His Majesty to guaranty the Constitution of 1812, indifference to which, to say the least . . . is the single point upon which anything like an Agreement of opinion has been found to exist in Spain? or is He to guaranty the antient despotism, the restoration of which, with all its accompaniments, appears to be the object of by far the largest party in the Country? or is it to be in behalf of some new system, struck out at a heat, at the winding up of affairs at Cadiz, that the faith of Great Britain is to be pledged, and that Her blood and treasure are to be forthcoming? or is it only to the undoubted right of the Spanish Nation to reform its own Government, that the sanction of His Majesty's guarantee is to be added? If such a guarantee were anything more than the mere affirmance of an abstract proposition, against whom would it have practically to operate ? clearly against the Spaniards themselves: and in the endless struggles which might be expected from the then distracted state of parties in that Country, against every party by turns ?

Could anything be more unbecoming than the assumption of such a right by a foreign Power ? Could anything be more intolerable to the Country with respect to which it was assumed ?

It is hardly necessary to add that while His Majesty must decline accepting such a right for Himself, he could not acknowledge it in any other Power.

The exercise of such a right must necessarily lead to an intermeddling with the affairs of the guaranteed State, such as to place it, in fact, at the mercy of the Power who gives the guarantee.

Russia, in former times, guaranteed the Constitution of Poland.

The result is known—and it was inevitable. The natural and necessary course of things must, in such a case, overbear even the most sincere and studied abstinence from interposition on the part of the guaranteeing Power.

There can be no doubt that His Majesty's Allies will feel how little such an arrangement would be compatible with the Engagements by which they stand bound to each other; to maintain the State of territorial possession established at the Peace, and the rights of independent Nations.

Printed in Temperley and Penson, *Foundations of British Foreign Policy* (Cambridge 1938), pp. 82–4.

15: CANNING'S POLICY. A Defence Answering Attacks Made on Him, Published after His Death by Lady Canning in the form of an Anonymous Pamphlet

Published in 1830

Canning succeeded Liverpool as Prime Minister in April 1827, but died in August. Between his death and the appointment of Palmerston, a disciple of Canning, as Foreign Secretary in Lord Grey's Government in November 1830, the conduct of foreign policy was in the hands of, first, Goderich and Dudley, and afterwards of Wellington and Aberdeen.

Wellington's government failed after the struggle for Catholic Emancipation at home, lost the initiative in foreign policy and played a negative and uncertain part during the war between Russia and Turkey, and during the establishment of the Greek State by the Treaty of Adrianople of September 1829 and the London Protocol of February 1830. In France, Charles X and Polignac were discussing ideas of re-drawing the map of Europe and revising the 1815 settlement, as well as, in May 1830, despatching an expedition to Algiers.

. . . It was Mr. Canning's policy to obtain for Great Britain the confidence and goodwill of the people of other nations, not, however, by flattering their prejudices, or encouraging their discontent, but by showing a fixed determination to act with impartial justice towards them. While he was at the helm, there was not one of the European governments which dared to provoke the vengeance of England, because they well knew that war with England would be a measure too

95

unpopular to hazard. Thus, Mr. Canning was enabled to hold language, and to carry measures in defiance of the principles and prejudices of some, and contrary to the wishes of the governments of all the great Continental Powers. By this means he obtained over these governments an influence which he employed not only to promote the interests of England, but the general prosperity of the world.

Alas! how different is our present position! Go to the North, and hear the terms of contempt and bitterness with which England is assailed by the Russian Government, for our vacillation—by the Russian people, for our illiberality. Go to Germany, and you may listen in vain for the praises which the name of England used to call forth when Canning ruled her destinies. Turkey complains of being betrayed. Greece considers us her enemy. Cross the Channel, and you will find in France the feelings of ancient rivalry, which Mr. Canning's policy had well nigh extinguished, revived with almost incredible virulence. Sail to Portugal, and there you will see that we are hated by all parties, and trusted by none. While the thousands exiled from their homes, in consequence of our change of policy, imprecate curses on British perfidy, and serve as a warning to all, not to place reliance on British protection. . . .

If the peace of Europe is broken, it will be because Great Britain has abdicated the " Umpire's " Throne, and has converted herself into an " adversary " of constitutional freedom. It was because " the professors of violent doctrines on both sides " dreaded England's taking part against them that their mutual excesses were restrained. But now that Great Britain is ranged on the side of absolutism, the friends of liberal institutions, feeling that they know the worst, are preparing for action. . . .

Let it not be supposed, that this commercial country can shut itself up within itself, and survey in tranquil serenity the struggles and commotions of our neighbours.

We have played too distinguished a part in latter times to be able to find a " refuge in littleness." If we do nothing to maintain our high character we shall speedily lose it, as well as what is far worse—the power of regaining it.

Let us not be deluded with the idea that our maritime preponderance does not excite the envy of other states. It is witnessed with the utmost jealousy—and if we once let the world see that we prefer a base submission to vengeance of our own insults, while we evince a heartless disregard of the oppression and the wrongs inflicted on our adherents, we shall be valueless as an ally; and every petty state will follow the example of Don Miguel,[1] in treating British subjects with injustice, and the remonstrances of their Government with contempt.

We cannot then withdraw from continental policy— the attempt, if long persevered in, would infallibly end in the ruin of our vital interests and the destruction of our commerce.

No one felt more entirely convinced of this than Mr. Canning; and therefore the leading object of his foreign policy was, to preserve the peace of the world, holding high the balance, and grasping, but not unsheathing the sword. It was for this end that he sought

[1] Since 1826 a struggle had been going on in Portugal between the " liberal " supporters of the young Queen Maria and the " absolutist " supporters of her uncle Dom Miguel. By 1830 Dom Miguel had established himself in Lisbon and in spite of British protests, had, in February and March, interfered with British subjects and ships.

to place this country in the position of an umpire; in order that, by restraining the passions of both parties, he might prevent their dreaded collision. He entirely succeeded in his endeavours, and at the period of his death, the bright aspect of the political horizon indicated no approaching storm.

Can anyone look at the horizon now, and say that no threatening clouds are to be seen . . . ?

> *An Authentic Account of Mr. Canning's Policy with respect to the Constitutional Charter of Portugal, in reply to* Observations on the Papers laid before Parliament (London 1830), pp. 46–50.

PART IV

THE PALMERSTONIAN PERIOD, 1830–65

PALMERSTON was Foreign Secretary from 1830 to 1841, and from 1846 to 1851, Home Secretary 1852–5, and Prime Minister 1855–8 and from 1859 until his death in 1865.

The next document is a dispatch to the British ambassador to Russia in answer to a suggestion by the Tsar " that some engagement should be entered into between England and the other three Great Powers who are Parties to the Treaty of July, with the view of providing for the contingency of an attack by France upon the liberties of Europe." The Treaty of London had been signed in July 1840 by England, Russia, Austria and Prussia to settle the problems raised in the Near East by the revolt of Egypt against Turkey, in which the Egyptians had had the support of France. Palmerston's personal views were less restrained than those expressed for the Tsar's benefit: in two private letters in July 1840 he had written: " Guizot (the French Ambassador in London) said that the French Government would now feel it necessary to be in force, in great force, in the Levant. Be it so. We shall not be daunted. . . . We shall go to work quietly in our own way, in presence of a superior force . . . just as undisturbed as if it were laid up in ordinary at Toulon. France knows full well that if that superior force should dare to meddle with ours, it is *war*; and she would be made to pay dearly for war so brought on." ". . . We none of us intend that France shall domineer over the other Powers of Europe, or even over England alone. Of all mistakes, in public affairs as well as in private, the greatest is to truckle to swagger and bully, or even to unjustifiable violence." [1]

[1] Sir H. L. Bulwer, *The Life of Viscount Palmerston*, 3rd Edition London, 1871, Vol. II, p. 315.

16: HENRY JOHN TEMPLE, VISCOUNT
PALMERSTON. Dispatch to the Marquis of
Clanricarde, the British Ambassador to Russia

11 January 1841

. . . One of the general principles which Her Majesty's
Government wish to observe as a guide for their conduct in dealing with the relations between England
and other States, is, that changes which foreign
Nations may chuse to make in their internal Constitution and form of Government, are to be looked upon
as matters with which England has no business to
interfere by force of arms, for the purpose of imposing
upon such Nations a Form of Government which they
do not wish to have, or for the purpose of preventing
such Nations from having Institutions which they
desire. These things are considered in England to be
matters of domestic concern, which every Nation ought
to be allowed to settle as it likes.

But an attempt of one Nation to seize and to appropriate to itself territory which belongs to another
Nation, is a different matter; because such an attempt
leads to a derangement of the existing Balance of
Power, and by altering the relative strength of States,
may tend to create danger to other Powers; and such
attempts therefore, the British Government holds
itself at full liberty to resist, upon the universally
acknowledged principle of self-defence.

Now, it is quite true, as stated by the Emperor, that

any Country, such as France, for instance, may, under the plea and pretext of altering its own Institutions, seek to overthrow the existing Governments of other countries, for the purpose of adding those Countries to its own Territories, or of associating them with its own aggressive system; and such proceedings would cease to be domestic changes of arrangement, and would assume the unquestionable character of external aggression.—Such attempts England has in former times on many occasions resisted; and it is highly probable that if a similar case were again to arise, England would again pursue a similar course.

But it is not usual for England to enter into engagements with reference to cases which have not actually arisen, or which are not immediately in prospect: and this for a plain reason. All formal engagements of the Crown, which involve the question of peace and war, must be submitted to Parliament; and Parliament might probably not approve of an engagement which should bind England prospectively to take up Arms in a contingency which might happen at an uncertain time, and under circumstances which could not as yet be foreseen.

It is true that His Imperial Majesty has spoken of an understanding which need not be recorded in any formal instrument; but upon which He might rely if the Turn of Affairs should render it applicable to events. But this course would not be free from objections. For, in the first place, it would scarcely be consistent with the spirit of the British Constitution for the Crown to enter into a binding engagement of such a nature, without placing it formally upon record, so that Parliament might have an opportunity of expressing its opinion thereupon, and this could only be done by some written Instrument; and to such a course the objection which I have alluded to above, would apply. But if the engagement were merely verbal though it would bind the Ministers who made it, it might be disavowed by their successors; and thus the Russian Government might be led to count upon a system of policy on the part of Great Britain which might not eventually be pursued.

Printed in Temperley and Penson, *Foundations of British Foreign Policy* (London 1938), pp. 136–7.

17: RICHARD COBDEN. The Spanish Marriages

September 1847

The most consistent and vigorous opponent of Palmerston was
Richard Cobden (1804–65). The next extract is quoted from his
life by John Morley, himself a later representative of many of
Cobden's views, who in 1914 resigned from Asquith's Government rather than be a member of a war administration.

". . . In all my travels," he wrote to Mr. Bright,
" three reflections constantly occur to me: how much
unnecessary solicitude and alarm England devotes to
the affairs of foreign countries; with how little knowledge we enter upon the task of regulating the concerns
of other people; and how much better we might employ our energies in improving matters at home." He
knew that the influential opinion of the country was
still against him, and that it would be long before it
turned. " Until that time," he said, in words which
may be usefully remembered by politicians who are
fain to reap before they have sown, " I am content to
be on this question as I have been on others in a
minority, and in a minority to remain, until I get a
majority."

While he was away that famous intrigue known as
the Spanish Marriages took place. The King of the
French, guided by the austere and devout Guizot, so
contrived the marriages of the Queen of Spain and her
sister, that in the calculated default of issue from the

Queen, the crown of Spain would go to the issue of her sister and the Duke of Montpensier, Louis Philippe's son. Cobden, as we shall see, did not believe that the King was looking so far as this. It was in any case a disgraceful and odious transaction, but events very speedily proved how little reason there was why it should throw the English Foreign Office into a paroxysm. Cobden was moved to write to Mr. Bright upon it:

" My object in writing again is to speak upon the Marriage question. I have seen with humiliation that the daily newspaper press of England has been lashing the public mind into an excitement (or at least trying to do so) upon the alliance of the Duke of Montpensier with the Infanta. I saw this boy and girl married, and as I looked at them, I could not help exclaiming to myself, ' what a couple to excite the animosity of the people of England and France! ' Have we not out-grown the days when sixty millions of people could be set at loggerheads by a family intrigue ? Yes, we have probably grown wiser than to repeat the War of Succession, but I see almost as great an evil as actual hostilities in the tone of the press and the intrigues of the diplomatists of England and France. They keep the two nations in a state of distrust and alienation, they familiarize us with the notion that war is still a possible event, and worse still, they furnish the pretext for continually augmenting our standing armaments, and thus oppressing and degrading the people with taxation, interrupting the progress of fiscal reforms, and keeping us in a hostile attitude ready for war.

"I began my political life by writing against this system of foreign interference, and every year's exper-ience confirms me in my early impression that it lies

at the bottom of our misgovernment at home. My
visit to Spain has strengthened, if possible, a hundred-
fold my conviction that all attempts of England to
control or influence the destinies, political and social,
of that country are worse than useless. They are mischievous alike to Spaniards and Englishmen. They
are a peculiar people not understood by us. They
have one characteristic, however, which their whole
history might have revealed to us, i.e., their inveterate
repugnance to all foreign influences and alliances, and
their unconquerable resistance to foreign control. No
country in Europe besides is so isolated in its prejudices
of race and caste. It has ever been so, whether in the
times of the Romans, of the Saracens, of Louis XIV, or
of Napoleon. No people are more willing to call in the
aid of foreign arms or diplomacy to fight their battles,
but they despise and suspect the motives of all who
come to help them, and they turn against them the
moment their temporary purpose is gained. As for any
other nation permanently swaying the destinies of
Spain, or finding in it an ally to be depended on
against other Powers, it would be as easy to gain such
an object with the Bedouins of the Desert, with whom,
by the way, the Spaniards have no slight affinity of
character. No one who knows the people, nobody who
has read their history, can doubt this: and yet our
diplomatists and newspaper-writers are pretending
alarm at the marriage of the youngest son of Louis
Philippe with the Infanta, on the ground of the possible future union of the two countries under one head,
or at least under one influence. Nobody knows the
absurdity of any such contingency better than Louis
Philippe. He feels, no doubt, that it is difficult enough
to secure *one* throne permanently for his dynasty, and

unless his sagacity be greatly over-rated, he would shrink from the possibility of one of his descendants ever attempting to wear at the same time the crowns of Spain and France. I believe the French King to have had but one object—to secure a rich wife for his younger son. He is perhaps a little avaricious in his old age, like most other men. But I care nothing for his motives or policy. Looking to the facts, I ask why should the French and English people allow themselves to be embroiled by such family manœuvres ? He may have been treacherous to our Queen, but why should kings and queens be allowed to enter into any marriage compacts in the name of their people ? You will perhaps tell me when you write that the bulk of the middle class, the reflecting portion of the people of England, do not sympathize with the London daily press on the subject of the Marriage question; and I know that there is a considerable portion of the more intelligent French people who do not approve of all that is written in the Paris papers. But, unhappily, the bulk of mankind do not think for themselves. The newspapers write in the name of the two countries, and to a great extent they form public opinion. Governments and diplomatists act upon the views expressed in the influential journals. . . . There is one way in which this system of interfering in the politics of Spain is especially mischievous. It prevents Spanish parties from being formed upon a purely domestic basis, and thus puts off the day when the politicians shall devote themselves to their own reforms. At present, all the intrigues of Madrid revolve round the diplomatic manœuvres of France and England. There is another evil arising out of it. It gives the bulk of the Spaniards a false notion of their own position. They are a proud people, they think all Europe is busy with their affairs, they hear of France and England being on the point of going to war about the marriage of one of their princesses, they imagine that Spain is the most important country in the world, and thus they forget their own ignorance, poverty, and political degradation, and of course do not occupy themselves in domestic reforms. If left to themselves, they would soon find out their inferiority, for they are not without a certain kind of common sense.

" I have always had an instinctive monomania against this system of foreign interference, protocolling, diplomatizing, etc., and I should be glad if you and our other Free Trade friends, who have beaten the daily broad-sheets into common sense upon another question, would oppose yourselves to the Palmerston system, and try to prevent the Foreign Office from undoing the good which the Board of Trade has done to the people. But you must not disguise from yourself that the evil has its roots in the pugnacious, energetic, self-sufficient, foreigner-despizing and pitying character of that noble insular creature, John Bull. Read Washington Irving's description of him fumbling for his cudgel always the moment he hears of any row taking place anywhere on the face of the earth, and bristling up with anger at the very idea of any other people daring to have a quarrel without first asking his consent or inviting him to take a part in it. . . ."

John Morley, *The Life of Richard Cobden* (London 1879), pp. 471-4.

18: LORD PALMERSTON. From Speech in House of Commons

1 March 1848

Palmerston was criticized not only for interfering too much in continental affairs but also, by a small section of opinion, for interfering too little, for instance in the support of Poland or Turkey against Russia. It was said of him, for instance, by Lord Dudley Stuart in 1837 " He has exhibited England as a bully and a coward, cruel and tyrannical to the weak, mean and abject before the strong."

A violent personal attack on Palmers on was made by the strongly anti-Russian Anstey in February 1848. Palmerston replied on March 1st and, after dealing at length with the detailed charges, ended his speech with the following statement of the principles governing his conduct up to 1848.

THE principle on which I have thought the foreign affairs of this country ought to be conducted is, the principle of maintaining peace and friendly understanding with all nations, as long as it was possible to do so consistently with a due regard for the interests, the honour, and the dignity of this country. My endeavours have been to preserve peace. All the Governments of which I have had the honour to be a member have succeeded in accomplishing that object.

The main charges brought against me are, that I did not involve this country in perpetual quarrels from one end of the globe to the other. There is no country that has been named, from the United States to the Empire of China, with respect to which part of the Hon. Member's charge has not been, that we have refrained from taking steps that might have plunged us into conflict with one or more of these Powers. On these occasions we have been supported by the opinion and approbation of Parliament and the public. We have endeavoured to extend the commercial relations of the country, or to place them where extension was not required, on a firmer basis and upon a footing of greater security. Surely in that respect we have not judged amiss, nor deserved the censure of the country; on the contrary I think we have done good service.

I hold, with respect to alliances, that England is a Power sufficiently strong, sufficiently powerful, to steer her own course, and not to tie herself as an unnecessary appendage to the policy of any other Government. I hold that the real policy of England— apart from questions which involve her own political interests, political or commercial—is to be the champion of justice and right; perserving that course with moderation and prudence, not becoming the Quixote[1] of the world, but giving the might of her moral sanction and support wherever she thinks justice is, and whenever she thinks that wrong has been done.

Sir, in pursuing that course, and in pursuing the more limited direction of our own particular interests, my conviction is, that as long as England keeps herself in the right—as long as she wishes to permit no injustice—as long as she wishes to countenance no wrong —as long as she labours at legislative interests of her own—and as long as she sympathizes with right and justice, she will never find herself altogether alone.

[1] Cf., Canning's speech at Plymouth, No. 13.

She is sure to find some other State of sufficient power, influence, and weight, to support and aid her in the course she may think fit to pursue. Therefore, I say that it is a narrow policy to suppose that this country or that is to be marked out as the eternal ally or the perpetual enemies. Our interests are eternal and perpetual, and those interests it is our duty to follow.

When we find other countries marching in the same courses, and pursuing the same objects as ourselves, we consider them as our friends, and we think for the moment that we are on the most cordial footing; when we find other countries that take a different view, and thwart us in that object we pursue, it is our duty to make allowance for the different manner in which they may follow out the same objects. It is our duty not to pass too harsh a judgment upon others, because they do not exactly see things in the same light as we see; and it is our duty not lightly to engage this country in the frightful responsibilities of war, because from time to time we may find this or that Power disinclined to concur with us in matters where their opinion and ours may fairly differ. That has been, as far as my faculties have allowed me to act upon it, the guiding principle of my conduct. And if I might be allowed to express in one sentence the principle which I think ought to guide our English Ministers, I would adopt the expression of Canning, and say that with every British Minister the interests of England ought to be the shibboleth of his policy.

Hansard, Third Series, Vol. XCVII, pp. 121-3.

19: DEBATE IN THE HOUSE OF COMMONS

21 July 1849

The Hungarian revolution of 1848 and its suppression by the Emperor Franz Joseph with the help of Russian forces aroused great enthusiasm for the cause of Hungarian independence among all English Liberals for many years afterwards.

The following extracts from a debate in the House of Commons on Russian intervention in Hungary illustrate the growing fear of Russia that was to create the atmosphere in which the Crimean War broke out. Ralph Bernal Osborne (1808–82, Liberal M.P. for Middlesex) and J. A. Roebuck (1801–79, Liberal M.P. for Sheffield) are characteristic of the Radical supporters of a policy of vigorous intervention in Europe. Their speeches are also typical of an uncritical enthusiasm for foreign causes that was not likely to be influenced by the opinions of eye-witnesses such as Lord C. Hamilton, who stated in the course of the debate: "Those who were acquainted with the nature of that constitution for which it was absurdly alleged the Hungarian nation had risen in arms, knew well that it was nothing more or less than a régime of tyranny, under which the peasants of Hungary were worse off than the peasantry of any other part of the Austrian Empire."

MR. BERNAL OSBORNE: . . . This was not a mere struggle for Hungarian independence. He looked upon this struggle that was going on in Europe as a struggle between the two principles of despotism and constitutional government. It was a struggle commenced in Hungary; but who knew where the struggle might not extend? When the last barrier was swept away, Hungary and the finest parts of the east of

Europe would become nothing more than slavish dependents of the Russian empire. He had given a vote for arbitration, in the abstract principle of which he perfectly agreed; but he would say that a time might arrive when he would prefer to fight the battle of European liberty in the Baltic rather than in the British Channel. . . .

MR. ROEBUCK: . . . His wish was, if possible, to make this a practical question; for he believed that however strongly their inclinations were expressed in that House, in the motion they would go for nothing, unless followed by some practical act on the part of Government. A mere opinion would never reach the country interested. The despotism to which he had alluded, would prevent Hungarians, Russians or Frenchmen, from hearing any words they might utter. Therefore he wished to see how far it was possible, without going counter to the people of England, to interfere practically in this question, and to lend our aid as a nation to this great question of international morality. He could not agree . . . that in all cases the Foreign Minister would be unpopular who involved England in a war. He did not think that a great or a wise sentiment. He maintained that the people of England liked that Minister and held him to their hearts who maintained the national honour. He would not believe in any school of politicians who took that low level of national morality, that we should bind up all our feelings in the interchange of commodities, or the sordid question of profit and loss. He believed that there was something more in the souls of the people than that—they had sympathies with the people of the world. . . . They had a desire to see good government

I   113

strengthened all over the world and to see the great
name of England used as a means of stopping the
advance of barbarian despotism, whether under the
banner of Russia or that of France. . . .

Suppose that the Russian army were victorious, and
that they crushed the Hungarian people, what would
be the effect ? We did not go round the Cape of Good
Hope to get to India now. Our highway to India was
through the Red Sea; and if the Russians entered
Constantinople and proceeded into Syria and Egypt,
that moment we should have war under the most dis-
advantageous circumstances. Therefore the people of
England were interested in this question. They were not
to shut their eyes and say—" Oh, we are a peaceable
people; we do not want war: we are afraid of war; we
want cotton spinning, and woollen spinning, and we
want the profits thereof." He acknowledged that we
wanted all these things; but he contended that we should
not have them unless we were a great and powerful
people.

LORD PALMERSTON: . . . It is most desirable that foreign
nations should know that, on the one hand, England
is sincerely desirous to preserve and maintain peace—
that we entertain no feelings of hostility towards any
nation in the world—that we wish to be on the most
friendly footing with all—that we have a deep interest
in the preservation of peace, because we are desirous
to carry on with advantage those innocent and peaceful relations of commerce . . . that we know must be
injured by the interruption of our friendly relations
with other countries: but, on the other hand, it is also
essential for the attainment of that object, and even
essential for the protection of that commerce to which

we attach so much importance, that it should be known and well understood by every nation on the face of the earth that we are not disposed to submit to wrong, and that the maintenance of peace on our part is subject to the indispensable condition that all countries shall respect our honour and our dignity, and shall not inflict any injury upon our interests.

Sir, I do not think that the preservation of peace is in any degree endangered by the expression of opinion with regard to the transactions in Hungary or other countries. . . .

There are cases like that which is now the subject of our discussion, of one Power having in the exercise of its own sovereign rights invited the assistance of another power; and, however we may lament that circumstance, however we may be apprehensive that therefrom consequences of great danger and evil may flow, still we are not entitled to interpose in any manner that will commit this country to embark in those hostilities. All we can justly do is to take advantage of any opportunities that may present themselves in which the counsels of friendship and peace may be offered to the contending parties. We have, on several occasions that have happened of late in Europe, been invited to " intermeddle " as it is called, in the affairs of other countries, although it has been said of this country, that it stands so low in public opinion in Europe, that we are treated with contempt both by governments and by nations. Certainly, the way in which that want of respect has been shown is singular, when from the north to the south, in cases of difficulty, not only between nations but internally between Governments and their own subjects, we have been asked and invited to interpose our friendly mediation in their affairs. We have on those occasions done our best to accomplish the object which we were called upon to fulfil. . . . Sir, to suppose that any Government of England can have any other wish or desire than to confirm and maintain peace between nations, and tranquillity and harmony between Governments and subjects, shows really a degree of ignorance and folly which I never supposed any public man could have been guilty of, which may do very well for a newspaper article, but which it astonishes me to find is made the subject of a speech in Parliament.

I agree with those who think—and I know there are many in this country who entertain the opinion—that there are two objects which England ought peculiarly to aim at. One is to maintain peace; the other is to count for something in the transactions of the world— that it is not fitting that a country occupying such a proud position as England—that a country having such various and extensive interests, should lock herself up in a simple regard to her own internal affairs, and should be a passive and mute spectator of everything that is going on around. It is quite true that it may be said, " Your opinions are but opinions, and you express them against our opinions, who have at our command large armies to back them—what are opinions against armies ? " Sir, my answer is, opinions are stronger than armies. Opinions, if they are founded in truth and justice, will in the end prevail against the bayonets of infantry, the fire of artillery, and the charges of cavalry. Therefore I say, that armed by opinion, if that opinion is pronounced with truth and justice, we are indeed strong, and in the end likely to make our opinions prevail; and I think that what is happening on the whole surface of the continent

of Europe, is a proof that this expression of mine
is a truth. Why, for a great many years the Governments of Europe imagined they could keep down
opinion by force of arms, and that by obstructing progressive improvement they would prevent that extremity of revolution which was the object of their constant
dread. We gave an opinion to the contrary effect, and
we have been blamed for it. We have been accused of
meddling with matters that did not concern us, and
of affronting nations and Governments by giving our
opinion as to what was likely to happen; but the result
has proved, that if our opinions had been acted upon,
great calamities would have been avoided. These very
Governments that used to say, " The man we hate,
the man we have to fear, is the moderate Reformer;
we care not for your violent Radical, who proposes
such violent extremes that nobody is likely to join him
—the enemy we are most afraid of is the moderate
Reformer, because he is such a plausible man that it is
difficult to persuade people that his counsels would
lead to extreme consequences—therefore let us keep
off, of all men, the moderate Reformer, and let us
prevent the first step of improvement, because that
improvement might lead to extremities and innovation." Those Governments, those Powers of Europe,
have at last learned the truth of the opinions expressed
by Mr. Canning, " That those who have checked improvement, because it is innovation, will one day or
other be compelled to accept innovation when it has
ceased to be improvement." I say, then, that it is our
duty not to remain passive spectators of events that in
their immediate consequences affect other countries,
but which in their remote and certain consequences
are sure to come back with disastrous effect upon us;

that, so far as the courtesies of international intercourse may permit us to do, it is our duty, especially when our opinion is asked, as it has been on many occasions on which we have been blamed for giving it, to state our opinions, founded on the experience of this country— an experience that might have been, and ought to have been, an example to less fortunate countries. At the same time, I am quite ready to admit that interference ought not to be carried to the extent of endangering our relations with other countries. . . . .

Hansard, Third Series, Vol. CVII, pp. 792, 800-2, 808-15.

20: DEBATE IN THE HOUSE OF COMMONS

24–28 June 1850

The Debate in the House of Commons from which extracts are given below gave an opportunity for Palmerston to review his policy as a whole and for his critics to attack it. It was a notable debate in which, in addition to Palmerston and Gladstone, Peel, Disraeli and Cobden all spoke.

The occasion for the motion by Palmerston's Radical supporter Roebuck was the dispute with Greece as a result of the claims made by " Don Pacifico " (a Portuguese Jew but a British subject by residence in Gibraltar), who alleged that his property had been destroyed by the mob in Athens. The debate, however, raised the whole question of intervention in the internal affairs of foreign countries. Palmerston had been largely responsible for establishing an independent Belgium after the revolution of 1830; in Portugal and Spain the situation appeared to English opinion to be in each case that of a struggle between young queens representing liberal opinions and their reactionary uncles, and in both countries Palmerston had given active diplomatic support and advice to the parties professing belief in constitutional principles. In 1847 he sent Lord Minto on a special mission to Italy to encourage the King of Sardinia in resistance to Austria, to give advice to the Pope and the Grand Duke of Tuscany and, generally, by his presence to embarrass the French and Austrians.

The essence of moderate support for Palmerston's policy was expressed later in the debate by A. Cockburn, the Liberal Member for Southampton and later Lord Chief Justice, as follows, when he described "that middle policy between absolutism and republicanism, encouraging constitutional governments, but not influencing to establish them by military force: using only our moral influence, taking the proud position which England is entitled to assume at the head of the constitutional nations of the world. The arbitrary rulers of foreign nations " he continues " may endeavour to destroy Her Majesty's Government; but rest assured of this—when the nations of the Continent have at length succeeded in establishing constitutional governments and in securing free institutions for themselves, and their voices can speak out, they will look back gratefully to the sympathy we have shown them in their time of suffering and distress; and the influence which we shall maintain amongst them will be commensurate with that sympathy."

THE motion moved by Roebuck on which the debate took place ran: " That the principles on which the Foreign Policy of Her Majesty's Government has been regulated, have been such as were calculated to maintain the honour and dignity of this country; and, in times of unexampled difficulty, to preserve peace between England and the nations of the world." It was carried by 310 votes to 264.

Hansard, Third Series, Vol. CXII.

LORD PALMERSTON:
(*a*) *Belgium*. I think that the arrangement which in 1815 had been thought conducive to the peace of Europe, and by which, through the union of Belgium with Holland, a Power of some consideration was to be formed in that particular part of Europe, interposed between Germany on the one hand and France on the other—I think that that arrangement, which originally, by those who framed it, was, and not without reason, expected to prove advantageous to the peace of Europe, has, by the course of events turned out to

have a contrary tendency. The people of Belgium and of Holland evidently could not coalesce; and if certain Powers of Europe had combined at that moment to compel a reunion between these separated portions of the Kingdom of the Netherlands, I doubt whether that reunion could have been effected without the immediate explosion of a war in Europe of the greatest magnitude; and I am quite sure that if it had been effected, it could not have lasted, and the foundation must have been laid thereby of future and inevitable disturbance. We carried out our opinion upon that point to a practical result. . . .

Why, if ever there was an experiment—call it so if you will—that fully and completely succeeded, the creation of Belgium into an independent State was that experiment.

(pp. 411–2)

(b) *Portugal.* Did it very much signify to England, in the abstract whether this young queen (Donna Maria) was to be Sovereign of Portugal, or whether Dóm Miguel . . . should remain upon the throne? Not much certainly; but we looked upon the question, not as a simple choice between one sovereign and the other, but—which it was in reality—as a question between absolute government on the one hand, and constitutional government on the other. But what interest, you will say, had we in that? Why, we might have had a selfish interest in favour of despotism; because it is manifest that if you want to exercise influence over a country, you are more likely to have it where the Government rests in a Court and a Cabinet, than where it rests in an assembly representing the nation. But we scorned that sort of influence in Portugal. We knew, in espousing the cause of a constitution, that that particular kind of influence on our part would cease; but we felt that we should reap other advantages, which would more than counter-balance any disadvantages arising from that source. We knew that the prosperity of Portugal was concerned in the issue—that the best chance for the cessation of the manifold abuses, administrative and others, which had so long prevailed to keep down Portugal in the scale of nations—that the best chance of applying a remedy to those evils, and of giving full development to the natural resources of Portugal, would consist in securing to it the inestimable advantages of a full constitution. . . .

(pp. 413–4)

(c) *Spain.* In Spain, as in Portugal, the question was between arbitrary rule and constitutional and parliamentary government, and in relation to Spain, as well as to Portugal, we thought that the interests of England in every point of view, commercial and political, would be benefited by the establishment of constitutional government.

If England has any interest more than another with reference to Spain, it is that Spain should be independent, that Spain should be Spanish. Spain for the Spaniards is the maxim upon which we proceed in our policy with regard to Spain. . . .

(pp. 417–8)

(d) *Italy.* With regard to our policy with respect to

Italy, I utterly deny the charges that have been brought against us, of having been the advocates, supporters, and encouragers of revolution. It has always been the fate of advocates of temperate reform and of constitutional improvement to be run at as the fomentors of revolution. It is the easiest mode of putting them down; it is the received *formula*. It is the established practice of those who are the advocates of arbitrary government to say, " Never mind real revolutionists; we know how to deal with them; your dangerous man is the moderate reformer; he is such a plausible man; the only way of getting rid of him, is to set the world at him, by calling him a revolutionist."

Now there are revolutionists of two kinds in this world. In the first place there are those violent, hot-headed, and unthinking men, who fly to arms, who overthrow established Governments; and who recklessly, without regard to consequences, and without measuring difficulties and comparing strength, deluge their country with blood, and draw down the greatest calamities on their fellow-countrymen. These are the revolutionists of one class. But there are revolutionists of another kind; blind-minded men, who, animated by antiquated prejudices, and daunted by ignorant apprehensions, dam up the current of human improvement; until the irresistible pressure of accumulated discontent breaks down the opposing barriers, and overthrows and levels to the earth, those very institutions which a timely application of renovating means would have rendered strong and lasting. . . . Under these circumstances, I am justified in denying that the policy which we pursued in Italy was that of exciting revolutions, and then abandoning the victims we had deluded. On the contrary, I maintain that we gave advice calculated to prevent revolutions, by reuniting opposite parties, and conflicting views. Ours was a policy of improvement and peace. . . .

(pp. 432–3)

(*e*) *Conclusion*. I believe that the principles on which we have acted are those which are held by the great mass of the people of this country. I am convinced that these principles are calculated, so far as the influence of England may properly be exercised with respect to the destinies of other countries, to conduce to the maintenance of peace, to the advancement of civilization, to the welfare and happiness of mankind. . . . It is a noble thing to be allowed to guide the policy and to influence the destinies of such a country; and, if ever it was an object of honourable ambition, more than ever must it be so at the moment at which I am speaking. For while we have seen . . . the political earthquake rolling Europe from side to side—while we have seen thrones shaken, shattered, levelled; institutions overthrown and destroyed—while in almost every country of Europe the conflict of civil war has deluged the land with blood, from the Atlantic to the Black Sea, from the Baltic to the Mediterranean; this country has presented a spectacle honourable to the people of England, and worthy of the admiration of mankind.

We have shown that liberty is compatible with order; that individual freedom is reconcilable with obedience to the law. We have shown the example of a nation, in which every class of society accepts with cheerfulness the lot which providence has assigned to it; while at the same time every individual of each class is constantly striving to raise himself in the social scale—not by injustice and wrong, not by violence and illegality, but by preserving good conduct, and by the steady and energetic exertion of the moral and intellectual faculties with which his Creator has endowed him. To govern such a people as this, is indeed an object worthy of the noblest man who lives in the land; and therefore I find no fault with those who may think any opportunity a fair one, for endeavouring to place themselves in so distinguished and honourable a position. But I contend that we have not in our foreign policy done anything to forfeit the confidence of the country. . . . I therefore fearlessly challenge the verdict which this House, as representing a political, a commercial, a constitutional country, is to give on the question now brought before it; whether the principles on which the foreign policy of Her Majesty's Government has been conducted, and the sense of duty which has led us to think ourselves bound to afford protection to our fellow subjects abroad, are proper and fitting guides for those who are charged with the Government of England; and whether, as the Roman, in days of old, held himself free from indignity, when he could say *Civis Romanus sum*; so also a British subject, in whatever land he may be, shall feel confident that the watchful eye and the strong arm of England, will protect him against injustice and wrong.

(pp. 443–7)

Mr. Gladstone: I cannot look upon all that has taken place during the four years which are the subject-matter of this Motion, without seeing a rash desire, a habitual desire, of interference, a disposition to make

125

the occasions of it, and, that which will always follow, a disposition, in making them, to look too slightly at the restraints imposed by the letter and the spirit of the law of nations. . . .

Sir, great as is the influence and power of Britain, she cannot afford to follow, for any length of time, a self-isolating policy. It would be a contravention of the law of nature and of God, if it were possible for any single nation of Christendom to emancipate itself from the obligations which bind all other nations, and to arrogate, in the face of mankind, a position of peculiar privilege. And now I will grapple with the noble Lord on the ground which he selected for himself, in the most triumphant portion of his speech, by his reference to those emphatic words *Civis Romanus sum.* He vaunted, amidst the cheers of his supporters, that under his administration an Englishman should be, throughout the world, what the citizen of Rome had been. What then, Sir, was a Roman citizen ? He was the member of a privileged caste; he belonged to a conquering race, to a nation that held all others bound by the strong arm of power. For him there was to be an exceptional system of law; for him principles were to be asserted, and by him rights were to be enjoyed, that were denied to the rest of the world. Is such, then, the view of the noble Lord, as to the relation that is to subsist between England and other countries. . . ?

I, for my part, am of opinion that England will stand shorn of a chief part of her glory and her pride if she shall be found to have separated herself, through the policy she preserves abroad, from the moral supports which the general and fixed convictions of mankind afford—if the day shall come in which she may continue to excite the wonder and the fear of other nations, but in which she shall have no part in their affection and their regard.

No, Sir, let it not be so: let us recognize, and recognize with frankness, the equality of the weak with the strong: the principles of brotherhood among nations, and of their sacred independence. . . . Let us refrain from all gratuitous and arbitrary meddling in the internal concerns of other States, even as we should resent the same interference if it were attempted to be practised towards ourselves.

(pp. 584, 586–7, 589–590)

SIR R. PEEL (after reviewing the foreign policy of his government in 1841–6 and comparing it with that of Russell and Palmerston continues): If you appeal to diplomacy, let me in the first place ask what is this diplomacy? It is a costly engine for maintaining peace. It is a remarkable instrument used by civilized nations for the purpose of preventing war. Unless it be used to appease the angry passions of individual men, to check the feelings that rise out of national resentments—unless it be used for that purpose it is an instrument not only costly but mischievous. If, then, your application of diplomacy be to fester every wound, to provoke instead of soothing resentments, to place a Minister in every Court of Europe for the purpose, not of fermenting quarrels, or of adjusting quarrels, but for the purpose of continuing an angry correspondence, and for the purpose of promoting what is supposed to be an English interest; of keeping up conflicts with the representatives of other Powers, then I say, that not only is the expenditure upon this

127

costly instrument thrown away, but this great engine, used by civilized society for the purpose of maintaining peace, is perverted into a cause of hostility and war. . . .

The principle for which I contend . . . is the principle for which every statesman of importance in this country for the last fifty years has contended—namely, non-interference with the domestic affairs of other countries, without some clear and unavoidable necessity arising from circumstances affecting the interests of our own country. . . . I say this, that the hon. and learned Gentleman (Mr. Roebuck) is calling upon me to affirm that principle which was contended against by Mr. Fox when it was employed in favour of arbitrary government; which was revised by Mr. Canning, and revised by Lord Castlereagh at the Congress of Vienna, when the combined Sovereigns attempted by force to check the progress of constitutional government. . . .

Then, what are we to declare ? That we will relinquish the principle of non-interference, and declare in favour of the principle of self-government . . . ? It is a most serious undertaking on the part of this House. If you do claim that right you must give a correlative right to other powers. Self-government! Who shall construe what is the basis of self-government ? We are living in the neighbourhood of a great republic—a republic which may be prosperous; which may calculate its power—which maintains the doctrine that legitimacy is inconsistent with self-government; that monarchy is inconsistent with self-government. If I claim the right to introduce my notion of self-government into an independent nation, can I deny that right of France to introduce its notion of self-government into countries opposed to republican institutions? Recollect our manifold relations with other countries in every corner of the globe. Recollect our position in North America. Recollect our monarchical colonies, in close contact with republicanism.... Does self-government extend beyond Europe? Does this right of self-government extend beyond it? We govern millions of people in India; are we to admit the right of other Powers to inculcate the right of self-government among them? Which is the wisest policy —to attempt to interfere with the institutions and measures of other countries not bordering on our own, out of an abstract love for constitutional government —or to hold that doctrine maintained by Mr. Fox, Mr. Pitt, Lord Granville, Mr. Canning, and Lord Castlereagh, that the true policy of this country is non-intervention in the affairs of others . . . ?

It is also my firm belief that you will not advance the cause of constitutional government by attempting to dictate to other nations. If you do, your intentions will be mistaken—you will rouse feelings upon which you do not calculate—you will invite opposition to Government; and beware that the time does not arrive when, frightened by your own influence, you withdraw your countenance from those whom you have excited, and leave upon their minds the bitter recollection that you have betrayed them. If you succeed, I doubt whether or not the institutions that take root under your patronage will be lasting. Constitutional liberty will be best worked out by those who aspire to freedom by their own efforts. You will only overload it by your help, by your principle of interference, against which I remonstrate—against which I enter my protest—to which I to-night will be no party. You are departing from the established policy

K 129

of England—you are involving yourselves in difficulties the extent of which you can hardly conceive—you are bestowing no aid on the cause of constitutional freedom, but are encouraging its advocates to look to you for aid, instead of to those efforts which can alone establish it, and upon the successful exertion of which alone it can be useful.

(pp. 689–93)

Among the critics of Palmerston's policy were the Queen and the Prince Consort, and they had been largely responsible for forcing him to resign in December 1851. The following two documents are the Queen's request to the Prime Minister for a statement of the principles of foreign policy, and part of the paper drawn up in reply by the new Foreign Secretary, Lord Granville.

21: QUEEN VICTORIA. To Lord John Russell

28 December 1851

THE Queen thinks the moment of the change in the person of Secretary of State for Foreign Affairs to afford a fit opportunity to have the principles upon which our Foreign Affairs have been conducted since the beginning of 1848 reconsidered by Lord John Russell and his Cabinet.

The Queen was fully aware that the storm raging at the time on the Continent rendered it impossible for any statesman to foresee with clearness and precision what development and direction its elements would take, and she consequently quite agreed that the line of policy to be followed, as the most conducive to the interests of England, could then only be generally conceived and vaguely expressed.

But although the Queen is still convinced that the general principles laid down by Lord John at that time for the conduct of our Foreign Policy were in themselves right, she has in the progress of the last three years become painfully convinced that the

131

manner in which they have been *practically applied* has worked out very different results from those which the correctness of the principles themselves had led her to expect. For when the revolutionary movements on the Continent had laid prostrate almost all its Governments, and England alone displayed that order, vigour, and prosperity which it owes to a stable, free, and good Government, the Queen, instead of earning the natural good results of such a glorious position, viz. consideration, goodwill, confidence, and influence abroad, obtained the very reverse, and had the grief to see her Government and herself treated on many occasions with neglect, aversion, distrust, and even contumely.

Frequently, when our Foreign Policy was called in question, it has been said by Lord John and his colleagues that the principles on which it was conducted were the right ones, and having been approved of by them, received their support, and that it was only the *personal manner* of Lord Palmerston in conducting the affairs which could be blamed in tracing the causes which led to the disastrous results the Queen complains of.

The Queen is certainly not disposed to defend the personal manner in which Lord Palmerston has conducted Foreign Affairs, but she cannot admit that the errors he committed were merely *faults in form and method*, that they were no more than acts of " inconsideration, indiscretion, or bad taste." The Queen considers that she has also to complain of what appeared to her deviations from the principles laid down by the Cabinet for his conduct, nay, she sees distinctly in their practical application a *personal and arbitrary perversion* of the very nature and essence of those principles. She has only to refer here to Italy,

QUEEN VICTORIA

Spain, Greece, Holstein, France, etc., etc., which afford ample illustrations of this charge.

It was one thing for Lord Palmerston to have attempted such substantial deviations; it will be another for the Cabinet to consider whether they had not the power to check him in these attempts.

The Queen, however, considering times to have now changed, thinks that there is no reason why we should any longer confine ourselves to the mere assertion of abstract principles, such as " non-intervention in the internal affairs of other countries," " moral support to liberal institutions," " protection to British subjects," etc., etc. The moving powers which were put in operation by the French Revolution of 1848, and the events consequent on it, are no longer so obscure; they have assumed distinct and tangible forms in almost all the countries affected by them (in France, in Italy, Germany, etc.), and upon the state of things now existing, and the experience gained, the Queen would hope that our Foreign Policy may be *more specifically defined*, and that it may be considered how the general principles are to be practically adapted to our peculiar relations with each Continental State.

The Queen wishes therefore that a regular programme embracing these different relations should be submitted to her, and would suggest whether it would not be the best mode if Lord John were to ask Lord Granville to prepare such a paper and to lay it before her after having revised it.

This would then serve as a safe guide for Lord Granville, and enable the Queen as well as the Cabinet to see that the Policy, as in future to be conducted, will be in conformity with the principles laid down and approved.

The Letters of Queen Victoria, First Series, Vol. II, pp. 351-2.

22: GEORGE LEVESON GOWER, EARL GRANVILLE; General Statement of Policy

12 January 1852

. . . . In the opinion of the present Cabinet, it is the duty and the interest of this country, having possessions scattered over the whole globe, and priding itself on its advanced state of civilization, to encourage moral, intellectual and physical progress among all other nations.

For this purpose the Foreign Policy of Great Britain should be marked by justice, moderation, and self respect, and this country should in her relations with other States do by others as it would be done by. While the Cabinet do not believe that all considerations of a higher character are to be sacrificed to the pushing of our manufactures by any means into every possible corner of the globe, yet considering the great natural advantages of our Foreign Commerce, and the powerful means of civilization it affords, one of the first duties of a British Gov(ernmen)t must always be to obtain for our Foreign Trade that security which is essential to its success. . . .

With regard to occurrences likely to have international consequences, no general rule can uniformly be applied. In each case, the Gov(ernmen)t must exercise its own discretion, whether it shall interfere at once, or remain aloof till its arbitration or good offices

134

be required. The latter course may often be advisable when, as at present, opinion abroad is in extremes, and the Foreign Policy of England has obtained, whether justly or unjustly, the reputation of interfering too much. It will also often be found advisable to combine with other great Powers, when no sacrifice of principle is required, to settle the disputes which may arise between other nations. . . .

The Cabinet is also of the opinion that new measures should be taken to secure the efficiency of those who enter into the diplomatic career, and who are promoted in that profession—that a stricter discipline should be established among the members of each mission, and that those persons who combine those personal qualities which engage respect and popularity with activity in obtaining information, and zeal in executing their instructions, should be selected to represent Her Majesty, at the different Courts.

Printed in Temperley and Penson, *Foundations of British Foreign Policy*, pp. 183–6.

23: RICHARD COBDEN. Mr. Cobden to the Reverend ——. From *1793 and 1853 in Three Letters*— Letter III

January 1853

Palmerston was also criticized by the Radical supporters of Free Trade and particularly by Richard Cobden and John Bright. From the time of his agitation for the Repeal of the Corn Laws Cobden had stressed the connection between Free Trade and peace. Both before and during the Crimean War he and Bright advised pacifist solutions to the problems of foreign policy, stressing both the moral and economic evils of war, although this cost them both their parliamentary seats in the General Election of 1857.

. . . But I must draw this long letter to a close.—What then is the practical deduction from the facts and arguments which I have presented? Why, clearly, that conciliation must proceed from ourselves. The people of this country must first be taught to separate themselves in feeling and sympathy from the authors of the late war[1], which was undertaken to put down principles of freedom. When the public are convinced, the Government will act; and one of the great ends to be attained, is an amicable understanding, if not a formal convention, between the two Governments, *whatever their form may be*, to prevent that irrational rivalry of warlike preparations which has been lately and is still carried on. One word of diplomacy exchanged upon

[1] *i.e.* The War of 1793-1815

136

this subject between the two countries will change the whole spirit of the respective governments. But this policy, involving a reduction of our warlike expenditure, will never be inaugurated by an aristocratic executive, until impelled to it by public opinion. Nay, as in the case of the repeal of the corn law,—*no minister can do it, except when armed by a pressure from without.*

I look to the agitation of the peace party to accomplish this end. It must work in the manner of the League,[1] and preach common sense, justice, and truth, in the streets and market places. The advocates of peace have found in the *peace congress* movement a common platform, to use an Americanism, on which all men who desire to avert war, and all who wish to abate the evil of our hideous modern armaments, may co-operate without compromising the most practical and " moderate " politician, or wounding the conscience of my friend Mr. Sturge, and his friends of the Peace Society—upon whose undying religious zeal, more than all besides, I rely for the eventual success of the peace agitation. The great advance of this party, within the last few years, as indicated most clearly by the attacks made upon them, which, like the spray dashed from the bows of a vessel, mark their triumphant progress, ought to cheer them to still greater efforts.

But the most consolatory fact of the times is the altered feelings of the great mass of the people since 1793. *There* lies our great advantage. With the exception of a lingering propensity to strike for the freedom of some other people, a sentiment partly traceable to a generous sympathy, and in some small degree, I fear, to insular pride and ignorance, there is little disposition

[1] The Anti-Corn Law League.

for war in our day. Had the popular tone been as sound in 1792, Fox and his friends would have prevented the last great war. But for this mistaken tendency to interfere by force on behalf of other nations, there is no cure but by enlightening the mass of the people upon the actual condition of the continental populations. This will put an end to the supererogatory commiseration which is sometimes lavished upon them, and turn their attention to the defects of their own social condition. I have travelled much, and always with an eye to the state of the great majority, who everywhere constitute the toiling base of the social pyramid; and I confess I have arrived at the conclusion that there is no country where so much is required to be done before the mass of the people become what it is pretended they are, what they ought to be, and what I trust they will yet be, as in England. There is too much truth in the picture of our social condition drawn by the Travelling Bachelor of Cambridge University,[1] and lately flung in our faces from beyond the Atlantic, to allow us any longer to delude ourselves with the idea that we have nothing to do at home, and may therefore devote ourselves to the elevation of the nations of the Continent. It is to this spirit of interference with other countries, the wars to which it has led, and the consequent diversion of men's minds (upon the Empress Catherine's principle) from home grievances, that we must attribute the unsatisfactory state of the mass of our people.

But to rouse the conscience of the people in favour of peace, the whole truth must be told them of the part they have played in past wars. In every pursuit in

---

[1] Joseph Kay, 1821–78, barrister, economist and writer on social and educational questions.

which we embark, our energies carry us generally in advance of all competitors. How few of us care to remember that, during the first half of the last century, we carried on the slave trade more extensively than all the world besides; that we made treaties for the exclusive supply of negroes; that ministers of state, and even royalty were not averse to profit by the traffic. But when Clarkson (to whom fame has not yet done justice) commenced his agitation against this vile commerce, he laid the sin at the door of the nation; he appealed to the conscience of the people, and made the whole community responsible for the crimes which the slave traders were perpetrating with their connivance; and the eternal principles of truth and humanity, which are ever present in the breasts of men, however they may be for a time obscured, were not appealed to in vain. We are now, with our characteristic energy, first and foremost in preventing, *by force*, that traffic which our statesmen sought to monopolize a century ago.

It must be even so in the agitation of the peace party. They will never rouse the conscience of the people, so long as they allow them to indulge the comforting delusion that they have been a peace-loving nation. We have been the most combative and aggressive community that has existed since the days of the Roman dominion. Since the revolution of 1688 we have expended more than fifteen hundred millions of money upon wars, not one of which has been upon our own shores, or in defence of our hearths and homes. " For so it is," says a not unfriendly foreign critic, " other nations fight at or near their own territory: the English everywhere." From the time of old Froissart, who, when he found himself on the English coast, exclaimed that he was among a people who " loved war

139

better than peace, and where strangers were well received," down to the day of our amiable and admiring visitor, the author of the *Sketch Book*, who, in his pleasant description of *John Bull*, has portrayed him as always fumbling for his cudgel whenever a quarrel arose among his neighbours, this pugnacious propensity has been invariably recognized by those who have studied our national character. It reveals itself in our historical favourites, in the popularity of the mad-cap Richard, Henry of Agincourt, the belligerent Chatham, and those monarchs and statesmen who have been most famous for their war-like achievements. It is displayed in our fondness for erecting monuments to warriors, even at the doors of our marts of commerce; in the frequent memorials of our battles, in the names of bridges, streets, and omnibuses; but above all in the display which public opinion tolerates in our metropolitan cathedral, whose walls are decorated with bas-reliefs of battle scenes, of storming of towns, and charges of bayonets, where horses and riders, ships, cannon, and musketry, realize by turns, in a Christian temple, the fierce struggle of the siege, and the battle-field.—I have visited, I believe, all the great Christian temples in the capitals of Europe; but my memory fails me, if I saw anything to compare with it. Mr. Layard has brought us some very similar works of art from Nineveh, but he has not informed us that they were found in Christian churches.

Nor must we throw upon the aristocracy the entire blame of our wars. An aristocracy never governs a people by opposing their ruling instincts. In Athens, a lively and elegant fancy was gratified with the beautiful in art; in Genoa and Venice, where the population were at first without territory, and consequently where commerce was the only resource, the path to power was on the deck of their merchantmen, or on 'Change. In England, where a people possessing a powerful physical organization, and an unequalled energy of character, were ready for projects of daring and enterprise, an aristocracy perverted these qualities to a century of constantly recurring wars. The peace party of our day must endeavour to turn this very energy to good account, in the same spirit in which Clarkson converted a nation of man-stealers into a Society of determined abolitionists. Far from wishing to destroy the energy, or even the combativeness, which has made us such fit instruments for the battlefield, we shall require these qualities for abating the spirit of war, and correcting the numberless moral evils from which society is suffering. Are not our people uneducated ? juvenile delinquents uncared for ? does not drunkenness still reel through our streets ? Have we not to battle with vice, crime, and their parent, ignorance, in every form ? And may not even charity display as great energy and courage in saving life, as was ever put forth in its destruction . . . ?

The Political Writings of Richard Cobden (London 1878), pp. 211–3.

Many members of the Government of Lord Aberdeen, formed in December 1852, were reluctant in 1854 to embark on war with Russia over disputes in the Near East trivial in themselves,[1] but Palmerston, who became Prime Minister in February 1855, had opinion in the country behind him, opinion which found expression in the Press and also in works of poets like Tennyson, who published *Maud* in 1855, and historians like Kinglake, who published *The Invasion of the Crimea* in 1863.

24: DEBATE IN THE HOUSE OF COMMONS
on the Queen's message announcing war with Russia

31 March 1854

LORD JOHN RUSSELL. Sir, in rising to move an answer to Her Majesty's Most Gracious Message, I have a deep sense of the solemn, I may say the awful, importance of the Motion that I am about to propose. It is now more than half a century since a Message of a

---

[1] In this connection the following story about Aberdeen himself is significant: " During his later years Lord Aberdeen was often haunted by melancholy thoughts. Some of his actions seemed strange even to those who knew him best. Among these was his persistent refusal to rebuild an ugly and dilapidated parish church on one of his estates. To all requests he returned a steady refusal, saying always ' I leave that for George ' (his son). Everyone thought his conduct very unusual and no one guessed the true reason for it. After his death a text was found, written and re-written by him on scraps of paper, which supplied the key to the mystery.

' And David said unto Solomon, My son, as for me, it was in my power to build a house unto the name of the Lord my God. But the word of the Lord came to me, saying, thou hast shed blood abundantly and has made great war: thou shalt not build an house unto my name, because thou hast shed much blood upon the earth in my sight.' (1 Chron. xxii. 7–8.) "
(Temperley; *England and the Near East—The Crimea* [London 1936], p. 385.)

similar import was brought to this House. For the period of nearly forty years this country has been in the enjoyment of the blessings of peace, and those blessings have been never more widely nor more extensively valued. The privileges of the people have been increased, their burdens have been diminished, and, with an increasing and prosperous commerce, wealth has been diffused throughout the country. . . .

I shall endeavour . . . to point to the course which Russia has pursued, and to show that, unless we are content to submit to the future aggrandisement of that Power, and, possibly, to the destruction of Turkey—whose integrity and independence have been so often declared essential to the stability of the system of Europe—we have no choice left us but to interpose by arms. . . .

[Her Majesty and the Emperor of the French] considered that the safety of Europe depended upon the maintenance of the equilibrium of which the integrity and independence of Turkey form a part. They considered that it would be impossible to maintain that integrity and independence if Russia was allowed unchecked and uninterrupted to impose her own terms upon Turkey. It was therefore decided by Her Majesty's Government . . . to advise Her Majesty to send down a Message to the Houses of Parliament, and at the same time to issue a declaration of war. That declaration of war has been issued. We can none of us be insensible to the gravity and importance of such a declaration—we should all have been glad to have avoided it; but I hold that, consistently with our position—consistently with our duties to Europe—consistently even with the general interests of this country, we cannot permit the aggrandisement of Russia to take any shape that her arms might enable it to assume. Sir, there are, I imagine, but few in this country who think that any other course was open to us. There are, I know, some who think that this country might remain altogether apart from the conflicts of other European nations; that we might be indifferent when the independence of a Power is assailed, when a country may be obliterated from the map of Europe, and some Power already great may obtain a fearful preponderance over the Powers of Europe. . . . But we, Sir, who are following the maxim which, since the time of William III has governed and actuated the councils of this country—we, who have believed that we have a part in the great question of the liberties and independence of Europe—we who believe that preponderance cannot safely be allowed to any one Power—we who believe it our duty to throw our weight into the scale in these conflicts—we who have seen this country rise to power, rise to reputation, rise I may also say, in moral greatness, by the assertion and maintenance of those doctrines—we who have seen the country support burdens and incur great sacrifices in the maintenance of these maxims—maxims which I believe to be connected not only with your honour and dignity, but with your very safety as a nation—we are not prepared to abandon our position in Europe, and we ask you, by agreeing to the address of tonight, to be firmly prepared to maintain it.

Hansard, Third Series, Vol. CXXXII, pp. 198–9.

MR. JOHN BRIGHT. If this phrase of the " balance of power " is to be always an argument for war, the pretext for war will never be wanting, and peace can never

be secure. Let anyone compare the power of this country with that of Austria now, and forty years ago. Will
anyone say that England, compared with Austria, is
not now three times as powerful as she was thirty or
forty years ago ? Austria has a divided people, bankrupt finances, and her credit is so low, that she cannot
draw a shilling out of her own territories; England has
a united people, national wealth rapidly increasing,
and a mechanical and productive power to which
that of Austria is as nothing. Might not Austria complain that we have disturbed the " balance of power "
because we are growing so much stronger from better
government, from the greater union of the people, from
wealth that is created by the hard labours and skill of
our population, and from the wonderful development
of the mechanical resources of the Kingdom, which is
seen on every side . . . ?

The United States may profit to a large extent by
the calamities which will befall us; whilst we, under
the miserable and lunatic idea that we are about to
set the worn-out Turkish empire on its legs, and permanently to sustain it against the aggressions of
Russia, are entangled in a war. Our trade will decay
and diminish—our people, suffering and discontented,
as in all former periods of war, will emigrate in increasing numbers to a country whose wise policy it is to
keep itself free from the entanglement of European
politics—to a country with whom rests the great question, whether England shall, for any long time, retain
that which she professes to value so highly—her great
superiority in industry and at sea. This whole notion
of " the balance of power " is a mischievous delusion
which has come down to us from past times; we ought
to drive it from our minds, and to consider the solemn

L 145

question of peace or war in more clear, more definite, and on far higher principles than any that are involved in the phrase, " the balance of power " . . .

The past events of our history have taught us that the intervention of this country in European wars is not only unnecessary, but calamitous; that we have rarely come out of such intervention having succeeded in the objects we fought for: that a debt of £800,000,000 sterling has been incurred by the policy which the noble Lord approves, apparently for no other reason than that it dates from the time of William III; and that, not debt alone has been incurred, but that we have left Europe at least as much in chains as before a single effort was made by us to rescue her from tyranny. I believe if this country, seventy years ago, had adopted the principle of non-intervention in every case where her interests were not directly and obviously assailed, she would have been saved from much of the pauperism and brutal crimes by which our Government and people have alike been disgraced. This country might have been a garden, every dwelling might have been of marble, and every person who treads its soil might have been sufficiently educated. We should indeed have had less of military glory. We might have had neither Trafalgar nor Waterloo; but we should have set a high example of a Christian nation, free in its isolation, courteous and just in its conduct towards all foreign States, and resting its policy on the unchangeable foundations of Christian morality.

Ibid., pp. 257–8, 267.

25: ALFRED, LORD TENNYSON. From *Maud*

Let it go or stay, so I wake to the higher aims
Of a land that has lost for a little her lust of gold,
And love of a peace that was full of wrongs and
    shames,
Horrible, hateful, monstrous, not to be told;
And hail once more to the banner of battle unroll'd!
Tho' many a light shall darken, and many shall weep
For those that are crush'd in the clashing of jarring
    claims,
Yet God's just wrath shall be wreak'd on a giant liar;
And many a darkness into the light shall leap,
And shine in the sudden making of splendid names,
And noble thought be freer under the sun.
And the heart of a people beat with one desire:
For the peace, that I deem'd no peace, is over and
    done,
And now by the side of the Black and the Baltic deep,
And deathful-grinning mouths of the fortress, flames
The blood-red blossom of war with a heart of fire.
Let it flame or fade, and the war roll down like a wind,
We have proved we have hearts in a cause, we are
    noble still,
And myself have awaked, as it seems, to the better
    mind;
It is better to fight for the good, than to rail at the ill;
I have felt with my native land, I am one with my
    kind,
I embrace the purpose of God, and the doom assign'd.

26. ALEXANDER WILLIAM KINGLAKE.

From *The Invasion of the Crimea*

ENGLAND has long been an enigma to the political students of the Continent, but after the summer of 1851 they began to imagine that they really at last understood her. They thought that she was falling from her place among nations; and indeed there were signs which might well lead a shallow observer to fancy that her ancient spirit was failing her. An army is but the limb of a nation, and it is no more given to a people to combine the possession of military strength with an unmeasured devotion to the arts of peace, than it is for a man to be feeble and helpless in the general condition of his body, and yet to have at his command a strong right arm for the convenience of self-defence. The strength of the right arm is as the strength of the man: the prowess of an army is as the valour and warlike spirit of the nation which gives it her flesh and blood. England, having suffered herself to grow forgetful of this truth, seemed, in the eyes of foreigners, to be declining. It was not the reduction of the military establishments which was the really evil sign: for—to say nothing of ancient times—the Swiss in Europe, and some of the States of the North American continent, have shown the world that a people which almost dispenses with a standing army may yet be among the most resolute and warlike of nations; but there was in England a general decrying of arms.

Well-meaning men harangued and lectured in this spirit. What they sincerely desired was a continuance of peace; but instead of taking the thought and acquiring the knowledge which might have qualified them to warn their fellow-countrymen against steps tending to a needless war, they squandered their indignation upon the deceased authors of former wars, and used language of such breadth that what they said was as applicable to one war as to another. At length they generated a sect called the " Peace Party," which denounced war in strong indiscriminate terms.

Moreover, at this time extravagant veneration was avowed for mechanical contrivances, and the very words which grateful nations had wrought from out of their hearts in praise of tried chiefs and heroes were plundered, as it were, from the warlike professions, and given to those who for their own gain could make the best goods. It was no longer enough to say that an honest tradesman was a valuable member of society, or that a man who contrived a good machine was ingenious. More was expected from those who had the utterance of the public feeling; and it was announced that " glory " and " honour "—nay, to prevent all mistake, " true honour " and " true glory "—were due to him who could produce the best articles of trade. At length, in the summer of 1851, it was made to appear to foreigners that this singular faith had demanded and obtained an outward sign of its State.[1] The foreigners were mistaken. The truth is that the English, in their exuberant strength and their carelessness about the strict import of words, are accustomed to indulge a certain extravagance in their demonstrations of public feeling; and this is the more

[1] i.e., in the Great Exhibition.

bewildering to foreign minds because it goes along with practical moderation and wisdom. What the English really meant was to give people an opportunity of seeing the new inventions and comparing all kinds of patterns, but, above all, to have a new kind of show, and bring about an immense gathering of people. Perhaps, too, in the secret hearts of many who were weary of tame life, there lurked a hope of animating tumults. This was all the English really meant. But the political philosophers of the Continent were re-solved to impute to the islanders a more profound intent. They saw in the festival a solemn renouncing of all such dominion as rests upon force. England, they thought, was closing her great career by a whimsical act of abdication; and it must be acknowledged that there was enough to confound men accustomed to lay stress upon symbols. For the glory of mechanic Arts, and in token of their conquest over nature, a cathedral of glass climbed high over the stately elms of Knights-bridge, enclosing them, as it were, in a casket the work of men's hands, and it was not thought wrong nor impious to give the work the sanction of a religious ceremony. It was by the Archbishop of Canterbury that the money-changers were brought back into the temple. Few protested. One man, indeed, abounding in Scripture, and inflamed with the sight of the glass Babel ascending to the skies, stood up and denounced the work, and foretold " wars " and " judgments." But he was a prophet speaking to the wrong genera-tion, and no one heeded him. Indeed, it seemed likely that the soundness of his mind would be questioned; and if he went on to foretell that within three years England would be engaged in a bloody war springing out of a dispute about a key and a silver star, he was probably adjudged to be mad, for the whole country at the time felt sure of its peaceful temper.

Certainly it was a hard task for the sagacity of a foreigner to pierce through these outward signs, and see that, notwithstanding them all, the old familiar "Eastern Question" might be so used as to make it rekindle the warlike ardour of England. Even for Englishmen, until long after the beginning of 1853, it was difficult to foresee how the country would be willing to act in regard to the defence of Turkey; and the representatives of foreign Powers accredited to St. James's might be excused if they assured their Courts that England was deep in pursuits which would hinder her from all due assertion of her will as a great European Power.

Thus foreigners came to believe that the English nature was changed, and that for the future the country would always be tame in Europe; and it chanced that, in the beginning of the year 1853, they were strengthened in their faith by observing the structure of the Ministry then recently formed; for Lord Palmerston, whose name had become associated with the idea of a resolute and watchful policy, was banished to the Home Office, and the Prime Minister was Lord Aberdeen, the same statesman who had held the seals of the Foreign Office in former years, when Austria was vainly entreating England to join with her in defending the Sultan. The Emperor Nicholas heard the tidings of Lord Aberdeen's elevation to the premiership with a delight which he did not suppress. Yet this very event, as will be seen, was a main link in the chain of causes which was destined to draw the Czar into war, and bring him in misery to the grave.

A. W. Kinglake, The Invasion of the Crimea, Vol. I
(3rd Edition, Edinburgh, 1863), pp. 78–82.

II

... The stake which England holds in the world makes it of deep moment to her to avert disorder among nations; and, on the other hand, her insular station in Europe, joined with the possession of more than sufficing empire in other regions of the world, keeps her clear of all thought of territorial aggrandisement in this quarter of the globe. And although it is the duty of all the rest of the great Powers as well as of England to endeavour towards the maintenance of of peace and order, yet, inasmuch as there is no other great State without some sort of lurking ambition which may lead it into temptation, the fidelity of the Continental guardians of the peace can always be brought into question. Suspicions of this kind are often fanciful, but the fears from which they spring are too well founded in the nature of things to be safely regarded as frivolous; and the result is, that the great island Power is the one which, by the well-informed statesmen of the Continent, is looked to as the surest safeguard against wrong. Europe leans, Europe rests, on this faith. So, the moment it is made to appear that for any reason England is disposed to abdicate, or to suspend for a while, the performance of her European duties, that moment the wrong-doer sees his opportunity and begins to stir. Those who dread him, missing the accustomed safeguard of England, turn whither they can for help, and, failing better plans of safety, they perhaps try hard to make terms with the spoiler. Monarchs find that to conspire for gain of territory, or to have other princes conspiring against them, is the alternative presented to their choice. The system of

Europe becomes decomposed, and war follows. Therefore, exactly in proportion as England values the peace
of Europe, she ought to abstain from every word and
from every sign which tends to give the wrong-doer a
hope of acquiescence. Unhappily this duty was not
understood by the more ardent friends of peace; and
they imagined that they would serve their cause by
entreating England to abstain from every conflict
which did not menace their own shores—nay, even by
permitting themselves to vow and declare that this was
the policy truly loved by the English race. Moreover,
by blending their praises of peace with fierce invective
against public men, they easily drew applause from
assembled multitudes, and so caused the foreigner to
believe that they really spoke the voice of a whole
people, or at all events of great masses, and that
England was no longer a Power which would interfere
with spoliation in Europe. The fatal effect which this
belief produced upon the peace of Europe has been
shown. But the evil produced by the excesses of the
Peace Party did not end there. It is the nature of
excesses to beget excesses of strange complexion; and
just as a too rigid sanctity has always been followed by
a too scandalous profligacy, so, by the law of reaction,
the doctrines of the Peace Party tended to bring into
violent life that keen warlike spirit which soon became
one of the main obstacles to the restoration of tranquillity. Therefore England, it must be acknowledged,
did much to bring on the war; first, by the want of
moderation and prudence with which she seemed to
declare her attachment to the cause of peace—and
afterwards by the exceeding eagerness with which she
coveted the strife.

Ibid., pp. 485 sqq.

27 October 1860

The cause of Italian unity was one that appealed to Liberals of all shades in England. Diplomatic encouragement was given by Lord John Russell, the Foreign Secretary in Palmerston's second Administration, to Garibaldi's successful action in invading the Kingdom of Naples and winning the crown for King Victor Emmanuel. The dispatch that follows was published shortly after it was written and received a popular reception both in England and in Italy. Odo Russell (later Lord Ampthill) wrote to his uncle from Rome on December 1st: " Ever since your famous dispatch of the 27th you are blessed night and morning by twenty millions of Italians. I could not read it myself without deep emotion, and the moment it was published in Italian, thousands of people copied it from each other to carry it to their homes and weep over it for joy and gratitude in the bosom of their families, away from brutal memories and greasy priests. . . ." (See Spencer Walpole: Life of Lord John Russell. ·London 1889. Vol. II, p. 328.)

. . . The large questions which appear to them [Her Majesty's Government] to be at issue are these: Were the people of Italy justified in asking the assistance of the King of Sardinia to relieve them from Governments with which they were discontented ? and was the King of Sardinia justified in furnishing the assistance of his arms to the people of the Roman and Neapolitan States ?

There appear to have been two motives which have

induced the people of the Roman and Neapolitan States to have joined willingly in the subversion of their Government. The first of these was, that the Governments of the Pope and the King of the Two Sicilies provided so ill for the administration of justice, the protection of personal liberty and the general welfare of their people, that their subjects looked forward to the overthrow of their rulers as a necessary preliminary to all improvement in their condition.

The second motive was, that a conviction had spread since the year 1849, that the only manner in which Italians could secure their independence of foreign control was by forming one strong Government for the whole of Italy. The struggle of Charles Albert in 1848, and the sympathy which the present King of Sardinia has shown for the Italian cause, have naturally caused the association of the name of Victor Emmanuel with the single authority under which the Italians aspire to live.

Looking at the question in this view, Her Majesty's Government must admit that the Italians themselves are the best judges of their own interests.

That eminent jurist Vattel, when discussing the lawfulness of the assistance given by the United Provinces to the Prince of Orange when he invaded England, and overturned the throne of James II, says, " The authority of the Prince of Orange had doubtless an influence on the deliberations of the States-General, but it did not lead them to the commission of an act of injustice; for when a people from good reasons take up arms against an oppressor, it is but an act of justice and generosity to assist brave men in the defence of their liberties."

Therefore, according to Vattel, the question resolves

itself into this: Did the people of Naples and of the Roman States take up arms against their Governments for good reasons?

Upon this grave matter Her Majesty's Government hold that the people in question are themselves the best judges of their own affairs. Her Majesty's Government do not feel justified in declaring that the people of Southern Italy had not good reasons for throwing off their allegiance to their former Governments; Her Majesty's Government cannot, therefore, pretend to blame the King of Sardinia for assisting them. There remains, however, a question of fact. It is asserted by the partizans of the fallen Governments that the people of the Roman States were attached to the Pope, and the people of the Kingdom of Naples to the Dynasty of Francis II, but that Sardinian Agents and foreign adventurers have by force and intrigue subverted the thrones of those Sovereigns.

It is difficult, however, to believe, after the astonishing events that we have seen, that the Pope and the King of the Two Sicilies possessed the love of their people. How was it, one must ask, that the Pope found it impossible to levy a Roman army, and that he was forced to rely almost entirely upon foreign mercenaries? How did it happen, again, that Garibaldi conquered nearly all Sicily with 2,000 men, and marched from Reggio to Naples with 5,000? How, but from the universal disaffection of the people of the Two Sicilies?

Neither can it be said that this testimony of the popular will was capricious or causeless. Forty years ago the Neapolitan people made an attempt regularly and temperately to reform their Government, under the reigning Dynasty. The Powers of Europe assembled at Lybach resolved, with the exception of England, to put down this attempt by force. It was put down, and a large foreign army of occupation was left in the Two Sicilies to maintain social order. In 1848 the Neapolitan people again attempted to secure liberty under the Bourbon Dynasty, but their best patriots atoned, by an imprisonment of ten years, for the offence of endeavouring to free their country. What wonder, then, that in 1860 the Neapolitans, mistrustful and resentful, should throw off the Bourbons, as in 1688 England had thrown off the Stuarts?

It must be admitted, undoubtedly, that the severance of the ties which bind together a Sovereign and his subjects is in itself a misfortune. Notions of allegiance become confused; the succession of the Throne is disputed; adverse parties threaten the peace of society; rights and pretensions are opposed to each other, and mar the harmony of the State. Yet it must be acknowledged on the other hand, that the Italian revolution has been conducted with singular temper and forbearance. The subversion of existing power has not been followed, as is too often the case, by an outburst of popular vengeance. The extreme views of democrats have nowhere prevailed. Public opinion has checked the excesses of the public triumph. The venerated forms of Constitutional Monarchy have been associated with the name of a Prince who represents an ancient and glorious Dynasty.

Such having been the causes and concomitant circumstances of the revolution of Italy, Her Majesty's Government can see no sufficient ground for the severe censure with which Austria, France, Prussia, and Russia have visited the acts of the King of Sardinia. Her Majesty's Government will turn their eyes rather to the gratifying prospect of a people building up the edifice of their liberties, and consolidating the work of their independence, amid the sympathies and good wishes of Europe.

Printed in Temperley and Penson, *Foundations of British Foreign Policy*, pp. 223–5.

28: LORD ROBERT CECIL. Essay on Foreign Policy

April 1864

In 1860 Lord Robert Cecil, later, as Marquess of Salisbury, to be Foreign Secretary and Prime Minister, began to publish regular political articles in the *Quarterly Review*.

The extract printed below is an attack on Palmerston's and Russell's foreign policy in its last stage—a stage which saw verbal encouragement unaccompanied by material help given to the Polish revolt in 1863, and to the Danes in their quarrel with Prussia and Austria over Schleswig-Holstein which ended in the war of 1864.

WHATEVER differences may exist as to the policy which this country ought to have pursued in the various conflicts by which Europe and America have been recently disturbed, few will be found to dispute that she occupies a position in the eyes of foreign Powers which she has never occupied before during the memory of any man now living. We have been brought up to believe that England's voice is of weight in the councils of the world. Our national pride has been fed by histories of the glorious deeds of our fathers, when single-handed they defied the conqueror to whom every other European nation had been compelled to humble itself. Resting upon these great deeds of past days, we have borne ourselves proudly in our dealings with other countries, speaking in the tone of those who have proved by action the weight and significance of their words. Until recently the rank we have thus assumed has been accorded to us readily. In spite of reduced armaments and of the predominance of the Quaker interest in our councils, the authority of England remained for a long time undiminished. Those who remembered the Great War refused to believe that England could not make good her threats or her promises if she thought fit; and, therefore, her representations in many negotiations of deep European moment were listened to with respect. Whatever the language in which they were couched, whatever the wisdom of the statesmen from whom they came, Foreign Ministers never forgot that they were backed up, in case of need, by the fleet that had baffled Napoleon and the army that had fought at Waterloo.

But this condition of things has lamentably changed. No one can be in the least degree conversant with the periodical literature of foreign countries, or hear ever so little of the common talk of foreign society, without being painfully aware that an entire revolution has taken place in the tone of foreign thought in regard to the position of England. Her influence in the councils of Europe has passed away. The reputation of material power upon which that influence was based has suddenly evaporated. It now fails to make even the faintest impression upon States that formerly yielded themselves absolutely to its spell. Our diplomatists are at least as active as they were at any former time. Their vigilance is as keen, their interference is as incessant, their language is bolder and far more insolent than it was in better times. But the impulse is gone which gave it force. That appearance of warlike

power which used to give dignity to its imperious tones
no longer imposes upon its hearers. Its vehemence of
language falls dead and impotent upon minds pene-
trated with the conviction that the storm which is
assailing them is nothing but words—brave words
possibly, but still only words. The language of speakers and writers out of doors faithfully echoes the views
that guide the statesmen of foreign Cabinets. Englishmen were, perhaps, never very popular on the
Continent. Satirists and wits have always amused
themselves with caricaturing the somewhat angular
peculiarities that mark our national character, and
the portrait was seldom flattering. But still the re-
proaches expressed or implied were of a kind that is
not very difficult to bear. Pride, uncouthness, fool-
hardiness, form the staple of the sarcasms levelled at
us by foreign writers. Undue roughness and violence
were the mark at which they were aimed. They were
derogatory rather to our claims to the polish of civilization than to any more sterling qualities. Sometimes
other blots were hit—our supposed perfidy, our selfishness, our shopkeeping propensities. But, whatever
else was said of us, no one ever thought of impugning
an Englishman's courage. If the Great War had done
little for our popularity, it had at least left deeply
graven on the minds of Continental populations that
we could fight. But all this is changed now. All the
respect for our national character which was founded
upon a belief in its bull-dog characteristics has dis-
appeared. Our courage is not only disbelieved, but it
is ridiculed as an imposture that has been found out.
English bravado and English cowardice are the common staple of popular caricatures. The Englishman
furnishes to Continental wits the same sort of standing

butt that the Yankee presented to us some three years ago. The estimate of the English character that is felt in every circle and class of society abroad, and expressed without reserve by the press, may be summed up in one phrase, as a portentous mixture of bounce and baseness.

It may be worth while for those who are the subject of such a change of view to investigate its causes. However satisfied we may be that it has no just foundation in any real alteration of the national character, our repute with other nations cannot be a matter of indifference to us. We will set aside the feelings which may be supposed to have inspired a Castlereagh or a Chatham. Such ideas may seem antiquated now, or at least, unsuitable for an era of octogenarian statesmanship.[1] But, upon the least ideal and most commercial views, it is not convenient to be despized. The defence of a high reputation is, after all, a cheap one. A nation which is known to be willing, as well as able, to defend itself will probably escape attack. Where the disposition to fight in case of need is wanting, or is dependent upon some casual and fleeting gust of passion, the political gamblers who speculate in war will naturally be inclined to invest in the venture of aggression. The policy which invites contempt seldom fails to earn a more substantial punishment. It is rarely permitted to take refuge in the cynical adage that hard words break no bones. Contempt is soon followed by open insult, and insult meekly borne draws injury quickly after it. And there is a point where injury becomes intolerable, and even the most submissive must turn. Indifference to reputation seems the cheapest and easiest policy while it is being pursued; but it

[1] Palmerston was 80 in 1864.

only deserves that character until the limit of tameness
has been reached. The time must come at last when
aggression must be resisted, and then, when it is too
late, the expensiveness of a name for cowardice forces
itself upon every apprehension. We shall enter, therefore, without any fear of being suspected of unduly
material prepossessions, upon a brief examination of
the foreign policy by which the Government have
brought the fame of England to the condition in which
it now finds itself. We fervently desire peace; but we
desire it in the only way in which it can be had. Peace
without honour is not only a disgrace, but, except as a
temporary respite, it is a chimera.

The reasons of this change in European opinion towards us, so humiliating to our feelings, so dangerous
to our security, are not difficult to find. Large bodies
of educated men are not often entirely wrong in their
judgments, though the truth in them is mixed up with
error. Our critics abroad are mistaken in believing
that the character of the English people is changed
from what it was in times that are now historical. The
inhabitants of these islands are as sensitive to the preservation of their honour and as keen to resent any
insult passed upon it as they have been at any previous
period. And yet it is not the less true that our policy
has really borne the character which has been affixed
to it abroad. It has been essentially a policy of cowardice. This word is often loosely used, and, in a mere
invective, may only be the imputation with which an
opponent tries to blacken a policy of moderation. We
have no intention of using it in so lax a sense. A policy
of moderation is one to which no Christian man could
raise an objection; and there are few countries bound
over in such heavy securities as this to do its duty in

that respect as a Christian nation. But a policy of moderation and a policy of cowardice, though often confounded in the angry strife of words, are in reality easily distinguished by those who do not wish to confound them. Consistency is the simple test that will unerringly separate true moderation from its base counterfeit. Courtesy of language, a willingness to concede, a reluctance to take offence, if they are impartially extended to all, will always, even when they are carried to excess, command respect and admiration. In the same way, a tribute, partly of fear, partly of honour, will always be paid to the combativeness that has no respect of persons. It is only when the two qualities of heroism and meekness are cunningly combined that they earn unmitigated contempt. There are occasions when the reproach of cowardice must be employed even by those who have the most earnest horror of bloodshed. If the word has a meaning, it is applicable to a policy which, according to the power of its opponent, is either valiant or submissive—which is dashing, exacting, dauntless to the weak, and timid and cringing to the strong. . . .

From *Essays by The Late Marquess of Salisbury, K.G.*, " Foreign Politics " (London 1905), pp. 151–6.

PART V

GLADSTONE AND LIBERAL PRINCIPLES IN FOREIGN POLICY, 1875–80

THE Crimean War and the Treaty of Paris that ended it in 1856 had not solved the Eastern Question. In 1875 revolts broke out in Bosnia and Bulgaria, leading, in 1876, to war between Serbia and Turkey, and re-opening the whole question of Turkey-in-Europe. This time it was the Conservatives who urged vigorous action against the Russians (who declared war on Turkey in April 1877) in favour of the Turks.

The events in the Balkans in 1875 called Gladstone from his retirement and he led a vigorous campaign in favour of the rights of small nations, addressing public meetings and writing pamphlets in which he expressed his views on foreign policy, views that found final expression in his speeches to his constituents in Midlothian in the General Election of 1880.

The pamphlet on " Bulgarian Horrors " was finished early in September 1876, and " from that time forward," Gladstone wrote later, "until the final consummation in 1879–80, I made the eastern question the main business of my life." The effects of Gladstone's agitation were remarkable. Gladstone wrote on 26th November " Yesterday night in the Tory town of Liverpool, when *Othello* was being acted, and the words were recited ' The Turks are drowned,' the audience rose in enthusiasm and interrupted the performance for some time with their cheering. These things are not without meaning."[1]

The meeting at St. James' Hall on December 8th 1876, was a great rally in favour of Gladstone's policy, attended by people from all parts of the country: Gladstone spoke for one and a half hours. The chairmen were the Duke of Westminster and Lord Shaftesbury, and among Gladstone's supporters were the historians Bryce, Freeman, Lecky, and J. R. Green, William Morris, Ruskin and Burne-Jones, Trollope and Browning, Darwin, Carlyle and the philosopher Herbert Spencer.

[1] See Morley, *Life of Gladstone*, Book VII, Chapter IV.

29: WILLIAM EWART GLADSTONE.

Bulgarian Horrors

1876

IT would not be practicable, even if it were honourable, to disguise the real character of what we want
from the government. It is a change of attitude and
policy, nothing less. We want them to undo and efface
that too just impression, which, while keeping their
own countrymen so much in the dark, they have succeeded in propagating throughout Europe, that we
are determined supporters of the Turk, and that, declaring his " integrity and independence " essential to
" British interests," we have winked hard, and shall
wink, if such be, harder still, according to the exigen-
cies of the case, alike at his crimes and at his impotence.
We want to place ourselves in harmony with the general sentiment of civilized mankind, instead of being
any longer, as we seem to be, the Evil Genius which
dogs, and mars, and baffles it. We want to make the
Turk understand that, in conveying the impression by
word and act to his mind, the British Government have
misunderstood, and, therefore, have misrepresented,
the sense of the British people.

But this change is dependent on an emphatic expression of the national sentiment, which is but beginning to be heard. It has grown from a whisper to a
sound; it will grow from a sound to a peal. . . . It is
melancholy, but it is also true, that we, who upon this
Eastern ground fought with Russia, and thought Austria slack, and Germany all but servile, have actually

for months past been indebted, and are even now indebted, to all or some of these very powers, possibly to Russia most among them, for having played the part which we think specially our own, in resistance to tyranny, in defending the oppressed, in labouring for the happiness of mankind. I say the time has come for us to emulate Russia by sharing in her good deeds, and to reserve our opposition until she shall visibly endeavour to turn them to evil account.

There is no reason to apprehend serious difficulty in the Councils of Europe on this subject. All the Powers, except ourselves, have already been working in this direction. Nor is there any ground to suppose that the Ottoman Government will tenaciously resist a scheme based on the intention to do all in its favour that its own misconduct, and the fearful crimes of its trusted agents have left possible. . . . The promises of a Turkish Ministry given simply to Europe are generally good; those given to its own subjects or concerning its own affairs are, without imputing absolute mendacity, of such fixed and demonstrated worthlessness, that any Ambassador or any State, who should trust them, must come under suspicion of nothing less than fraud by wilful connivance. The engagement of a Turkish Ministry, taken in concert with Europe, that Bulgaria or any other province, shall now settle and hereafter conduct its own local government and affairs, would carry within itself that guarantee of its own execution. The only question is, whether it would be given or withheld. I am disposed to believe it would be given, not withheld; and for this reason, I know of no case in which Turkey has refused to accede to the consent of United Europe, nay, even of less than United Europe, if Europe was not in actual schism

168

with itself under unwise or factious influences. In the matter of Greece, in the Union of the Principalities[1] after the Crimean War, and in the conduct of its relations (for example, with Persia and with Egypt,) there has been abundant proof that the Ottoman Party is no more disposed than other governments, in the homely phrase, to drive its head against a brick wall. It has known how to yield, not ungracefully, to real necessity, without provoking violence. . . .

But I return to, and I end with, that which is the Omega as well as the Alpha of this great and most mournful case. An old servant of the Crown and State, I entreat my countrymen, upon whom far more than perhaps any other people of Europe, it depends, to require, and to insist, that our Government, which has been working in one direction, shall work in the other, and shall apply all its vigour to concur with the other States of Europe in obtaining the extinction of the Turkish executive power in Bulgaria. Let the Turks now carry away their abuses in the only possible manner, namely by carrying off themselves. Their Zaptiehs and their Mudirs, their Bimbashis and their Yusbachis, their Kaimakams and their Pashas, one and all, bag and baggage, shall, I hope, clear out from the province they have desolated and profaned. This thorough riddance, this most blessed deliverance, is the only reparation we can make for the memory of those heaps on heaps of dead; to the violated purity alike of matron, of maiden, and of child; to the civilization that has been affronted and shamed; to the laws of God, or, if you like, of Allah; to the moral sense of mankind at large. There is not a criminal in a European gaol, there is not a cannibal in the South

[1] The Principalities of Moldavia and Wallachia, united to form Roumania.

Sea Islands, whose indignation would not rise and overboil at the recital of what has been done, which has too late been examined, but which remains unavenged; which has left behind all the foul and all the fierce passions that produced it, and which may again spring up, in another murderous harvest, from the soil soaked and reeking with blood, and in the air tainted with every imaginable deed of crime and shame. That such things should be done once is a damning disgrace to the portion of our race which did them; that a door should be left open for their even-so-barely possible repetition would spread that shame over the whole. . . .

W. E. Gladstone, *Bulgarian Horrors and the Question of the East* (London 1876), pp. 57–62.

30: WILLIAM EWART GLADSTONE.
Speech at St. James' Hall

8 December 1876

The meeting at St. James' Hall on December 8th 1876, was a great rally in favour of Gladstone's policy, attended by people from all parts of the country: Gladstone spoke for one and a half hours. The chairmen were the Duke of Westminster and Lord Shaftesbury, and among Gladstone's supporters were the historians Bryce, Freeman, Lecky, and J. R. Green, William Morris, Ruskin and Burne-Jones, Trollope and Browning, Darwin, Carlyle and Herbert Spencer.

. . . I do not object to the language of those who say that Russia ought to be jealously watched. As to the Emperor of Russia, I look upon him as a gentleman and a Sovereign who has distinguished his reign by some of the noblest acts in the annals of civilization. If I speak of the Russian people I believe their hearts to be just as susceptible to generous emotions as those of any other people, and I believe they have during the present year been signally and generously swayed by those emotions. I admit, however, that wherever there is an official class and a great standing army there exist the materials out of which may come intrigues and designs of aggrandisement. I think it is our duty, with the temptations that Russia derives from her neighbourhood to Turkey, that she should be jealously and carefully watched. But I hold that the best mode of watching Russia or Austria is to become competitors with them for the affections of the Christian populations of the East of Europe. (Cheers.) That is my specific and that is equivalent to saying, " Let us do exactly the opposite of everything that has been done by the British Government during the last twenty years." Do not let us denounce the Servians and say their war is about the most wicked war upon record. (Cheers.) Do not let us hold, as was held by the Prime Minister, that the atrocities in Bulgaria were the consequence of what he called an invasion of Bulgaria. Do not let us teach that the rebellion in Bosnia and the rebellion in Herzogovina were the works of foreign emissaries. By these proceedings, and others like them, we are alienating and estranging the hearts of these people, and we are driving them with all the power at our command into the hands and into the arms of Russia. . . . I have stated that we are not here to lay down plans for the government of those Provinces, and to teach a policy to Lord Salisbury or to anybody else; but I will venture to place a model before his eyes, and that is the model supplied by Mr. Canning in the case of Greece. That is a subject which has in some degree passed from the memory of England, such is the rapid succession of public interests and public events. But it has not passed from the memory of Greece, and the recollection of that distinguished man is a star of hope in the firmament of the oppressed populations in those countries allied with the Greek races that have not yet obtained even the first beginnings of their freedom. (Cheers.) What was the character of the policy of Mr. Canning ? It consisted entirely in these three things. He first sought to acquire the confidence of the Greeks and to teach them to look to England as their protector. He did acquire it by the simplest process in the world—namely, by showing that he was ready to receive it. They had sympathy with us that they could not have with Russia, because although they have a closer contact in religion with Russia, yet with respect to that great question of civil and social institutions upon which so much of the happiness of life depends, it must always be recollected that these Greeks, these Slavs, these Roumanians, have one great point in common—their social and political opinions are entirely popular, liberal, perhaps democratic. Mr. Canning challenged and obtained their confidence by the most formal proceeding they were capable of taking—committing solemnly to Great Britain the charge of their infant happiness as a state. What did Mr. Canning do upon that? He instantly assumed a bold initiative. . . . Having assumed this initiative, what was his next proceeding? It was to invoke that aid of Russia (Hear, Hear). He invited the concert of Europe, but before doing so the Government of which he was Foreign Minister sent the Duke of Wellington to St. Petersburgh, and in 1826 he obtained the cordial aid of Russia. England and Russia carried on the work together. They solicited the aid of Europe. They obtained the aid of France. Now, I say that chapter in our history is one of the most satisfactory on which we can look back, and the vital and distinguishing point of that chapter is the generous confidence, I may also say the prudent confidence, which led Mr. Canning to seek the aid of Russia as beyond and above all things necessary in order to a good settlement [*sic*] of the question of the establishment of Greek liberty. (Cheers.) . . .

We bring that model into painful contrast with the policy that has been pursued this year. We may well say in the words of Shakespeare:

" Look on this picture and on this."

Most different are they indeed; but yet, it is not, I
hope, too late to return from the worse path to the
better. . . . It is indeed strange. A great work of
liberation is proceeding in the East. One would have
thought that the simple announcement that there was
such a work going on would have implied that
England was the first in its prosecution. (Hear, Hear.)
What course are we to take? Are we to resist it?
Are we to abstain? Are we to acquiesce? No, I say;
but let us enter into it with vigour of heart and purpose; promote it with all our soul and with all our
might. Is not this the business of England . . . ? We
talk of traditional policy. It is the traditional policy of
this country to support the Turk. I know not where
that policy was in 1826, when Mr. Canning formed his
alliance with the Emperor of Russia, or in 1827, when
the battle of Navarino was fought. But this I know,
that there is a higher and broader traditional policy;
that traditional policy was not complicity with guilty
power, but was sympathy with suffering weakness.
(Cheers.) Cast your eye over Europe and see whether
that is not the fact. We see a liberated and a united
Italy. (Cheers.) We never spent one life on the
Italian's coast, yet he regards us as having powerfully
promoted the emancipation of his country. Look at
Belgium, where, not by fighting, but by the masterly
policy in the main of Lord Palmerston, you have a
free State whose Government and institutions may
challenge comparison with the whole civilized world.
I am far from saying we have taken out a commission
of universal knight-errantry. But this is not a case
where we are thrown simply on the general principles
of benevolence. This is a case where we have given a

conditional support to the Turkish Power, and where the conditions have been forgotten and betrayed. It is a case, therefore, of positive obligation; and under the slightest pressure of that obligation I say that if long suffering and long oppressed humanity in these Provinces is at length lifting itself from the ground and trying again to contemplate the heavens, it is our business to assist the work; it is our business to acknowledge our obligation, to take part in the burden; and it is our privilege to claim for our country a share in the honour and in the fame. This acknowledgement of duty, this attempt to realize honour, is what we, at least, shall endeavour to obtain from our government; and to nothing less than this, I believe, shall we who are here assembled be, under any circumstance, persuaded to say " Content."

The Times, Saturday 9 December 1876.

Gladstone's views were opposed not only by Lord Beaconsfield and his Government but also by the Queen herself and those sections of public opinion (especially in London) recorded in the popular song that gave its name to " Jingoism ". But a group of Radicals, of whom Sir Charles Dilke was the chief spokesman, also felt that they could not follow Gladstone. " He marvelled," Dilke said in a speech to his constituents, " to see Radicals, for years the enemies of Russian autocracy, propose the immediate adoption of the policy of Canon Liddon [Canon of St. Paul's and an enthusiastic Gladstonian] and of the Emperor Alexander," and he wrote later " Although I was the first politician to make a speech upon the Bulgarian massacres I afterwards refused to follow Mr. Gladstone into what was called the " atrocity agitation ", because I feared that we should find ourselves plunged into a war with Turkey in alliance with Russia, of which I should have disapproved." Dilke had first-hand knowledge of Russia.[1]

31 : QUEEN VICTORIA. Memorandum

7 September 1877

BALMORAL, 7th Sept. 1877.—The Turco-Russian War is unexampled in its savageness, while its commencement was most iniquitous, being merely the result of the Emperor of Russia's declaring he could *not* accept a slap in the face (" *un soufflet* ") from the Turks, when they refused the proposals of the Conference. For this he has plunged his *own* nation as well

[1] See Stephen Gwynne and Gertrude Tuckwell, *The Life of Sir Charles Dilke* (London 1917), Vol. I, Chapter XIV.

as the Turkish Empire into *one* of the most *bloody wars* ever known, and which *no one* thought *possible* in this century. Under the cloak of RELIGION and under the pretence of obtaining just treatment for the so-called " Christians " of the principalities, but who are far worse than the Mussulmans, and who moreover had been *excited* to revolt by General Ignatieff, who prevented regular troops being sent out to quell the revolt, leading thereby to the so-called " Bulgarian atrocities " as the irregular troops were sent out, this *war of extermination* (for that it is) has been iniquitously commenced!

The question *now* arises whether in the *interests of humanity*, justice, and of the *British Empire*, this is to be allowed to go on to the bitter end; *merely* to *remain neutral*, and to avoid *all interference* ?

The Queen is *most decidedly* of opinion that this should *not be*. When it is clear that Russia is not inclined to make even an offer for peace, but to press on for two campaigns, the Queen thinks we *ought* to *declare* that, having taken part in all the negotiations previous to the war, we feel *determined* to put *an end* to so horrible a *slaughter*, which the longer it lasts the more savage it will become, and the more difficult to stop. We should then propose *certain* terms *recapitulating* the disinterested *protestations* of *Russia*, and should at the same time say that, *if these* are rejected, we shall support Turkey in defence of her capital, and in *preventing* her *extermination*.

We should state this to the *other Powers*, *asking them* to *join us* in *preventing* further bloodshed *either* by *enforcing our terms* by negotiation or else by *force* of *arms*. That we shall be *drawn* into the *conflict* if it goes on is *certain*, and that it will be far less serious and far less likely to cause a general European war if we pronounce ourselves in time.

The Cabinet should be asked to agree beforehand to *this line* of action when the time comes, and no fear of the Opposition, which has done its worst, should deter this country from doing her duty to humanity, and to her own Empire, which would be most seriously jeopardized by a continuation of our present policy.

The Letters of Queen Victoria, Second Series, Vol. II (London 1926), pp. 567–8.

32: BENJAMIN DISRAELI, EARL OF BEACONS-FIELD. Speech in Debate on Queen's Speech

House of Lords, 17 January 1878

NOW, my Lords, let me say one word upon a point on which the noble Earl (Granville) has dwelt much, and that is " conditional neutrality "—a neutrality conditional upon British interests being regarded and maintained. The noble Earl says . . . that the greatest of British interests is peace. Well, that was a felicitous expression, but it was an expression of rhetoric; but the noble Earl takes it to be a statistical fact, as if he found it in a Blue Book. The noble Earl thereon says that if peace is a British interest, it is also a European interest—it is an Austrian interest, it is an Italian interest, it is a French interest—in short, it is a universal interest. But the noble Earl rode off upon a mere trick of rhetoric, because we know very well when we talk of " British interests " we mean material British interests—interests of that character which are sources of the wealth or securities for the strength of the country. We do not want to be informed that the cardinal virtues are British interests. We possess and and endeavour to exercise them, but they have not their peculiar character which the British interests that we refer to possess. Then we are told that it is a contracted and selfish view of affairs to suppose our interests peculiar to this country, or, if they are peculiar, that we ought to be silent on the subject, and put them away in a corner. All I can say is, that if our conduct in this subject in defining what this country is interested in brings the imputation of selfishness, selfishness cannot be justly imputed to England alone. I do not know that there is any other country that has not very frankly declared that it has acted, and is acting, on the same principle. . . .

There are two kinds of isolation. There is an isolation that comes from decay, that comes from infirmity, that is a sign of impending insignificance—and all those symptoms which denote a falling or an expiring State. But there is also an isolation for a State which may arise from qualities very different—from self-confidence, from extreme energy, from abounding resources, and, above all from the inspiration of a great cause. This country has before this been isolated. In the early years of this century it was isolated: but how and why was it isolated ? It was isolated at the commencement of this century because among the craven communities of Europe it alone asserted and vindicated the cause of national independence. It was a great cause which your forefathers then maintained; and however depressed trade may be, whatever may be the circumstances brought forward to enervate the national mind—whatever may be the considerations introduced to prevent you from acting as your forefathers then acted—it may be your duty to follow in their footsteps. If that cause were again at stake, if there were a Power that threatened the peace of the world with a predominance fatal to public liberty and national independence, I feel confident that your Lordships would not be afraid of the charge of being isolated if you stood alone in maintaining such a cause and in fighting for such precious interests.

Hansard, Third Series, Vol. ccxxxvii, pp. 34–5, 39–40.

33: LORD BEACONSFIELD. From a Letter to Queen Victoria

8 March 1878

. . . Lord Beaconsfield is of opinion, that, throughout the transactions of the last two years, much too much consideration has been given to the disposition of other Powers. England is quite strong enough, when the nation is united as it is now, to vindicate and assert her own rights and interests. There have been terrible opportunities lost, and terrible acts of weakness committed, by us during these two years, but the nation was perplexed, bewildered, and half-hearted. The nation is so no longer. She is fresh, united, and full of resources, and a state of affairs must be substituted for that which has been destroyed and displaced. We must think less of Bismarks and Andrassys and Gortchakoffs,[1] and more of our own energies and resources. We must rebuild, and on stronger foundations than before, for doubtless they were nearly worn out. Your Majesty will soon have a navy superior to all the navies united of the world, and, in a short time, an army most efficient, not contemptible in number, and with a body of officers superior to that of any existing force. . . .

G. E. Buckle, *The Life of Benjamin Disraeli, Earl of Beaconsfield*, Vol. VI (London 1920), p. 256.

[1] Bismarck was the German Chancellor; Andrassy and Gortchakoff were the Austro-Hungarian and Russian Foreign Ministers respectively.

34: SIR CHARLES DILKE. *The Eastern Question*
1878

I INVITE you to recognize in the present war a conflict between two corrupt and cruel governments, with neither of which can Liberals feel sympathy, but behind one of which are ranged powerful forces of the future. . . .

. . . What is the Russian power with which the Liberals of England are to strike alliance? It is the power which has been throughout history the most constant upholder of absolutism in Europe. It is the only European power which has to this day no representative system, and which continues to be an absolute autocracy of the purest type. It is the power which crushes Poland; the power which crushed Hungary for Austria. . . .

. . . Looking, then, to all the facts, I think that we are justified, not, indeed, in fear of Russia, but in a certain measure of suspicion. So far as liberals are concerned, an absence of cordial sympathy with such a Government seems natural. The *Spectator* has been the most strongly anti-Turkish of our leading journals, yet the *Spectator* of November 4th [1877] confirms my view upon this point. It speaks of the Russian Government as being " leavened with barbarism." " The Court, judged by its record throughout history, is undoubtedly tainted with faithlessness; the Executive, military and civil, is very careless to human suffering. . . . For ourselves, we believe that Russian faithlessness in promises and Russian callousness when provoked, and Russian ambition, are sound reasons for watching Russia—for keeping ourselves prepared, and for acting, should it become necessary, with energy and fearlessness." I repeat, then, that when asked to support Russia the Liberal party is asked to support a power which, since it was first admitted to the European family has been the permanent and the principal opponent of Liberal ideas. That power at the end of the last century committed acts precisely similar to those in Bulgaria which have lately made infamous the name of the Turks. In the present day, and under the government of the so-called Liberal Emperor who now rules the country, education is stationary, if it has not actually gone back, protectionism in trade is rampant, and from Central Asia foreign goods and foreign travellers are almost absolutely excluded. From the whole Russian Empire all foreign books are excluded except those which are permitted by the Holy Synod. The enlightened Government which is to be the future friend of English Liberals stops all printed matter at the frontier. No one under the rank of general can receive a newspaper from abroad by post. . . . Official Russia is eaten up by a gangrene of venality and corruption. Turkey having adopted a constitution, Russia and Monaco are the only two remaining autocracies in Europe. In Russia every man still lives at the mercy of the secret Imperial police. This is the country which is to be the Liberal's friend.

Sir Charles Wentworth Dilke, Bart., M.P., *The Eastern Question* (London 1878), pp. 35, 67–8, 81–2.

Although the Congress of Berlin in 1878 provided a temporary answer to the Eastern Question, Gladstone continued his assertion of the principles on which he thought foreign policy should be based. The General Election of 1880 provided an opportunity, and extracts from two of his speeches in his constituency of Midlothian are printed below.

35: W. E. GLADSTONE. Speech at West Calder

27 November 1879

THE first thing is to foster the strength of the Empire by just legislation and economy at home, thereby producing two of the great elements of national power—namely, wealth, which is a physical element, and union and contentment, which are moral elements—and to reserve the strength of the Empire, to reserve the expenditure of that strength, for great and worthy occasions abroad. Here is my first principle of foreign policy: good government at home.

My second principle of foreign policy is this: that its aim ought to be to preserve to the nations of the world—and especially, were it but for shame, when we recollect the sacred name we bear as Christians, especially to the Christian nations of the world— the blessings of peace. That is my second principle. . . .

In my opinion the third sound principle is this: to strive to cultivate and maintain, ay, to the very uttermost, what is called the Concert of Europe; to keep the

Powers of Europe in union together. And why? Because by keeping all in union together you neutralize and fetter and bind up the selfish aims of each. I am not here to flatter either England or any of them. They have selfish aims, as, unfortunately, we in late years have too sadly shown that we, too, have had selfish aims; but then, common action is fatal to selfish aims. Common action means common objects; and the only objects for which you can unite together the Powers of Europe are objects connected with the common good of them all. That, Gentlemen, is my third principle of foreign policy.

My fourth principle is—that you should avoid needless and entangling engagements. You may boast about them; you may brag about them. You may say you are procuring consideration for the country. You may say that an Englishman can now hold up his head among the nations. You may say that he is now not in the hands of a Liberal Ministry, who thought of nothing but pounds, shillings, and pence. But what does all this come to, gentlemen? It comes to this, that you are increasing your engagements without increasing your strength; and if you increase engagements without increasing strength, you diminish strength, you abolish strength; you really reduce the Empire and do not increase it. You render it less capable of performing its duties; you render it an inheritance less precious to hand on to future generations. My fifth principle is this, gentlemen, to acknowledge the equal rights of all nations. You may sympathize with one nation more than another. Nay, you must sympathize in certain circumstances with one nation more than another. You sympathize most with those nations, as a rule, with which you have the closest connexion in language, in blood, and in religion, or whose circumstances at the time seem to give the strongest claim to sympathy. But in point of right all are equal, and you have no right to set up a system under which one of them is to be placed under moral suspicion or espionage, or to be made the constant subject of invective. If you do that, but especially if you claim for yourself a superiority, a pharisaical superiority over the whole of them, then I say you may talk about your patriotism if you please, but you are a misjudging friend of your country, and in undermining the basis of the esteem and respect of other people for your country you are in reality inflicting the severest injury upon it. I have now given you, gentlemen, five principles of foreign policy. Let me give you a sixth, and then I have done.

And that sixth is, that in my opinion foreign policy, subject to all the limitations that I have described, the foreign policy of England should always be inspired by the love of freedom. There should be a sympathy with freedom, a desire to give it scope, founded not upon visionary ideas, but upon the long experience of many generations within the shores of this happy isle, that in freedom you lay the firmest foundations both of loyalty and order; the firmest foundations for the development of individual character, and the best provision for the happiness of the nation at large. In the foreign policy of this country the name of Canning ever will be honoured. The name of Russell ever will be honoured. The name of Palmerston ever will be honoured by those who recollect the erection of the kingdom of Belgium, and the union of the disjoined provinces of Italy. It is that sympathy, not a sympathy with disorder, but, on the contrary, founded upon the deepest and most profound love of order—it is that sympathy which, in my opinion, ought to be the very atmosphere in which a Foreign Secretary of England ought to live and to move. . . .

W. E. Gladstone, *Political Speeches in Scotland, November-December 1879* (Rev. ed., Edinburgh 1880), pp. 115-7.

36: W. E. GLADSTONE. Speech at Edinburgh

17 March 1880

THERE is an allegation abroad that what is called the " Manchester School " is to rule the destinies of this country if the Liberals come into power. . . . What is called the Manchester School has never ruled the foreign policy of this country—never during a Conservative Government, and never especially during a Liberal Government. Do not let me be supposed to speak of what is called the Manchester School, or sometimes the Peace Party, as if I were about to cast disrespect upon them. I respect them even in what I think to be their great and serious error. I think it is like many errors in our mixed condition. It is not only a respectable, it is even a noble error. Abhorring all selfishness of policy, friendly to freedom in every country of the earth, attached to the modes of reason and detesting the ways of force, this Manchester School has sprung prematurely to the conclusion that wars may be considered as having closed their melancholy and miserable history, and that the affairs of the world may henceforth be conducted by methods more adapted to the dignity of man, more suited both to his strength and to his weakness, less likely to lead him out of the ways of duty, to stimulate his evil passions, to make him guilty before God for inflicting misery on his fellow creatures. But no Government of this country could ever accede to the management and control of affairs without finding that that dream of a Paradise upon earth was rudely dispelled by the shock of experience. However we may detest war—and you cannot detest it too much—there is no war—except one, the war for liberty—that does not contain in it elements of corruption, as well as of misery, that are deplorable to recollect and to consider; but however deplorable wars may be, they are among the necessities of our condition; and there are times when justice, when faith, when the welfare of mankind requires a man not to shrink from the responsibility of under-taking them. And if you undertake wars, so also you are often obliged to undertake measures which may lead to war.

[*Mr. Gladstone then went on to discuss the British guarantee to Belgium in 1870.*]

We felt called on to enlist ourselves on the part of the British nation as advocates and as champions of the integrity and independence of Belgium. And if we had gone to war, we should have gone to war for freedom, we should have gone to war for public right, we should have gone to war to save human happiness from being invaded by tyrannous and lawless power. . . . And though I detest war . . . in such a war as that, while the breath in my body is continued to me, I am ready to engage. I am ready to support it, I am ready to give all the help and aid I can to those who carry this country to it.

Well, gentlemen, pledged to support the integrity

and independence of Belgium, what did we do? We proposed to Prussia to enter into a new and solemn treaty with us to resist the French Emperor if the French Emperor attempted to violate the sanctity of freedom in Belgium; and we proposed to France to enter into a similar treaty to preserve exactly the same measures against Prussia. . . . And we undertook that, in concert with the one, or in concert with the other, whichever the case might be, we would pledge all the resources of this Empire, and carry it into war for the purpose of resisting mischief and maintaining the principles of European law and peace. I ask you whether it is not ludicrous to apply the doctrine or the imputation that we belong to the Manchester School, or to a Peace Party, we who made these engagements to go to war with France if necessary, or to go to war with Prussia if necessary, for the sake of the independence of Belgium.

W. E. Gladstone, *Political Speeches in Scotland, March and April 1880* (rev. ed., Edinburgh 1880), pp. 30–3.

PART VI

THE END OF ISOLATION

IN the eighteen-nineties the new Imperialism and the growing importance to international relations of non-European affairs presented British policy with new problems. At the same time, the growth of the industrial and military power of Germany made British supremacy no longer self-evident. The period 1895–1904 marks the end of isolation. Although Lord Salisbury, Prime Minister 1895–1901 and Foreign Secretary for most of that period, adhered to a policy of isolation, Joseph Chamberlain, his Colonial Secretary and the leading exponent of imperialism, began to influence foreign policy in a different direction.

37: ROBERT CECIL, MARQUESS OF SALISBURY. Speech at Annual Meeting of the Primrose League

Albert Hall, 4 May 1898

IF we could look simply upon the world as it presents itself to us, if we could merely count our colonies and our possessions and our growing enormous trade, we might, indeed, look forward to the future without disquietude. We know that we shall maintain against all comers that which we possess, and we know, in spite of the jargon about isolation, that we are amply competent to do so. (Cheers.) But that will not secure the peace of the world.

You may roughly divide the nations of the world as the living and the dying. On one side you have great countries of enormous power growing in power every year, growing in wealth, growing in dominion, growing in the perfection of their organization. Railways have given to them the power to concentrate upon any one point the whole military force of their population and to assemble armies of a magnitude and power never dreamt of in the generations gone by. Science has placed in the hands of those armies weapons ever growing in their efficacy of destruction, and, therefore, adding to the power—fearfully to the power—of those who have the opportunity of using them. By the side of these splendid organizations, of which nothing seems to diminish the forces and which present rival claims

which the future may only be able by a bloody arbitra-
ment to adjust—by the side of these there are a number of communities which I can only describe as
dying. . . . They are mainly communities that are not
Christian, but I regret to say that is not exclusively the
case, and in these states disorganization and decay are
advancing almost as fast as concentration and increasing power are advancing in the living nations that
stand beside them. Decade after decade they are
weaker, poorer, and less provided with leading men or
institutions in which they can trust, apparently drawing
nearer and nearer to their fate and yet clinging with
strange tenacity to the life which they have got.
. . . The society, and official society, the Administration, is a mass of corruption, so that there is no firm
ground on which any hope of reform or restoration
could be based, and in their various degrees they are
presenting a terrible picture to the more enlightened
portion of the world—a picture which, unfortunately,
the increase in the means of our information and communication draws with darker and more conspicuous
lineaments in the face of all the nations, appealing to
their feelings as well as to their interests, calling upon
them to bring forward a remedy. How long this state
of things is likely to go on, of course, I do not attempt
to prophesy. All I can indicate is that that process is
proceeding, that the weak States are becoming weaker
and the strong States are becoming stronger. . . . For
one reason or another—from the necessities of politics
of under the pretence of philanthropy—the living
nations will gradually encroach on the territory of the
dying, and the seeds and causes of conflict among
civilized nations will speedily appear. . . . These
things may introduce causes of fatal difference between

the great nations whose mighty armies stand opposite threatening each other. These are the dangers, I think, which threaten us in the period that is coming on. It is a period which will tax our resolution, our tenacity, and Imperial instincts to the utmost. Undoubtedly we shall not allow England to be at a disadvantage in any re-arrangement that may take place. (Cheers.) On the other hand, we shall not be jealous if desolation and sterility are removed by the aggrandisement of a rival in regions to which our arms cannot extend. . . . Do not abate your efforts because you think your task is done. Your task is ever living, and it never was more important than now, as is indicated by the threatening circumstances of the world outside to which I have alluded. . . .

The Times, Thursday 5 May 1898.

38: JOSEPH CHAMBERLAIN. Speech to Birmingham Liberal Unionist Association

13 May 1898

OURS is a democratic Government. We gain all our strength from the confidence of the people (hear, hear), and we cannot gain strength or confidence unless we show confidence in return, and therefore, to my mind, there is no longer any room for the mysteries and the reticencies of the diplomacy of fifty years ago. You must tell the people what you mean and where you are going if you want them to follow you. (Hear, hear.) I do not mean to say that I can tell you all the details of secret negotiations. . . . But the plain issue and the main principles and the particulars of the problems with which we have to deal—those might be stated in language to be understood of the people, and I would take the judgement of the people just as soon upon them as I would take that of the wisest diplomatist in the world.

Now the first point that I want to impress upon you is this. It is the crux of the situation. Since the Crimean War, nearly fifty years ago, the policy of this country has been a policy of strict isolation. We have had no allies—I am afraid we have had no friends. (Laughter.) This is not due altogether to the envy which is undoubtedly felt at our success; it is due in part to the suspicion that we are acting in our own selfish interests, and were willing that other people should draw the chestnuts out of the fire for us; that we would take no responsibilities, whilst we were glad enough to profit by the work of others. In this way we have avoided entangling alliances, we have escaped many dangers; but we must accept the disadvantages that go with such a policy. As long as the other great Powers of Europe were also working for their own hand, and were separately engaged, I think the policy we have pursued—consistently pursued—was undoubtedly the right policy for this country. (Hear, hear.) But now in recent years a different complexion has been placed upon the matter. A new situation has arisen, and it is right the people of this country should have it under their consideration. All the powerful States of Europe have made alliances, and as long as we keep outside these alliances, as long as we are envied by all, and as long as we have interests which at one time or another conflict with the interests of all, we are liable to be confronted at any moment with a combination of Great Powers so powerful that not even the most extreme, the most hotheaded politician, would be able to contemplate it without a certain sense of uneasiness. . . .

The Times, Saturday 14 May 1898.

39: JOSEPH CHAMBERLAIN. Speech at Luncheon in County Assembly Rooms, Leicester

30 November 1899

Bᴜᴛ there is something more which I think any far-seeing English statesman must have long desired, and that is that we should not long remain permanently isolated on the continent of Europe; I think that the moment that aspiration was formed it must have appeared evident to everybody that the natural alliance is between ourselves and the great German Empire. (Loud cheers.)

It is not with German newspapers that we desire to have an understanding or alliance; it is with the German people; and I may point out to you that at bottom the character, the main character, of the Teutonic race differs very slightly indeed from the character of the Anglo-Saxon (cheers), and the same sentiments which bring us into close sympathy with the United States of America may also be evoked to bring us into closer sympathy and alliance with the Empire of Germany. What do we find? We find our system of justice, we find our literature, we find the very base and foundation on which our language is established, the same in the two countries, and if the union between England and America is a powerful factor in the cause of peace, a new Triple Alliance between the Teutonic race and the two great branches of the Anglo-Saxon race will be a still more potent influence in the future of the world. (Cheers.)

The Times, Friday 1 December 1899.

197

40: LORD SALISBURY. Memorandum

29 May 1901

Chamberlain's suggestion of an alliance with Germany in 898–9 came to nothing; so did a proposal in 1901 that England should join the Triple Alliance of Germany, Austria and Italy. Some of the reasons for this refusal are given in the following document, a memorandum written by Salisbury for Lord Lansdowne, who succeeded him at the Foreign Office when age prevented him from continuing to combine the posts of Prime Minister and Foreign Secretary.

THIS is a proposal for including England within the bounds of the Triple Alliance. I understand its practical effect to be:

1. If England were attacked by two Powers— say France and Russia—Germany, Austria, and Italy would come to her assistance.

2. Conversely, if either Austria, Germany, or Italy were attacked by France and Spain, England must come to the rescue.

Even assuming that the Powers concerned were all despotic, and could promise anything they pleased, with a full confidence that they would be able to perform the promise, I think it is open to much question whether the bargain would be for our advantage. The liability of having to defend the German and Austrian frontiers against Russia is heavier than that of *having to defend the British Isles against France*. Even, therefore, in its most naked aspect the bargain would be a bad

198

one for this country. Count Hatzfeldt[1] speaks of our
" *isolation* " as constituting a serious danger for us.
Have we ever felt that danger practically? If we had suc-
cumbed in the revolutionary war, our fall would not
have been due to our isolation. We had many allies,
but they would not have saved us if the French Emperor had been able to command the Channel. Except
during his reign we have never even been in danger;
and, therefore, it is impossible for us to judge whether
the "isolation" under which we are supposed to
suffer, does or does not contain in it any elements of
peril. It would hardly be wise to incur novel and most
onerous obligations, in order to guard against *a danger
in whose existence we have no historical reason for believing*.

But though the proposed arrangement, even from
this point of view, does not seem to me admissible,
these are not by any means the weightiest objections
that can be urged against it. The fatal circumstance is
that *neither we nor the Germans are competent to make the
suggested promises*. The British Government cannot
undertake to declare war, for any purpose, unless it is
a purpose of which the electors of this country would
approve. If the Government promised to declare war
for an object which did not commend itself to public
opinion, the promise would be repudiated, and the
Government would be turned out. I do not see how,
in common honesty, we could invite other nations to
rely upon our aids in a struggle which must be formidable and probably supreme, when we have no
means whatever of knowing what may be the humour
of our people in circumstances which cannot be foreseen. We might, to some extent, divest ourselves of
the full responsibility of such a step, by *laying our
Agreement with the Triple Alliance before Parliament* as

[1] German Ambassador in London.

soon as it is concluded. But there are very grave objections to such a course, and I do not understand it to be recommended by the German Ambassador.

The impropriety of attempting to determine by a *secret contract* the future conduct of a Representative Assembly upon an issue of peace or war would apply to German policy as much as to English, only that the German Parliament would probably pay more deference to the opinion of their Executive than would be done by the English Parliament. But *a promise of defensive alliance with England would excite bitter murmurs in every rank of German society*—if we may trust the indications of German sentiment, which we have had an opportunity of witnessing during the last two years.

It would not be safe to stake any important national interest upon the fidelity with which, in case of national exigency, either country could be trusted to fulfil the obligations of the Alliance, if the Agreement had been concluded without the assent of its Parliament.

Several times during the last sixteen years Count Hatzfeldt has tried to elicit from me, in conversation, some opinion as to the probable conduct of England, if Germany or Italy were involved in war with France. I have always replied that no English Minister could venture on such a forecast. The course of the English Government in such a crisis must depend on the view taken by public opinion in this country, and public opinion would be largely, if not exclusively, governed by the nature of the *casus belli*.

British Documents on the Origins of the War, edited by G. P. Gooch and Harold Temperley, Vol. II (London 1927), pp. 68-9.

When the Liberals returned to power in 1905, they took over a foreign policy that had been radically changed by the Anglo-Japanese Alliance of 1902 and the *Entente* with France in 1904. At the same time the German Government had, by their naval laws of 1898 and 1900, begun to challenge British supremacy at sea.

The next two documents are extracts from reviews of the situation: first, a private one by Sir Edward Grey, the Foreign Secretary, for the President of the United States, and, second, a policy-making memorandum by Sir Eyre Crowe, then Senior Clerk and later Permanent Under-Secretary of State at the Foreign Office.

41:   SIR EDWARD GREY. From a letter to President Theodore Roosevelt

December 1906

Now, a word as to our policy. It is not anti-German. But it must be independent of Germany. We wish to keep and strengthen the *Entente* with France, who is now very peaceful, and neither aggressive nor restless. She also plays the game fairly, and as long as she trusts one she is a good friend. The weak point is that she might some day have a scare that we intended to change. I think Germany has already tried more than once to make her imagine this.

In our view, the *Entente* with France means good and easy relations for both of us with Italy and Spain. This means that peace and quietness are assured among the four Western Powers of Europe. To complete this foundation, we wish to make an arrangement with Russia that will remove the old traditions of enmity, and ensure that, if we are not close friends, at any rate we do not quarrel.

If all this can be done, we shall take care that it is not used to provoke Germany, or to score off her, if she will only accept it, and not try to make mischief.

If, on the other hand, by some misfortune or blunder our *Entente* with France were to be broken up, France will have to make her own terms with Germany. And Germany will again be in a position to keep us on bad terms with France and Russia, and to make herself predominant upon the Continent. Then, sooner or later, there will be war between us and Germany, in which much else may be involved.

It is in German diplomacy alone that one now meets with deliberate attempts to make mischief between other countries by saying poisoned things to one about another. It is the lees left by Bismarck that still foul the cup. The economic rivalry (and all that) with Germany do not give much offence to our people, and they admire her steady industry and genius for organization. But they do resent mischief making. They suspect the Emperor of aggressive plans of *Weltpolitik*, and they see that Germany is forcing the pace in armaments in order to dominate Europe, and is thereby laying a horrible burden of wasteful expenditure upon all the other Powers.

The long and the short of the matter is that, to secure peace, we must maintain the *Entente* with France, and attempts from outside to shake it will only make it stronger.

Austria, at present, is no danger and no problem

except to herself. What questions may arise if she cannot settle her internal difficulties is another story.

I can give you no forecast of Japanese policy. They have been quite satisfactory allies; cautious and not exacting. But they are very reserved, and I do not feel that I know the working of their minds on questions outside the alliance itself.

As for ourselves.

We should detest war anywhere. This is not because we have grown weak or cowardly, but because we have had enough war for one generation. Before the Boer war, we were spoiling for a fight. We were ready to fight France about Siam, Germany about the Kruger telegram, and Russia about any thing. Any Government here, during the last ten years of last century, could have had war by lifting a finger. The people would have shouted for it. They had a craving for excitement and a rush of blood to the head. Now, this generation has had enough excitement, and has lost a little blood, and is sane and normal. Its instincts are, I think, healthy. . . .

Printed in G. M. Trevelyan, *Grey of Fallodon* (London 1937), pp. 114-5.

42: SIR EYRE CROWE. From Memorandum on the Present State of British Relations with France and Germany

Foreign Office, 1 January 1907

THE general character of England's foreign policy is determined by the immutable conditions of her geographical situation on the ocean flank of Europe as an island State with vast oversea colonies and dependencies, whose existence and survival as an independent community are inseparably bound up with the possession of preponderant sea power. The tremendous influence of such preponderance has been described in the classical pages of Captain Mahan. No one now disputes it. Sea power is more potent than land power, because it is as pervading as the element in which it moves and has its being. Its formidable character makes itself felt the more directly that a maritime State is, in the literal sense of the word, the neighbour of every country accessible by sea. It would, therefore, be but natural that the power of a State supreme at sea should inspire universal jealousy and fear, and be ever exposed to the danger of being overthrown by a general combination of the world. Against such a combination no single nation could in the long run stand, least of all a small island kingdom not possessed of the military strength of a people trained to arms, and dependent for its food supply on oversea commerce.

The danger can in practice only be averted—and history shows that it has been so averted—on condition that the national policy of the insular and naval State is so directed as to harmonize with the general desires and ideals common to all mankind, and more particularly that it is closely identified with the primary and vital interests of a majority, or as many as possible, of the other nations. Now, the first interest of all countries is the preservation of national independence. It follows that England, more than any other non-insular Power, has a direct and positive interest in the maintenance of the independence of nations, and therefore must be the natural enemy of any country threatening the independence of others and the natural protector of the weaker communities.

Second only to the ideal of independence, nations have always cherished the right of free intercourse and trade in the world's markets, and in proportion as England champions the principle of the largest measure of general freedom of commerce, she undoubtedly strengthens her hold on the interested friendship of other nations, at least to the extent of making them feel less apprehensive of naval supremacy in the hands of a free trade England than they would in the face of a predominant protectionist Power. This is an aspect of the free trade question which is apt to be overlooked. It has been well said that every country, if it had the option, would, of course, prefer itself to hold the power of supremacy at sea, but that, this choice being excluded, it would rather see England hold that power than any other state.

History shows that the danger threatening the independence of this or that nation has generally arisen, at least in part, out of the momentary predominance of a neighbouring State at once militarily powerful, economically efficient, and ambitious to extend its frontiers or spread its influence, the danger being directly proportionate to the degree of its power and efficiency, and to the spontaneity or " inevitableness " of its ambitions. The only check on the abuse of political predominance derived from such a position has always consisted in the opposition of an equally formidable rival, or of a combination of several countries forming leagues of defence. The equilibrium established by such a grouping of forces is technically known as the balance of power, and it has become almost an historical truism to identify England's secular policy with the maintenance of this balance by throwing her weight now in this scale and now in that, but ever on the side opposed to the political dictatorship of the strongest single State or group at a given time.

If this view of British policy is correct, the opposition into which England must inevitably be driven to any country aspiring to such a dictatorship assumes almost the form of a law of nature. . . .

By applying this general law to a particular case, the attempt might be made to ascertain whether, at a given time, some powerful and ambitious State is or is not in a position of natural and necessary enmity towards England; and the present position of Germany might, perhaps be so tested. Any such investigation must take the shape of an inquiry as to whether Germany is, in fact, aiming at a political hegemony with the object of promoting purely German schemes of expansion, and establishing a German primacy in the world of international politics at the cost and to the detriment of other nations.

British Documents on the Origins of the War, 1914–1918, edited by G. P. Gooch and Harold Temperley, Vol. III (London 1928), pp. 402–3.

In 1907 a settlement of outstanding differences was achieved between Britain and Russia, but this, and the growing desire of the French to strengthen the *Entente*, aroused much criticism among the supporters of Grey's own party. Thus he had to face not only Conservative criticism that his policy was too weak, but also Liberal criticism that he was committing the country too deeply against Germany. The next extracts are examples of this Liberal reaction, the first to the Anglo-Russian negotiations of 1907, and second to the co-operation with the French against German threats to Morocco at the time of the Agadir crisis in the summer of 1911. They are followed by a reflection of Government policy by the journalist J. A. Spender, the leading supporter in the Press of Grey's viewpoint.

43: *The Proposed Anglo-Russian Agreement*

Letter to *The Times*

11 June 1907

Sir,

Speaking on behalf of ourselves and, we believe, a large body of public opinion, we desire to express to you our apprehension at the report that an agreement is being arranged between our Foreign Office and the Government of St. Petersburg.

We regard any alliance, understanding, or agreement with the present Russian Government as equivalent to taking sides against the Russian people in its struggle for constitutional rights and freedom. We think any such agreement is likely to diminish our prestige as the supporter of liberty throughout the world, and to prejudice the Russian people against us when they are strong enough to offer us the national alliance to which we look forward.

For this reason we regard any arrangement now concluded as dangerous and insecure, and, even if the Russian Government succeeds in suppressing popular liberties, we are unable to place confidence in their pledges for the future, judging from their disregard of past pledges in the case of the Black Sea and Manchuria. Nor does an agreement with regard to Asia only appear to us a matter of urgent importance when we consider how unlikely any hostile movement on the part of Russian forces must necessarily be for some years to come.

We consider that the proposed agreement will have the effect of strengthening the Russian credit and enabling the Government to appeal successfully to Europe for another loan over which representatives of the Russian people will have no control, and which will be employed only to strengthen the position of the autocracy against them.

We also fear that, relying on this improved credit and closer relations between the Governments, the English people may be tempted to invest largely in Russian Government stock—an investment likely to influence our political attitude towards Russia and other powers, as already seen in the case of France.

Finally, we protest against maintaining any but the most distant diplomatic relations with a Government which is, with good reason, suspected of connivance at the recent massacres of Jews, the devastation of the Caucasus and Baltic provinces, and the prison tortures in Riga. In all these cases, if the atrocities were not directed by the St. Petersburg Government, it is certain that the Government officials who carried them out suffered no penalty, but in many cases were rewarded by promotion.

On these grounds we cannot but condemn an arrangement which, for a very dubious and temporary advantage, places this country in a false position with regard to a liberation movement which, so far as we can forecast the future, is likely to exert the highest influence on the European history of the present century.

Yours faithfully,

L. A. Atherley-Jones, K.C., M.P., J. Ramsay Macdonald, M.P., Will Thorne, M.P., Justin McCarthy, G. Bernard Shaw, George Cadbury, Robert Spence Watson, Edward G. Browne (Professor of Arabic and formerly Lecturer in Persian, Cambridge), Walter Crane, Alice Stopford Green, Olive Meynell, Stopford A. Brooke, Arthur Sidgwick (Fellow of Corpus Christi College, Oxford), John Galsworthy, R. B. Cunninghame Graham, John A. Hobson, T. Fisher Unwin.

The Times, Tuesday 11 June 1907.

44: C. P. SCOTT. Letter from Manchester Liberal Federation to Sir Edward Grey

12 January 1912

WE have been instructed by the Executive Committee of the Manchester Liberal Federation to write to you on their behalf in order to express to you the deep concern of the members of the Federation, and of Liberals generally in Manchester, at recent developments of the foreign policy of the Government.

They were dismayed to learn that in the recent negotiations between the French and German Governments on the subject of Morocco, this country was so intimately involved that had war broken out between France and Germany, we must in all probability have become a party to it. They fail to recognize that any British interest of such magnitude was at stake as to justify war or the threat of war, and they are unable to discover that there is anything in the treaty obligations of this country which can be construed as obliging us to support France by force of arms in a quarrel not our own.

They would therefore appeal to the Government, which in foreign as in domestic policies they trust to sustain a Liberal policy, now to make it absolutely clear to the French government that we hold ourselves under no obligation either of treaty or of honour to support French diplomacy in any future controversy,

by the might of the armed forces of this country, or by
any such diplomatic action as might imply such assistance in the last resort, but that this country holds
itself perfectly free to take such action as it may think
that the circumstances of the occasion demand when
any difficulty arises. In other words, they would urge
the Government to make it plain to the French Government that the " *Entente* " or friendly understanding
with France . . . is not to be understood as an alliance,
and that it leaves us perfectly free to enter into similar
close and cordial relations with other European powers
and notably with Germany.

Printed in J. L. Hammond, *C. P. Scott of the Manchester
Guardian* (London 1934).

45: J. A. SPENDER. *The Foundations of British Policy*

1912 (reprinted from *The Westminster Gazette*)

WE have all the requisites for making ourselves respected, provided we keep within the limits which Nature and circumstances impose upon the power of every nation. But to do this we must resist the interpretation of our treaty obligations which would commit us to military operations in Europe outside our interests and beyond our power of effective action. In a previous chapter I defined the supreme British interest in a sentence I will venture to repeat. It is *to have a navy which will be equal to any possible combinations against us and a policy which will keep the probable combinations against us to what we can meet without a gross inflation of expenditure on armaments.* Such a policy will necessarily be defensive and pacific. It will not regard this country as having a Providential mission to redress the balance of power in Europe. It will tend, as far as possible, to avoid entanglement in European quarrels. It will seek to make sea-power as acceptable as possible to other nations, and, if it cannot remove their theoretical grievance, it will seek to avoid causes of practical complaint. Such a policy will endeavour to establish with Germany relations at least as good as Russia, in spite of her alliance with France, succeeds in maintaining with Germany.

J. A. Spender, *The Foundations of British Policy* (London 1912), p. 56.

PART VII

THE WAR WITH GERMANY 1914–18

THE Liberal and Labour criticisms of Grey, though much diminished, had not ceased on the eve of the outbreak of war as the speeches of Mr. Ponsonby (then Liberal member for Stirling) and Mr. Rowntree (Liberal member for York) in the debate from which extracts are printed below, show.

However, respect for the guarantee that had been given by Britain to Belgium in 1839 and repeated in 1870 aroused almost universal support for entry into the war once it was conclusively shown that Germany had violated Belgian neutrality.

46: DEBATE IN THE HOUSE OF COMMONS

3 August 1914

SIR EDWARD GREY: Last week I stated that we were working for peace not only for this country, but to preserve the peace of Europe. To-day events move so rapidly that it is exceedingly difficult to state with technical accuracy the actual state of affairs, but it is clear that the peace of Europe cannot be preserved. Russia and Germany, at any rate, have declared war upon each other.

Before I proceed to state the position of His Majesty's Government, I would like to clear the ground so that, with regard to the present crisis, the House may know exactly under what obligations the Government is, or the House can be said to be, in coming to a decision on the matter. First of all let me say, very shortly, that we have consistently worked with a single mind, with all the earnestness in our power, to preserve peace. The House may be satisfied on that point. We have always done it. During these last years, as far as His Majesty's Government are concerned, we would have no difficulty in proving that we have done so. Throughout the Balkan crisis,[1] by general admission, we worked for peace. The co-operation of the Great Powers of Europe was successful in working for peace

[1] The Balkan Wars of 1912–3, when Grey took the initiative in organizing discussions in London between the representatives of the four powers.

in the Balkan crisis. It is true that some of the Powers had great difficulty in adjusting their points of view. It took much time and labour and discussion before they could settle their differences, but peace was secured, because peace was their main object, and they were willing to give time and trouble rather than accentuate differences rapidly.

In the present crisis, it has not been possible to secure the peace of Europe; because there has been little time, and there has been a disposition—at any rate in some quarters on which I will not dwell—to force things rapidly to an issue, at any rate, to the great risk of peace, and, as we now know, the result of that is that the policy of peace, as far as the Great Powers generally are concerned, is in danger. I do not want to dwell on that, and to comment on it, and to say where the blame seems to us to lie, which Powers were most in favour of peace, which were most disposed to risk or endanger peace, because I would like the House to approach this crisis in which we are now, from the point of view of British interests, British honour, and British obligations, free from all passion, as to why peace has not been preserved. . . .

I come first, now, to the question of British obligations. I have assured the House—and the Prime Minister has assured the House more than once—that if any crisis such as this arose, we should come before the House of Commons and be able to say to the House that it was free to decide what the British attitude should be, that we would have no secret engagement which we should spring upon the House, and tell the House that, because we had entered into that engagement, there was an obligation of honour upon the country. I will deal with that point to clear the ground first.

There has been in Europe two diplomatic groups, the Triple Alliance and what came to be called the "Triple *Entente*," for some years past. The Triple *Entente* was not an Alliance—it was a Diplomatic group. . . .

In this present crisis, up till yesterday, we have also given no promise of anything more than diplomatic support—up till yesterday no promise of more than diplomatic support. Now I must make this question of obligation clear to the House. I must go back to the first Moroccan crisis of 1906. That was the time of the Algeciras Conference, and it came at a time of very great difficulty to His Majesty's Government when an election was in progress, and Ministers were scattered over the country, and I—spending three days a week in my constituency and three days at the Foreign Office—was asked the question whether if that crisis developed into war between France and Germany we would give armed support. I said then that I could promise nothing to any foreign Power unless it was subsequently to receive the whole-hearted support of public opinion here if the occasion arose. I said, in my opinion, if war was forced upon France then on the question of Morocco—a question which had just been the subject of agreement between this country and France, an agreement exceedingly popular on both sides—that if out of that agreement war was forced on France at that time, in my view public opinion in this country would have rallied to the material support of France.

I gave no promise, but I expressed that opinion during the crisis, as far as I remember, almost in the same words, to the French Ambassador and the German Ambassador at the time. I made no promise, and I used no threats; but I expressed that opinion. That position was accepted by the French Government, but they said to me at the time—and I think very reasonably—" If you think it possible that the public opinion of Great Britain might, should a sudden crisis arise, justify you in giving to France the armed support which you cannot promise in advance, you will not be able to give that support, even if you wish to give it, when the time comes, unless some conversations have already taken place between naval and military experts." There was force in that. I agreed to it, and authorized those conversations to take place, but on the distinct understanding that nothing which passed between military or naval experts should bind either Government, or restrict in any way their freedom to make a decision as to whether or not they would give that support when the time arose. . . .

The Agadir crisis came—another Morocco crisis—and throughout that I took precisely the same line that had been taken in 1906. But subsequently, in 1912, after discussion and consideration in the Cabinet it was decided that we ought to have a definite understanding in writing, which was to be only in the form of an unofficial letter, that these conversations which took place were not binding upon the freedom of either Government; and on 22 November, 1912, I wrote to the French Ambassador the letter which I will now read to the House, and I received from him a letter in similar terms in reply. The letter which I have to read now is the record that, whatever took place between military and naval experts, they were not binding engagements upon the Government:

" My dear Ambassador—from time to time in recent years

the French and British naval and military experts have consulted together. It has always been understood that such consultation does not restrict the freedom of either Government to decide at any future time whether or not to assist the other by armed force. We have agreed that consultation between experts is not and ought not to be regarded as an engagement that commits either Government to action in a contingency that has not yet arisen and may never arise. The disposition, for instance, of the French and British Fleets respectively at the present moment is not based upon an engagement to co-operate in war.

" You have, however, pointed out that, if either Government had grave reason to expect an unprovoked attack by a third power, it might become essential to know whether it could in that event depend upon the armed assistance of the other.

" I agree that, if either Government had grave reason to expect an unprovoked attack by a third power, or something that threatened the general peace, it should immediately discuss with the other whether both Governments should act together to prevent aggression and to preserve peace, and, if so, what measures they would be prepared to take in common. . . ."

That is the starting-point for the Government with regard to the present crisis. I think it makes it clear that what the Prime Minister and I said to the House of Commons was perfectly justified, and that, as regards our freedom to decide in a crisis what our line should be, whether we should intervene or whether we should abstain, the Government remained perfectly free and, *a fortiori*, the House of Commons remains perfectly free. That I say to clear the ground from the point of view of obligation. I think it was due to prove our good faith to the House of Commons that I should give that full information to the House now, and say what I think is obvious from the letter I have just read, that we do not construe anything which has previously taken place in our diplomatic relations with other Powers in this matter as restricting the freedom of Government to decide what attitude they should take now, or restrict the freedom of the House of Commons to decide what their attitude should be.

Well, Sir, I will go further, and I will say this: The situation in the present crisis is not precisely the same as it was in the Morocco question. In the Morocco question it was primarily a dispute which concerned France—a dispute which concerned France and France primarily—a dispute, as it seemed to us, affecting France, out of an agreement subsisting between us and France, and published to the whole world, in which we engaged to give France diplomatic support   No doubt we were pledged to give nothing but diplomatic support; we were, at any rate, pledged by a definite public agreement to stand with France diplomatically in that question.

The present crisis has originated differently. It has not originated with regard to Morocco. It has not originated as regards anything with which we had a special agreement with France; it has not originated with anything which primarily concerned France. It has originated in a dispute between Austria and Servia. I can say this with the most absolute confidence—no Government and no country has less desire to be involved in war over a dispute with Austria and Servia than the Government and the country of France. They are involved in it because of their obligation of honour under a definite alliance with Russia. Well, it is only fair to say to the House that that obligation of honour cannot apply in the same way to us. We are not parties to the Franco-Russian Alliance. We do not even know the terms of that Alliance. So far I have, I think, faithfully and completely cleared the ground with regard to the question of obligation.

I now come to what we think the situation requires of us. For many years we have had a long-standing friendship with France (An hon. Member: " And with Germany! "). I remember well the feeling in the House—and my own feeling—for I spoke on the subject, I think, when the late Government made their agreement with France—the warm and cordial feeling resulting from the fact that these two nations, who had had perpetual differences in the past, had cleared these differences away. I remember saying, I think, that it seemed to me that some benign influence had been at work to produce the cordial atmosphere that had made that possible. But how far that friendship entails obligation—it has been a friendship between the nations and ratified by the nations—how far that entails an obligation let every man look into his own heart, and his own feelings, and construe the extent of the obligation for himself. I construe it myself as I feel it, but I do not wish to urge upon anyone else more than their feelings dictate as to what they should feel about the obligation. The House, individually and collectively, may judge for itself. I speak my personal view, and I have given the House my own feeling in the matter.

The French Fleet is now in the Mediterranean, and the Northern and Western coasts of France are absolutely undefended. The French Fleet being concentrated in the Mediterranean the situation is very different from what it used to be, because the friendship which has grown up between the two countries has given them a sense of security that there was nothing to be feared from us. The French coasts are absolutely undefended. The French Fleet is in the Mediterranean, and has for some years been concentrated there because of the feeling of confidence and friendship which has existed between the two countries. My own feeling is that if a foreign fleet engaged in a war which France had not sought, and in which she had not been the aggressor, came down the English Channel and bombarded and battered the undefended coasts of France, we could not stand aside and see this going on practically within sight of our eyes with our arms folded, looking on dispassionately, doing nothing! I believe that would be the feeling of this country. There are times when one feels that if these circumstances actually did arise, it would be a feeling which would spread with irresistible force throughout the land.

But I also want to look at the matter without sentiment, and from the point of view of British interests, and it is on that that I am going to base and justify what I am presently going to say to the House. If we say nothing at this moment, what is France to do with her Fleet in the Mediterranean? If she leaves it there, with no statement from us as to what we will do, she leaves her Northern and Western coasts absolutely undefended, at the mercy of a German fleet coming down the Channel, to do as it pleases in a war which is a war of life and death between them. If we say nothing, if may be that the French Fleet is withdrawn from the Mediterranean. We are in the presence of a European conflagration; can anybody set limits to the consequences that may arise out of it? Let us assume that to-day we stand aside in an attitude of neutrality, saying, " No, we cannot undertake and engage to help either party in this conflict." Let us suppose the

French Fleet is withdrawn from the Mediterranean; and let us assume that the consequences—which are already tremendous in what has happened in Europe even to countries which are at peace—in fact, equally whether countries are at peace or at war—let us assume that out of that come consequences unforeseen, which make it necessary at a sudden moment that, in defence of vital British interests, we should go to war: and let us assume—which is quite possible— that Italy, who is now neutral—(Hon. Members: " Hear, Hear! ")—because, as I understand, she considers that this war is an aggressive war, the Triple Alliance being a defensive alliance her obligation did not arise—let us assume that consequences which are not yet foreseen—and which perfectly legitimately consulting her own interests—make Italy depart from her attitude of neutrality at a time when we are forced in defence of vital British interests ourselves to fight, what then will be the position in the Mediterranean ? It might be that at some critical moment those consequences would be forced upon us because our trade routes in the Mediterranean might be vital to this country. . . .

We have great and vital interests in the independence—and integrity is the least part—of Belgium. If Belgium is compelled to submit to allow her neutrality to be violated, of course the situation is clear. Even if by agreement she admitted the violation of her neutrality, it is clear she could only do so under duress. The smaller States in that region of Europe ask but one thing. Their one desire is that they should be left alone and independent. The one thing they fear is, I think, not so much that their integrity but that their independence should be interfered with. If in this war which is before Europe the neutrality of one of those countries is violated, if the troops of one of the combatants violate its neutrality and no action be taken to resist it, at the end of the war, whatever the integrity may be, the independence will be gone.

I have one further quotation from Mr. Gladstone as to what he thought about the independence of Belgium. . . . Mr. Gladstone said:

" We have an interest in the independence of Belgium which is wider than that which we may have in the literal operation of the guarantee. It is found in the answer to the question whether under the circumstances of the case, this country endowed as it is with influence and power, would quietly stand by and witness the perpetration of the direst crime that ever stained the pages of history, and thus become participators in the sin."

No, Sir, if it be the case that there has been anything in the nature of an ultimatum to Belgium, asking her to compromise or violate her neutrality, whatever may have been offered to her in return, her independence is gone if that holds. If her independence goes, the independence of Holland will follow. I ask the House from the point of view of British interests, to consider what may be at stake. If France is beaten in a struggle of life and death, beaten to her knees, loses her position as a great Power, becomes subordinate to the will and power of one greater than herself—consequences which I do not anticipate, because I am sure that France has the power to defend herself with all the energy and ability and patriotism which she has shown so often—still, if that were to happen, and if Belgium fell under the same dominating influence, and then Holland, and then Denmark, then would not Mr.

Gladstone's words come true, that just opposite to us there would be a common interest against the unmeasured aggrandizement of any Power?

It may be said, I suppose, that we might stand aside, husband our strength, and that whatever happened in the course of this war at the end of it intervene with effect to put things right, and to adjust them to our own point of view. If, in a crisis like this, we run away from those obligations of honour and interest as regards the Belgian Treaty, I doubt whether, whatever material force we might have at the end, it would be of very much value in face of the respect that we should have lost. And do not believe, whether a great Power stands outside this war or not, it is going to be in a position at the end of it to exert its superior strength. For us, with a powerful Fleet, which we believe able to protect our commerce, to protect our shores, and to protect our interests, if we are engaged in war, we shall suffer but little more than we shall suffer even if we stand aside.

We are going to suffer, I am afraid, terribly in this war whether we are in it or whether we stand aside. Foreign trade is going to stop, not because the trade routes are closed, but because there is no trade at the other end. Continental nations engaged in war—all their populations, all their energies, all their wealth, engaged in a desperate struggle—they cannot carry on the trade with us that they are carrying on in times of peace, whether we are parties to the war or whether we are not. I do not believe for a moment, that at the end of this war, even if we stood aside and remained aside, we should be in a position, a material position to use our force decisively to undo what had happened in the course of the war, to prevent the whole of the west of Europe opposite to us—if that has been the

224

result of the war—falling under the domination of a single Power, and I am quite sure that our moral position would be such as to have lost us all respect. I can only say that I have put the question of Belgium somewhat hypothetically, because I am not yet sure of all the facts, but, if the facts turn out to be as they have reached us at present, it is quite clear that there is an obligation on this country to do its utmost to prevent the consequences to which those facts will lead if they are undisputed.

I have read to the House the only engagements that we have yet taken definitely with regard to the use of force. I think it is due to the House to say that we have taken no engagement yet with regard to sending an Expeditionary armed force out of the country. Mobilization of the Fleet has taken place; mobilization of the Army is taking place; but we have as yet taken no engagement, because I do feel that in the case of a European conflagration such as this, unprecedented, with our enormous responsibilities in India and other parts of the Empire, or in countries of British occupation, with all the unknown factors, we must take very carefully into consideration the use which we make of sending an Expeditionary Force out of the country until we know how we stand. . . .

The most awful responsibility is resting upon the Government in deciding what to advise the House of Commons to do. We have disclosed our mind to the House of Commons. We have disclosed the issue, the information which we have, and made clear to the House, I trust, that we are prepared to face that situation, and that should it develop as probably it may develop, we will face it. We worked for peace up to the last moment, and beyond the last moment. How hard,

Q

how persistently, and how earnestly we strove for peace last week, the House will see from the Papers that will be before it.

But that is over, as far as the peace of Europe is concerned. We are now face to face with a situation and all the consequences which it may yet have to unfold. We believe we shall have the support of the House at large in proceeding to whatever the consequences may be and whatever measures may be forced upon us by the development of facts or action taken by others. I believe the country, so quickly has the situation been forced upon it, has not had time to realize the issue. It perhaps is still thinking of the quarrel between Austria and Servia, and not the complications of this matter which have grown out of the quarrel between Austria and Servia. Russia and Germany we know are at war. We do not yet know officially that Austria, the ally whom Germany is to support, is yet at war with Russia. We know that a good deal has been happening on the French frontier. We do not know that the German Ambassador has left Paris.

The situation has developed so rapidly that technically, as regards the condition of the war, it is most difficult to describe what has actually happened. I wanted to bring out the underlying issues which would affect our own conduct, and our own policy, and to put them clearly. I have put the vital facts before the House, and if, as seems not improbable, we are forced, and rapidly forced, to take our stand upon those issues, then I believe, when the country realizes what is at stake, what the real issues are, the magnitude of the impending dangers in the west of Europe, which I have endeavoured to describe to the House, we shall be supported throughout, not only by the House of

Commons, but by the determination, the resolution, the courage, and the endurance of the whole country.

Hansard, Fifth Series, Vol. LXV, pp. 1809–27.

MR. PONSONBY: I feel that I cannot remain seated at what I feel to be the most tragic moment I have yet seen. We are on the eve of a great war, and I hate to see people embarking on it with a light heart. The war fever has already begun. I saw it last night when I walked through the streets. I saw bands of half-drunken youths waving flags, and I saw a group outside a great club in St. James's Street being encouraged by members of the club from the balcony. The war fever has begun, and that is what is called patriotism! I think we have plunged too quickly, and I think the Foreign Secretary's speech shows that what has been rankling all these years is a deep animosity against German ambitions. The balance of power is responsible for this—this mad desire to keep up an impossibility in Europe, to try and divide the two sections of Europe into an armed camp, glaring at one another with suspicion and hostility and hatred, and arming all the time, and bleeding the people to pay for armaments. Since I have been in this House I have every year protested against the growth in the expenditure upon armaments. Every year it has mounted up, and old women of both sexes have told us that the best way to maintain peace is to prepare for war. This is what they have led us to—those who were foolish enough to believe it. It bled the people in order to furnish new ships and new guns, to grind all the people who devote their energy, their labour and their enterprise to one sole object, the preparation for war, war will take place. . . .

Ibid., pp. 1841–2.

MR. ROWNTREE: I cannot believe that it is impossible yet to obtain from Germany the two assurances that the Foreign Secretary specially desired—the assurances with respect to the integrity of Belgium. I know it is a difficult thing to maintain the integrity of a country. I remember not long ago that we guaranteed the integrity of Persia, and yet we have seen that integrity done away with by Russia, and we have been able to do very little to support the promise that we made. I do appeal to the Foreign Secretary, and the Prime Minister, who, after all, stand higher in the public estimation of Europe and the world than almost any other statesmen, not to give way yet in their efforts for peace. For whom are we going to fight? We are going to fight for Russia. We shall argue that it is chiefly because of France, and yet we know that it is for Russia that we are going to fight. I agree with my honourable Friend the Member for Burnley (Mr. Morrell) that that is not the civilization that England wishes to fight for at the present time. I cannot help thinking that if this government is going to increase the power of Russia at the expense of Germany, she will find in the near future that her difficulties are largely increased. I think of the frontier of India, I think of Afghanistan, and I think of Persia. We are going to increase enormously the power of Russia, and I think we shall have these difficulties to face at a very early day. Ay! and do not let us forget that when we go to war against Germany we go to war against a people who, after all, hold largely the ideals which we hold. I do not mean the bueaucracy, I do not mean the military element, but the German civilization is in many ways near the British civilization. We think of their literature, we think of what they have done for progressive religious thought, we think of what they have done for philosophy, and we say that these are not the men we want to fight.

Ibid., pp. 1845–6.

47: HENRY HERBERT ASQUITH. Speech in House of Commons, in Committee, on Vote of Credit for War

6 August 1914

I AM entitled to say, and I do so on behalf of this country—I speak not for a party, I speak for the country as a whole—that we made every effort any Government could possibly make for peace. But this war has been forced upon us. What is it we are fighting for? Everyone knows, and no one knows better than the Government, the terrible, incalculable suffering, economic, social, personal and political, which war, and especially a war between the Great Powers of the world, must entail. There is no man amongst us sitting upon this bench in these trying days—more trying perhaps than any body of statesmen for a hundred years have had to pass through—there is not a man amongst us who has not, during the whole of that time, had clearly before his vision the almost unequalled suffering which war, even in a just cause, must bring about, not only to the peoples who are for the moment living in this country and in the other countries of the world, but to posterity and to the whole prospects of European civilization. Every step we took with that vision before our eyes, and with a sense of responsibility which it is impossible to describe. Unhappily, if in spite of all our efforts to keep the peace, and with what fully and overpowering consciousness of the result, if the issue be decided in favour of war, we have, nevertheless thought it the duty as well as the interest of this country to go to war, the House may be well assured it was because we believe, and I am certain the country will believe, that we are unsheathing our sword in a just cause.

If I am asked what we are fighting for I reply in two sentences. In the first place to fulfill a solemn international obligation, an obligation which, if it had been entered into between private persons in the ordinary concerns of life, would have been regarded as an obligation not only of law but of honour, which no self-respecting man could have repudiated. I say, secondly we are fighting to vindicate the principle which, in these days when force, material force, sometimes seems to be the dominant influence and factor in the development of mankind, we are fighting to vindicate the principle that small nationalities are not to be crushed, in defiance of international good faith, by the arbitrary will of a strong and overmastering Power.

Hansard, Fifth Series, Vol. LXV, pp. 2978–9.

Asquith stated the aims for which Britain was, in his view, fighting, early in the war. By 1917, however, the length and scale of the war were producing a reaction against its continuance and demands for a more specific statement of war aims and a negotiated peace. One of the most important of these demands came from the former Conservative Foreign Secretary, Lord Lansdowne and aroused much criticism from those politicians of both parties who were supporting the Coalition Government in its conduct of the war.

48: H. H. ASQUITH on War Aims

(1) *Dublin. 25 September 1914.*

Forty-four years ago, at the time of the war of 1870, Mr. Gladstone used these words. He said: " The greatest triumph of our time will be the enthronement of the idea of public right as a governing idea of European politics." Nearly fifty years have passed. Little progress, it seems, has yet been made towards the great and beneficent change, but it seems to me to be now at this moment to be as good a definition as we can have of our European policy. The idea of public right. What does it mean when translated into concrete terms ? It means, first and foremost, the clearing of the ground by the definite repudiation of militarism as the governing factor in the relations of States, and of the future moulding of the European world. It means next that room must be found and kept for the independent existence and the free development of smaller nationalities, each with a corporate consciousness of its own. Belgium, Holland, Switzerland, and

232

the Scandinavian countries, Greece, and the Balkan States—they must be recognized as having exactly as good a title as their more powerful neighbours—more powerful in strength and wealth—to a place in the sun. And it means finally, or it ought to mean, perhaps, by a slow and gradual process, the substitution for force, for the clash of competing ambition, for the groupings and alliances and a precarious equipoise, of a real European partnership based upon the recognition of equal right, and established and enforced by common will. A year ago that would have sounded like a Utopian idea. It is probably one that may not, or will not, be realized either to-day or to-morrow. If and when this war is decided in favour of the Allies it will at once come within the range and before long within the grasp of European statesmanship.

The Times, 26 September 1914.

(2) *Guildhall. 9 November 1914.*
We shall never sheathe the sword which we have not lightly drawn until Belgium recovers in full measure all and more than all that she has sacrificed, until France is adequately secured against the menace of aggression, until the rights of the smaller nationalities of Europe are placed upon an unassailable foundation and until the military domination of Prussia is wholly and finally destroyed. That is a great task worthy of a great nation.

The Times, 10 November 1914.

49: LORD LANSDOWNE. Letter to *Daily Telegraph* on Co-ordination of Allies' War Aims

29 November 1917

SIR—We are now in the fourth year of the most dreadful war the world has ever known; a war in which, as Sir W. Robertson has lately informed us, " the killed alone can be counted by the million, while the total number of men engaged amounts to nearly 24 millions." Ministers continue to tell us that they scan the horizon in vain for the prospect of a lasting peace. And without a lasting peace we all feel that the task we have set ourselves will remain unaccomplished.

But those who look forward with horror to the prolongation of the war, who believe that its wanton prolongation would be a crime, differing only in degree from that of the criminals who provoked it, may be excused if they too scan the horizon in the hope of discerning there indications that the outlook may not after all be as hopeless as is supposed.

The obstacles are indeed formidable enough. We are constantly reminded of them. It is pointed out with force that while we have not hesitated to put forward a general description of our war aims, the enemy have, though repeatedly challenged, refused to formulate theirs, and have limited themselves to vague and apparently insincere professions of readiness to negotiate with us.

234

The force of the argument cannot be gainsaid, but it is directed mainly to show that we are still far from agreement as to the territorial questions which must come up for settlement in connection with the terms of peace. These are, however, by no means the only questions which will arise, and it is worth while to consider whether there are not others, also of first-rate importance, with regard to which the prospects of agreement are less remote.

Let me examine one or two of these. What are we fighting for? To beat the Germans? Certainly. But that is not an end in itself. We want to inflict signal defeat on the Central Powers, not out of mere vindictiveness, but in the hope of saving the world from a recurrence of the calamity which has befallen this generation.

What, then, is it we want when the war is over? I know of no better formula than that more than once made use of, with universal approval, by Mr. Asquith in the speeches which he has from time to time delivered. He has repeatedly told his hearers that we are waging war in order to obtain reparations and security. Both are essential, but of the two security is perhaps the more indispensable. In the way of reparation much can no doubt be accomplished, but the utmost effort to make good all the ravages of this war must fall short of completeness, and will fail to undo the grievous wrong which has been done to humanity. It may, however, be possible to make some amends for the inevitable incompleteness of the reparation if the security afforded is, humanly speaking, complete. To end the war honourably would be a great achievement; to prevent the same curse falling upon our children would be a greater achievement still.

This is our avowed aim, and the magnitude of the issue cannot be exaggerated. For, just as this war has been more dreadful than any war in history, so we may be sure would the next war be more dreadful than this. The prostitution of science for purposes of pure destruction is not likely to stop short. Most of us, however, believe that it should be possible to secure posterity against the repetition of such an outrage as that of 1914. If the powers will, under a solemn pact, bind themselves to submit future disputes to arbitration, if they will undertake to outlaw, politically and economically, any one of their number which refuses to enter into such a pact, or to use their joint military and naval forces for the purpose of coercing a power which breaks away from the rest, they will, indeed, have travelled far along the road to security.

We are, at any rate, right to put security in the front line of our peace demands, and it is not unsatisfactory to note that in principle there seems to be complete unanimity upon this point. . . . [After quoting from President Wilson, the German Chancellor, a Papal Note, Count Czernin, Mr. Balfour, etc., Lord Lansdowne continues:]

That we shall have to secure ourselves against the fiscal hostility of others, that we shall have to prevent the recurrence of conditions under which, when the war broke out, we found ourselves short of essential commodities, because we had allowed certain industries, and certain sources of supply, to pass entirely under the control of our enemies, no one will doubt, subject however to this reservation, that it will surely be for our own interest that the stream of trade should, so far as our own fiscal interests permit, be allowed to flow strong and uninterrupted in its natural channels.

There remains the question of territorial claims. . . . Some of our original desiderata have probably become unattainable. Others would probably now be given a less prominent place than when they were first put forward. Others again, notably the reparation due to Belgium, remain, and must always remain, in the front rank, but when it comes to the wholesale re-arrangement of the map of South-Eastern Europe we may well ask for a suspension of judgment and for the elucidation which a frank exchange of views between the Allied Powers can alone afford. . . .

Let me end by explaining why I attach so much importance to these considerations. We are not going to lose this war, but its prolongation will spell ruin to the civilized world, and an infinite addition to the load of human suffering already weighs upon it. Security will be invaluable to a world that has the vitality to profit by it, but what will be the value of the blessings of peace to nations so exhausted that they can scarcely stretch out a hand with which to grasp them ?

In my belief, if the war is to be brought to a close in time to avert a world-wide catastrophe it will be brought to a close because on both sides the peoples of the countries involved realize that it has already lasted too long. . . .

An immense stimulus would probably be given to the peace party in Germany if it were understood:

(1) That we do not desire the annihilation of Germany as a Great Power;

(2) That we do not seek to impose upon her people any form of Government other than that of their own choice;

(3) That, except as a legitimate war measure, we have no desire to deny to Germany her place among the great commercial communities of the world;

(4) That we are prepared, when the war is over, to examine in concert with other powers the groups of international problems, some of them of recent origin, which are connected with the question of " the freedom of the seas ";

(5) That we are prepared to enter into an international pact under which ample opportunities would be afforded for the settlement of international disputes by peaceful means. . . .

If it be once established that there are no insurmountable difficulties in the way of agreement upon these points, the political horizon might perhaps be scanned with better hope by those who pray, but can at this moment hardly venture to expect, that the new year may bring us a lasting and honourable peace.

Printed in an article by Lord Lansdowne's son in *The Nineteenth Century and After*, No. DCLXXXV (March 1934), " The ' Peace Letter ' of 1917," pp. 380-4.

PART VIII

THE PEACE OF 1919

THE next three extracts deal with the Peace Settlement of 1919, when Lloyd George, the Prime Minister, led the British Delegation at the Conference of Paris.

The " Fontainebleau Memorandum " was perhaps his most important contribution to the Conference, a plea for the modification of the more extreme French demands. But in the General Election at the end of 1918, Lloyd George had also given promises of severe treatment for Germany and for the Kaiser which his supporters had not forgotten. The second extract is from the statement he made in the House of Commons when he had been summoned back from the Conference by a threatened revolt by some of his conservative supporters.[1]

[1] The revolt found expression in a telegram to Lloyd George from Kennedy Jones, Colonel Lowther and others, which included the following passage: " The greatest anxiety exists throughout the country at the persistent reports from Paris that the British delegates instead of formulating the complete financial claim of the Empire are merely considering what amount can be extracted from the enemy. . . .

" Our constituents have always expected—and still expect—that the first action of the Peace Delegates would be, as you repeatedly stated in your election speeches, to present the bill in full, to make Germany acknowledge the debt, and then to discuss ways and means of obtaining payment.

" Although we have the utmost confidence in your intention to fulfil your pledges to the country, may we, as we have to meet innumerable inquiries from our constituents, have your assurance that you have in no way departed from your original intention." (Lloyd George, *The Truth about the Peace Treaties*, p. 563.)

This also gave him an opportunity of dealing with the question of British intervention against the Bolsheviks.

The third extract is from one of the most influential of the attacks on the Treaty. Keynes himself was a member of the British Delegation at Paris as representative of the Treasury.

50: DAVID LLOYD GEORGE. *Some Considerations for the Peace Conference Before They Finally Draft Their Terms.* (The " Fontainebleau Memorandum.")

25 March 1919

WHEN nations are exhausted by wars in which they have put forth all their strength and which leave them tired, bleeding and broken, it is not difficult to patch up a peace that may last until the generation which experienced the horrors of the war has passed away. Pictures of heroism and triumph only tempt those who know nothing of the sufferings and terrors of war. It is therefore comparatively easy to patch up a peace which will last for thirty years.

What is difficult, however, is to draw up a peace which will not provoke a fresh struggle when those who have had practical experience of what war means have passed away. History has proved that a peace, which has been hailed by a victorious nation as a triumph of diplomatic skill and statesmanship, even of moderation in the long run, has proved itself to be shortsighted and charged with danger to the victor. The peace of 1871 was believed by Germany to ensure not only her security but her permanent supremacy. The facts have shown exactly the contrary. France itself has demonstrated that those who say you can make Germany so feeble that she will never be able to hit back

are utterly wrong. Year by year France became
numerically weaker in comparison with her victorious
neighbour, but in reality she became ever more
powerful. She kept watch on Europe; she made
alliances with those whom Germany had wronged or
menaced; she never ceased to warn the world of its
danger and ultimately she was able to secure the overthrow of the far mightier power which had trampled
so brutally upon her. You may strip Germany of her
colonies, reduce her armaments to a mere police force
and her navy to that of a fifth-rate power; all the same
in the end if she feels that she has been unjustly treated
in the peace of 1919 she will find means of exacting
retribution from her conquerors. The impression, the
deep impression, made upon the human heart by four
years of unexampled slaughter will disappear with the
hearts upon which it has been marked by the terrible
sword of the great war. The maintenance of peace
will then depend upon there being no causes of exasperation constantly stirring up the spirit of patriotism,
of justice or of fair play. To achieve redress our terms
may be severe, they may be stern and even ruthless,
but at the same time they can be so just that the
country on which they are imposed will feel in its
heart that it has no right to complain. But injustice,
arrogance, displayed in the hour of triumph, will never
be forgotten or forgiven.

For these reasons I am, therefore, strongly averse to
transferring more Germans from German rule to the
rule of some other nation than can possibly be helped.
I cannot conceive any greater cause of future war than
that the German people, who have certainly proved
themselves one of the most vigorous and powerful
races in the world, should be surrounded by a number

of small States, many of them consisting of people who have never previously set up a stable government for themselves, but each of them containing large masses of Germans clamouring for reunion with their native land. The proposal of the Polish Commission that we should place 2,100,000 Germans under the control of a people which is of a different religion and which has never proved its capacity for stable self-government, throughout its history, must in my judgment, lead sooner or later to a new war in the East of Europe. What I have said about the Germans is equally true of the Magyars. There will never be peace in South-Eastern Europe if every little state now coming into being is to have a large Magyar Irredenta within its borders. I would therefore take as a guiding principle of the peace that as far as is humanly possible the different races should be allocated to their motherlands, and that this human criterion should have precedence over considerations of strategy or economics or communications, which can usually be adjusted by other means. Secondly, I would say that the duration for the payments of reparation ought to disappear if possible with the generation which made the war.

But there is a consideration in favour of a long-sighted peace which influences me even more than the desire to leave no causes justifying a fresh outbreak thirty years hence. There is one element in the present condition of nations which differentiates it from the situation as it was in 1815. In the Napoleonic war the countries were equally exhausted, but the revolutionary spirit had spent its force in the country of its birth, and Germany had satisfied legitimate popular demands for the time being by a series of economic changes which were inspired by courage, foresight and high statesmanship. Even in Russia the Czar had effected great reforms which were probably at that time even too advanced for the half savage population. The situation is very different now. The revolution is still in its infancy. The supreme figures of the Terror are still in command in Russia. The whole of Russia is filled with the spirit of revolution. There is everywhere a deep sense not only of discontent, but of anger and revolt amongst the workmen against pre-war conditions. The whole existing order in its political, social and economic aspects is questioned by the masses of the population from one end of Europe to the other. In some countries, like Germany and Russia, the unrest takes the form of open rebellion; in others, like France, Great Britain and Italy, it takes the shape of strikes and of general disinclination to settle down to work—symptoms which are just as much concerned with the desire for political and social change as with wage demands.

Much of this unrest is healthy. We shall never make a lasting peace by attempting to restore the conditions of 1914. . . .

The greatest danger that I see in the present situation is that Germany may throw in her lot with Bolshevism and place her resources, her brains, her vast organizing power at the disposal of the revolutionary fanatics whose dream it is to conquer the world for Bolshevism by force of arms. This present Government in Germany is weak; it has no prestige; its authority is challenged; it lingers merely because there is no alternative but the Spartacists, and Germany is not ready for Spartacism as yet. . . .

. . . If we are wise, we shall offer to Germany a peace, which, while just, will be preferable for all sensible men to the alternative of Bolshevism. I would, therefore, put it in the forefront of the peace that once she accepts our terms, especially reparation, we will open to her the raw materials and markets of the world on equal terms with ourselves, and will do everything possible to enable the German people to get upon their legs again. We cannot both cripple her and expect her to pay.

Finally, we must offer terms which a responsible Government in Germany can expect to be able to carry out. If we present terms to Germany which are unjust, or excessively onerous, no responsible Government will sign them. . . .

From every point of view, therefore, it seems to me that we ought to endeavour to draw up a peace settlement as if we were impartial arbiters, forgetful of the passions of the war. This settlement ought to have three ends in view. First of all it must do justice to the Allies by taking into account Germany's responsibility for the origin of the war and for the way in which it was fought. Secondly, it must be a settlement which a responsible German Government can sign in the belief that it can fulfil the obligations it incurs. Thirdly, it must be a settlement which will contain in itself no provocations for future wars, and which will constitute an alternative to Bolshevism, because it will commend itself to all responsible opinion as a fair settlement of the European problem.

II

It is not, however, enough to draw up a just and far-sighted peace with Germany. If we are to offer Europe an alternative to Bolshevism we must make the League of Nations into something which will be both a safeguard to those nations who are prepared for fair dealing with their neighbours, and a menace to those who would trespass on the rights of their neighbours, whether they are imperialist empires or imperialist Bolshevists. An essential element, therefore, in the peace settlement is the constitution of the League of Nations as the effective guardian of international right and international liberty throughout the world. If this is to happen the first thing to do is that the leading members of the League of Nations should arrive at an understanding between themselves in regard to armaments. *To my mind it is idle to endeavour to impose a permanent limitation of armaments upon Germany unless we are prepared similarly to impose a limitation upon ourselves.* I recognize that until Germany has settled down and given practical proof that she has abandoned her imperialist ambitions, and until Russia has also given proof that she does not intend to embark upon a military crusade against her neighbours, *it is essential that the leading members of the League of Nations should maintain considerable forces both by land and sea in order to preserve liberty in the world. But if they are to present an united front to the forces both of reaction and revolution, they must arrive at such an agreement in regard to armaments among themselves as would make it impossible for suspicion to arise between the members of the League of Nations in regard to their intentions towards one another. If the League is to do its work for the world it will only be because the members of the League trust it themselves and because there are no apprehensions, rivalries and jealousies in the matter of armaments between them.* The first condition of success for the League of Nations is, therefore, a firm understanding between the British Empire and the United States of America and France and Italy that there will be no competitive building up of fleets or armies between them. Unless this is arrived at before the Covenant is signed the League of Nations will be a sham and a mockery. It will be regarded, and rightly regarded, as a proof that its principal promoters and patrons repose no confidence in its efficacy. But once the leading members of the League have made it clear that they have reached an understanding which will both secure to the League of Nations the strength which is necessary to enable it to protect its members and which at the same time will make misunderstanding and suspicion with regard to competitive armaments impossible between them its future and its authority will be ensured. It will then be able to ensure an essential condition of peace that not only Germany, but all the smaller States of Europe undertake to limit their armaments and abolish conscription. If the small nations are permitted to organize and maintain conscript armies running each to hundreds of thousands, boundary wars will be inevitable and all Europe will be drawn in. *Unless we secure this universal limitation we shall achieve neither lasting peace, nor the permanent observance of the limitation of German armaments which we now seek to impose.*

I should like to ask why Germany, if she accepts the terms we consider just and fair, should not be admitted to the League of Nations, at any rate as soon as she has established a stable and democratic Government. Would it not be an inducement to her both to sign the terms and to resist Bolshevism ? Might it not be safer that she should be inside the League than that she should be outside it ?

Finally, I believe that until the authority and effectiveness of the League of Nations has been demonstrated, the British Empire and the United States

247

ought to give to France a guarantee against the possibility of a new German aggression. France has special reason for asking for such a guarantee. She has twice been attacked and twice invaded by Germany in half a century. She has been so attacked because she has been the principal guardian of liberal and democratic civilization against Central European autocracy on the Continent of Europe. It is right that the other great Western democracies should enter into an undertaking which will ensure that they stand by her side in time to protect her against invasion, should Germany ever threaten her again or until the League of Nations has proved its capacity to preserve the peace and liberty of the world.

Printed in David Lloyd George, *The Truth about the Peace Treaties*, Vol. I (London 1938), pp. 404–11.

51: LLOYD GEORGE. Statement to the House of Commons

16 April 1919

MR. LLOYD GEORGE: In rising to move the Adjournment of the House, I shall ask the indulgence of Members to make some observations about the present situation. My first impulse, when I returned from the Peace Conference, was to await the much advertised criticism that I had been told to expect, but inquiries—diligent inquiries—proved to me that it was not forthcoming. The reason assigned, in particular quarters is rather a remarkable one—that I must not expect criticism until, at any rate, the House has been informed as to what the Delegates have been doing. Coming from such quarters, I should not have thought that fact would be regarded as the slightest basis for any criticism. But I am fully aware that there is a good deal of impatience in the world for peace—some of it very natural impatience. I propose to address myself to the really sincere, honest impatience which is felt throughout all lands.

The task with which the Peace Delegates have been confronted has indeed been a gigantic one. No Conference that has ever assembled in the history of the world has been confronted with problems of such variety, of such complexity, of such magnitude, and of such gravity. The Congress of Vienna was the nearest approach to it. You had then to settle the affairs of Europe. It took eleven months. But the problems at the Congress of Vienna, great as they were, sink into insignificance compared with those which we have had to attempt to settle at the Paris Conference. It is not one continent that is engaged—every continent is affected. With very few exceptions, every country in Europe has been in this War. Every country in Asia is affected by the War, except Tibet and Afghanistan. There is not a square mile of Africa that has not been engaged in the War in one way or another. Almost the whole of the nations of America are in the War, and in the far islands of the Southern Seas there are islands that have been captured, and there are hundreds of thousands of men who have come to fight in this great world struggle. There has never been in the whole history of this globe anything to compare to it. Ten new States have sprung into existence, some of them independent, some of them semi-independent, some of them may be Protectorates, and, at any rate, although you may not define their boundaries, you must give indications of them. The boundaries of fourteen countries have to be re-cast.

That will give some idea of the difficulties, purely of a territorial character, that have engaged our attention. But there are problems equally great and equally important, not of a territorial character, but all affecting the peace of the world, all affecting the well-being of men, all affecting the destiny of the human race, and every one of them of a character where, if you make blunders, humanity may have to pay. Armaments, economic questions, which are the life of commerce and trade, questions of international waterways and railways, the question of indemnities—not an easy one, and not going to be settled by telegram—and international arrangements for labour practically never attempted before! Thanks very largely to the skill and real statesmanship displayed by my right hon. Friend the Member for the Gorbals Division of Glasgow (Mr. Barnes),[1] and thanks also to the assistance which he has had from some hon. and right hon. Gentlemen opposite, and from others who are in the Trade Union movement, a great world scheme has been adopted. And there is that great organization— a great experiment, but an experiment upon which the whole future of the globe for peace hangs—the Society of Nations.

All, and each of them separately, would occupy months. A blunder might precipitate universal war— it may be near, it may be distant. And all nations, almost every nation on earth, engaged in the consideration of all these problems! We were justified in taking some time. In fact, I do not mind saying that it would have been imperative in some respects that we should have taken more time but for one fact, and that is that we are setting up a machine which is capable of readjusting and correcting possible mistakes. That is why the League of Nations, instead of wasting time, has saved the time of the Conference. We had to shorten our labours and work crowded hours, long and late, because, whilst we were trying to build, we saw in many lands the foundations of society crumbling into dust, and we had to make haste. I venture to say that no body of men ever worked harder, and that no body of men have ever worked in better harmony. I am doubtful whether any body of men with a difficult task

---

[1] Mr. G. N. Barnes had been Labour representative in the War Cabinet, and was a member of the British delegation to the Peace Conference; the reference is to the establishment of the International Labour Office.

have worked under greater difficulties—stones clatter-
ing on the roof, and crashing through the windows,
and sometimes wild men screaming through the
keyholes. I have come back to say a few things, and
I mean to say them. (AN HON. MEMBER: " Save you
from your friends! ") I quite agree, and when enormous issues are depending upon it, you require calm
deliberation. I ask it for the rest of the journey. The
journey is not at an end. It is full of perils, perils for
this country, perils for all lands, perils for the people
throughout the world. I beg, at any rate, that the men
who are doing their best should be left in peace to do
it, or that other men should be sent there.

Those are merely artificial difficulties. They are
difficulties that are more trying to the temper than to
the judgement. But there are intrinsic difficulties of
an extraordinary character. You are dealing with a
multitude of nations, most of them with a problem of
its own, each and every one of them with a different
point of view, even where the problems are common,
looking from a different angle at questions—sometimes, perhaps, with different interests; and it requires
all the tact, all the patience, and all the skill that we
can command to prevent different interests from
developing into conflicting interests. I want this
House and the country to bear that in mind. I believe
that we have surmounted those difficulties, but it has
not been easy. There were questions one never heard
of which have almost imperilled the peace of Europe
while we were sitting there.

I should like to put each Member of this House
under an examination. I am certain that I could not
have passed it before I went to the Peace Conference.
How many Members have heard of Teschen ? I do

not mind saying that I had never heard of it, but Teschen very nearly produced an angry conflict between two Allied States[1] and we had to interrupt the proceedings to try and settle the affairs at Teschen. There are many questions of that kind where commissions have had to be sent, and where we have had to smooth difficulties, in order to enable us to get on with the bigger problems of the War. And those questions are important. They are questions of small States. It was the quarrel for small States that made the great War. The difficulties of the Balkans—I believe they disturbed Europe, they created the atmosphere of unrest which began the trouble, they aroused the military temper, and I am not at all sure they did not excite the blood lust in Europe. One of the features of the present situation is that, owing to the break-up of great Empires, Central Europe is being broken into small States, and the greatest care must be taken that no cause of future unrest shall be created by the settlements which we make. I have given the House some of the difficulties with which we are confronted.

In addition to them we have had before us the complete break-up of three ancient empires—Russia, Turkey and Austria. I should like to say, before I come to the other work of the Conference, a few words about Russia. I have read, and I have heard of very simple remedies produced by both sides. Some say, " Use force! " Some say, " Make peace! " It is not easy; it is one of the most complex problems ever dealt with by any body of men. One difficulty is that there is no Russia. Siberia is broken off. There is the Don, one of the richest provinces of Russia, the Caucasus, and then there is some organization controlling

[1] Poland and Czechoslovakia.

Central Russia; but there is no body that can say it is a *de facto* Government for the whole of Russia. Apart, then, from all questions of whether you could, under any circumstances, recognize the Bolshevik Government, you cannot recognize it as the *de facto* Government of Russia. You have that vast country in a state of complete chaos, confusion, and anarchy. There is no authority that extends over the whole. Boundaries advance and boundaries recede. One day a large territory is governed by one authority, and the next day by another. It is just like a volcano; it is still in fierce eruption, and the best you can do is to provide security for those who are dwelling on its remotest and most accessible slopes, and arrest the devastating flow of lava, so that it shall not scorch other lands.

It is very easy to say about Russia, " Why do you not do something ? " I would like to ask each man consecutively what would he have done. To begin with, let me say at once, there is no question of recognition. It has never been discussed—it was never put forward, and never discussed for the reasons I have given. I can give two or three more. There is no Government representing the whole of Russia. The Bolshevik Government has committed against Allied subjects great crimes which have made it impossible to recognize it, even if it were a civilized Government, and the third reason is that at this very moment they are attacking our friends in Russia. What is the alternative ? Does anyone propose military intervention ? I want to examine that carefully and candidly. I will not say before the House, but before any individual commits his conscience to such an enterprise, I want him to realize what it means. First of all there is the fundamental principle of all foreign policy in this country—a very sound principle—that you should never interfere in the internal affairs of another country, however badly governed; and whether Russia is Menshevik or Bolshevik, whether it is reactionary or revolutionary, whether it follows one set of men or another, that is a matter for the Russian people themselves. We cannot interfere, according to any canon of good government, to impose any form of government on another people, however bad we may consider their present form of government to be. The people of this country thoroughly disapprove of Tsarism—its principles, its corruption, and its oppression—but it was not our business to put it down. This is a question for Russia itself. We certainly disagree—I believe I may say every man in this House wholly disagrees fundamentally—with all the principles upon which the present Russian experiment is based. We deplore its horrible consequences—starvation, bloodshed, confusion, ruin, and horror. But that does not justify us in committing this country to a gigantic military enterprise in order to improve the conditions in Russia.

Let me speak in all solemnity, and with a great sense of responsibility. Russia is a country which it is very easy to invade, but very difficult to conquer. It has never been conquered by a foreign foe, although it has been successfully invaded many times. It is a country which it is easy to get into, but very difficult to get out of. You have only to look at what has happened in the last few years to the Germans. They rolled up the Russian armies, they captured millions of Russian prisoners, they took Russian guns. The Russians had no ammunition, there was barely anyone to resist them, and at last the Russian Army fled, leaving their guns in the field. There was no Russian Army. Neither M. Kerensky nor any of his successors could get together 10,000 disciplined men, and yet the Germans, to the last moment, whilst their front was broken in France, while their country was menaced with invasion, while they themselves were being overwhelmed with disaster, had to keep a million of men in Russia; and why? Because they had entangled themselves in the morass, and could not get out of it. Let that be a warning. At that time the Bolshevik Army was comparatively feeble. May I put it in another way?

If we conquered Russia—and we could conquer it— you would be surprised at the military advice which is given us as to the number of men who would be required, and I should like to know where they are to come from. But supposing you had them. Supposing you gathered together an overwhelming army, and you conquered Russia. What manner of government are you going to set up there? You must set up a government which the people want; otherwise it would be an outrage of all the principles for which we have fought in this War. Does anyone know for what government they would ask, and if it is a government we do not like, are we to reconquer all Russia in order to get a government we do like?

Look at it in another way. We have an Army of Occupation. I know what it costs. You cannot immediately leave Russia until you have restored order. It will take a long time to restore order in Russia. It is not a highly organized community. Has anyone reckoned up what an Army of Occupation would cost in Russia? The Rhine is accessible; it is not so very far from Great Britain. But what about Russia, with its long lines of communication, with its deficient transport, and its inadequate resources.

I read how hon. Members in this House showed a natural anxiety to control the expenditure in this country on railways and canals. But my right hon. Friend (Sir Eric Geddes), with all his energy, could not in a quarter of a century spend as much money on railways and canals in Britain as a single year of military enterprise in Russia would cost. I share the horror of all the Bolshevik teachings, but I would rather leave Russia Bolshevik until she sees her way out of it than see Britain bankrupt. And that is the surest road to Bolshevism in Britain. I only want to put—and I must put quite frankly to the House—I should not be doing my duty as head of the Government unless I stated quite frankly to the House my earnest conviction—that to attempt military intervention in Russia would be the greatest act of stupidity that any Government could possibly commit. But then I am asked if that be the case, why do you support Koltchak, Denikin, and Kharkow? I will tell the House with the same frankness as I put the other case. When the Brest-Litoff treaty was signed, there were large territories and populations in Russia that had neither hand nor part in that shameful pact, and they revolted against the Government which signed it.

Let me say this. They raised armies at our instigation and largely, no doubt, at our expense. That was an absolutely sound military policy. For what happened? Had it not been for those organizations that we improvized, the Germans would have secured all the resources which would have enabled them to break the blockade. They would have got through to the grain of the Don, to the minerals of the Urals, and to the oils of the Caucasus. They could have supplied themselves with almost every commodity of which four or five years of rigid blockade had deprived them, and which was essential to their conducting the War. In fact, the Eastern Front was reconstructed—not on the Vistula. It was reconstructed at a point that hurled the German Armies to their own destruction, and, when they got there, deprived them of all the things they had set out to seek. What happened? Bolshevism threatened to impose, by force of arms, its domination on those populations that had revolted against it, and that were organized at our request. If we, as soon as they had served our purpose, and as soon as they had taken all the risks, had said, " Thank you; we are exceedingly obliged to you. You have served out purpose. We need you no longer. Now let the Bolshevists cut your throats," we should have been mean—we should have been thoroughly unworthy indeed of any great land. As long as they stand there, with the evident support of the populations—because wherever the populations are not behind them every organized effort to resist Bolshevism has failed—in the Ukraine, where the population is either indifferent or, perhaps, friendly, we have there populations like those in Siberia, the Don, and elsewhere, who are opposed to Bolshevism—they are offering a real resistance. It is our business, since we asked them to take this step, since we promised support to them if they took this step, and since by taking this stand they contributed largely to the triumph of the Allies, it is our business to stand by our friends. Therefore, we are not sending troops, but we are supplying goods. Everyone who knows Russia knows that, if she is to be redeemed, she must be redeemed by her own sons. All that they ask is—seeing that the Bolsheviks secured the arsenals of

Russia—that they should be supplied with the necessary arms to enable them to fight for their own protection and freedom in the land where the Bolshevists are anti-pathetic to the feeling of the population. Therefore I do not in the least regard it as a departure from the fundamental policy of Great Britain not to interfere in the internal affairs of any land that we should support General Denikin, Admiral Koltchak, and General Kharkoff.

MR. CLEMENT EDWARDS: Are you supplying them with food ?

THE PRIME MINISTER: I do not think so. They are not asking for it; they are asking for equipment, and we are supplying them. As far as food is concerned, they are very well off. The Don is a very rich country, and we have not heard that there is any suffering in those parts. What more are we doing ? This is so important a part of the policy of the Allies that I am bound to take up some time in order to explain it. The next item in our policy is what I call to arrest the flow of the lava—that is, to prevent the forcible eruption of Bolshevism into Allied lands. For that reason, we are organizing all the forces of the Allied countries bordering on Bolshevist territory from the Baltic to the Black Sea—Poland, Czecho-Slovakia, and Roumania. There is no doubt that the populations are anti-Bolshevist. I had the pleasure of meeting Mr. Paderewski the other day. He had just come from Poland, and he told me that the Polish population were bitterly anti-Bolshevist. The Czecho-Slovakian statesmen—a very able body of men—told me exactly the same thing about Bohemia, and the same observation applies to

Roumania. If Bolshevism attacks any of our Allies, it is our business to defend them.

For that reason, we are supplying all these countries with the necessary equipment to set up a real barrier against an invasion by force of arms. The Bolshevists may menace or they may not. Whether they do so or not, we should be ready for any attempt to overrun Europe by force. That is our policy. But we want peace in Russia. The world will not be pacified so long as Russia is torn and rent by civil war. We made one effort. I make no apology for that. That was an effort to make peace among the warring sections, not by recognizing any Government, but by inducing them to come together, with a view to setting up some authority in Russia which would be acceptable to the whole of the Russian people, and which the Allies could recognize as the Government of that great people. We insisted that it was necessary they should cease fighting before they started to negotiate. With one accord, I regret to say, they refused to assent to this essential condition, and, therefore, the effort was not crowned with success.

LIEUTENANT-COMMANDER KENWORTHY: Did not the Soviet Republic accede?

THE PRIME MINISTER: No; they would not accede to the request that they should cease fighting. On the contrary, they suggested that we were doing it purely because our friends were getting the worst of it. That fact itself shows that the time has not yet arrived for securing the pacification of Russia by means of any outside pressure. I do not despair of a solution being found. There are factors in the situation even now which are promising. Reliable information which we have received indicates that while the Bolshevist forces are apparently growing in strength, Bolshevism itself is rapidly on the wane. It is breaking down before the relentless pressure of economic facts. This process must inevitably continue. You cannot carry on a great country upon rude and wild principles such as those which are inculcated by the Bolsheviks. When Bolshevism, as we know it and as Russia to her sorrow has known it, disappears, then the time will come for another effort at re-establishing peace in Russia. But that time is not yet. We must have patience, and we must have faith. You are dealing with a nation which has been misgoverned for centuries, and been defeated and trampled to the ground, largely, let us admit, owing to the corruption, the inefficiency, and the treachery of its own governors. Its losses have been colossal. All that largely accounts for the real frenzy that seized upon a great people. That is why a nation which has gone through untold horrors has abandoned itself for the moment to fantastic and hysterical experiments. But there are unmistakable signs that Russia is emerging from the trouble. When that time comes, when she is once more sane, calm, and normal, we shall make peace in Russia. Until we can make peace in Russia, it is idle to say that the world is at peace. . . .

I should now like to say something about the general question of the peace. After very prolonged discussions, not an hour of which was wasted, the representatives of the Great Powers have arrived at a complete understanding on the great fundamental questions that affect peace with Germany. We have formulated our demands, and I hope that by the end of next week they will be presented. I should like to say one or two

words about the very unfortunate attempts which have
been made to sow dissension, distrust and suspicion
between the nations whose solidarity and good will
towards each other is essential to the whole of civilization. I cannot conceive at the present moment a worse
crime than to attempt to sow strife, distrust and suspicion between those people whose good will, whose
co-operation, whose common action, whose common
sacrifice, have just saved the world from disaster.
Those things can be done in our domestic politics, and
no great harm ensues, even though it be due to false
rumours and misrepresentations. You can do them
with impunity, but to do them now, in the very greatest crisis of the world's history, when nothing can save
the world but keeping the nations together, is an outrage. No discussions could ever have been more
friendly. Never was a greater desire shown to understand each other's point of view and to make allowance
for that point of view.

The idea that America and Europe have been at
hopeless variance is untrue. No one could have treated
more sympathetically the peculiar problem and the
special susceptibilities of Europe, with long and bitter
memories of national conflicts, than President Wilson.
Nor have we during the whole of these Conferences
ever forgotten the poignant fact that most of the sufferings and sacrifices of this War were borne by the heroic
land in whose capital the conditions of peace have been
determined. We have not forgotten that France
within living memory, has been rent and torn by the
same savage enemy. We have not forgotten that she
is entitled not merely to security against a repetition of
attack, but that she is entitled to a keener sense of
security against it. Upon all the questions which have

come before us we have come to conclusions which are unanimous.

What about publicity? We considered that question and we came to the unanimous conclusion that to publish those terms before they are discussed with the enemy would be a first-class blunder. I know there have been criticisms, and there has been rather silly talk about secrecy. No Peace Conference ever held has given so much publicity to its proceedings. I am not referring to unauthorized reports. I am referring to official communications. Honestly I would rather have a good Peace than a good Press.

May I give one or two reasons why we came to the conclusion not to publish the terms before they are discussed. No peace terms, no measure of any kind ever devised or promulgated—can satisfy everyone. I am not referring to mere political and personal attack, or to worked-up effects. I am thinking of honest criticisms inspired by higher and more sincere motives. There are some people who will say, "You have gone too far." There will be others who will say, "You have not gone far enough." There will probably be people in each country who will suggest that the interests of their country have been sacrificed to those of some other country, and if all that can be published who will benefit by it? No one but the enemy. Supposing there were men in this country who thought our peace terms were too severe, there would be speeches and there would be leading articles. Those are the speeches and those are the articles that would be published in Germany as if British public opinion were opposed to our terms, because we have gone too far. It would encourage resistance. Let me put the other side—the effect in

Germany. I want to make peace. Supposing the terms proposed by Bismarck to the French had been published in France before they had been discussed by Jules Favre, what would have happened? The Communists would have been strengthened by the adhesion of men who, for patriotic reasons and in a momentary impulse, without considering the best thing, looking over a period of twenty years or longer, would have supported even anarchy in preference to what they considered harsh terms. France could not have made peace. To publish the terms prematurely before they were discussed, before the enemy had a full opportunity of considering them, would be to raise difficulties in the way of peace, and we mean to take every action that is necessary to prevent publication.

But there are two or three things I can say about it. Before the War was over, we stated our peace terms. On behalf of the Government, I made a considered statement—which was considered by every member of the Cabinet and by the Trade Union Conference—of what we conceived to be the terms on which we could make peace with the enemy. That was last year. At that time those terms received the adhesion of every section of opinion in this country. There was no protest from any quarter. A few days afterwards President Wilson proposed his famous " Fourteen Points," which practically embodied the same proposals. I am referred to my speeches before the last election. There are some who suggest that at the last election I and my colleagues were rushed into declarations of which now we are rather ashamed, and wish to get out of. I do not wish to get out of them in the least. These declarations were adopted by, I think, every political leader of every section. . . .

We want peace. We want a peace which will be just, but not vindictive. We want a stern peace, because the occasion demands it. The crime demands it. But its severity must be designed, not to gratify vengeance, but to vindicate justice. Every clause and term in those conditions must be justified on that ground. Above all, we want to protect the future against a repetition of the horrors of this War, by making the wrongdoer repair the wrong and the loss which he has inflicted by his wanton aggression, by punishing any individual who is responsible, by depriving the nations that have menaced the peace of Europe for half a century with a flourishing sword— by depriving them of their weapon—(An Hon. Member: " What about the Kaiser ? ")—I stand by all my pledges—by avoiding conditions which would create a legitimate sense of wrong, which would excite national pride needlessly to seek opportunities for redress, and by giving the most permanent security to the nations of the earth to federate for a firm purpose of maintaining right.

I want to say one other thing, because I am going back, if the House wants me to—unless it prefers some other choice. (Hon. Members: " No, no! ") There are many " eligible offers." But whoever goes there is going to meet the emissaries of the enemy, the enemy with whom we have been confronted for five years, and who has inflicted terrible wounds upon humanity. Whoever goes there must go knowing that he has the fullest confidence of Parliament behind him. I know that Parliament can repudiate the treaty when it is signed. I do not want to contemplate that. It would be difficult to do when once the British signatures are attached, but Parliament can do it. So, before anyone goes there, Parliament must feel that, at any rate, it knows that whoever is there will carry out his pledges to the utmost of his power and his gifts. You cannot always clear up misconceptions. When you see mis-statements you cannot instantly write, and say that they are not true, that they are inaccurate. You cannot always be leaving the Conference to come home to clear up this or that. You cannot conduct negotiations under those conditions. . . .

I now come back to the general question, and I apologize for taking up so much time on the other matter. There is a general feeling that people want peace. I have talked to business men; I have talked to many soldiers awaiting demobilization; and the general word, if I can just express it shortly, is, " Hurry up; we want peace." Another request which I have heard from French soldiers whom I met in the devastated areas was, " Give us a good peace." That is the thing that the people of this country are out for. Revenge—they do not understand it; they are out for justice. The world wants to get back quickly to work, and it wants to get to work under better conditions than it had before the War. From all countries, without exception—and I have now seen men of many lands—I heard the echo of that resolve on the part of the worker, fixed deep in their hearts everywhere, and I am proud that Britain has been the first to take action on that line. I should like to say something of the profound impression which is created in every country by the quiet way in which Britain is setting her house in order—by conference, by conciliation, by legislation, and not by warring anarchy and force—and they all say, " Is not this characteristic of British tradition ? " It is having its effect right through the world. There was a great labour orator, I think the greatest on the Continent of Europe, who spoke on Friday at the Labour Conference. He was detailing all the labour conditions that had stirred the working men everywhere, and he said, " There are two methods of dealing with the situation. One is the Russian method, and the other is the English method." I felt a thrill of pride for my country when I heard that. It is essential that the ordinary machinery of commerce and industry should be set going. You cannot do without them. There are men in every trade with their hands on the lever waiting for the announcement. It is essential that the enormous expenditure of war should be cut down ruthlessly, and as soon as possible. That is why peace is necessary, otherwise the fruits of industry will be squandered.

One of the most beneficent results of peace, in my judgment, will be that the great continental menace of armaments will be swept away. The country that has kept Europe armed for forty years is to be reduced to an army which is just adequate to police her cities and her villages, and with her fleet, which was a sort of terror to us—a hidden terror—she will now have just enough to protect her commerce, and no more. We must profit by that. Europe must profit by it, and not Germany alone. I know there is a good deal of talk about the recrudescence of the military power of Germany, and you get paragraphs about what Germany is going to do—she is going to release her fleet, and she is going to have great armies. That is not the danger. The fact is that, with difficulty, can she gather together 80,000 armed men to preserve order. Her guns have been taken away from her—her weapons of offence on the sea, on the land, and in the air.

That is not the danger. The world is going to pieces. A very keen observer who has just come from Central Europe said to me, " I have seen a world going to pieces—men helpless, half-starved, benumbed; no fight in them, no revolution, because the men have no heart." Two British soldiers crossing a square in Vienna saw a hungry child. They took out a biscuit, and cast it to the child. You have seen when you throw a bit of bread on the ground how birds flock from every part, birds that you have never seen before. Well, hundreds of children came from nowhere, they clawed for that food, and it was with difficulty that these two British soldiers escaped with their lives!

COMMANDER KENWORTHY: The blockade?

THE PRIME MINISTER: That which I have described is the real danger. The gaunt spectre of hunger is stalking throughout the land. The Central Powers and Russia have overtaxed their strength in the conflict. They are lying prostrate, broken, and all these movements of Spartacists, and Bolsheviks, and revolutionaries in each of these countries are more like the convulsions of a broken-backed creature, crushed in a savage conflict. It is in these conditions, and with this material, that we are making peace. Nations with military ambitions have received a cruel lesson, nay, Europe itself has suffered more in the last five years than ever in the whole of its past history. The lesson has been a sharper one than ever. It has been administered to vaster multitudes of human beings than ever. The people have a more intelligent appreciation of what it means than ever. For that reason the opportunity of organizing the world on the basis of peace is

268

such a one as has never been presented to the world before, and in this fateful hour it is the supreme duty of statesmen in every land—of the Parliaments upon whose will statesmen depend, of those who guide and direct the public opinion which is the making of all— not to soil this triumph of right by indulging in the angry passions of the moment, but to consecrate the sacrifices of millions to the permanent redemption of the human race from the scourge and agony of war.

Hansard, Fifth Series, Vol. CXIV, pp. 2936–45, 2950, 2954–6.

52: JOHN MAYNARD KEYNES. From *The Economic Consequences of the Peace*, 1919

For one who spent in Paris the greater part of the six months which succeeded the Armistice an occasional visit to London was a strange experience. England still stands outside Europe. Europe's voiceless tremors do not reach her. Europe is apart and England is not of her flesh and body. But Europe is solid with herself. France, Germany, Italy, Austria, and Holland, Russia and Roumania and Poland, throb together, and their structure and civilization are essentially one. They flourished together, they have rocked together in a war, which we, in spite of our enormous contributions and sacrifices (like, though in a less degree than, America), economically stood outside, and they may fall together. In this lies the destructive significance of the Peace of Paris. If the European Civil War is to end with France and Italy abusing their momentary victorious power to destroy Germany and Austria-Hungary now prostrate, they invite their own destruction also, being so deeply and inextricably intertwined with their victims by hidden psychic and economic bonds. At any rate an Englishman who took part in the Conference of Paris and was during those months a member of the Supreme Economic Council of the Allied Powers, was bound to become, for him a new experience, a European in his cares and outlook. There, at the nerve centre of the

European system, his British preoccupations must largely fall away and he must be haunted by other and more dreadful spectres. Paris was a nightmare, and every one there was morbid. A sense of impending catastrophe overhung the frivolous scene; the futility and smallness of man before the great events confronting him; the mingled significance and unreality of the decisions; levity, blindness, insolence, confused cries from without—all the elements of ancient tragedy were there. Seated indeed amid the theatrical trappings of the French Saloons of State, one could wonder if the extraordinary visages of Wilson and of Clemenceau, with their fixed hue and unchanging characterisation, were really faces at all and not the tragic-comic masks of some strange drama or puppet-show. . . .

The progress of the General Election of 1918 affords a sad, dramatic history of the essential weakness of one who draws his chief inspiration not from his own true impulses, but from the grosser effluxions of the atmosphere which momentarily surrounds him. The Prime Minister's natural instincts, as they so often are, were right and reasonable. He himself did not believe in hanging the Kaiser or in the wisdom or the possibility of a great indemnity. On the 22nd of November he and Mr. Bonar Law issued their Election Manifesto. It contains no allusion of any kind either to the one or to the other, but, speaking, rather, of Disarmament and the League of Nations, concludes that " our first task must be to conclude a just and lasting peace, and so to establish the foundations of a new Europe that occasion for further wars may be for ever averted." In his speech at Wolverhampton on the eve of the Dissolution (November 24), there is no word of Reparation or Indemnity. On the following day at

Glasgow, Mr. Bonar Law would promise nothing. "We are going to the Conference," he said, "as one of a number of allies, and you cannot expect a member of the Government, whatever he may think, to state in public before he goes into that Conference, what line he is going to take in regard to any particular question." But a few days later at Newcastle (November 29) the Prime Minister was warming to his work: "When Germany defeated France she made France pay. That is the principle which she herself has established. There is absolutely no doubt about the principle, and that is the principle we should proceed upon—that Germany must pay the costs of the war up to the limit of her capacity to do so." But he accompanied this statement of principle with many "words of warning" as to the practical difficulties of the case: "We have appointed a strong Committee of experts, representing every shade of opinion, to consider this question very carefully and to advise us. There is no doubt as to the justice of the demand. She ought to pay, she must pay as far as she can, but we are not going to allow her to pay in such a way as to wreck our industries." At this stage the Prime Minister sought to indicate that he intended great severity, without raising excessive hopes of actually getting the money, or committing himself to a particular line of action at the Conference. It was rumoured that a high city authority had committed himself to the opinion that Germany could certainly pay £20,000 million and that this authority for his part would not care to discredit a figure of twice that sum. The Treasury officials, as Mr. Lloyd George indicated, took a different view. He could, therefore, shelter himself behind the wide discrepancy between the opinions of his different advisers, and regard the precise figure of Germany's capacity to pay as an open question in the treatment of which he must do his best for his country's interests. As to our engagements under the Fourteen Points he was always silent.

On November 30, Mr. Barnes, a member of the War Cabinet, in which he was supposed to represent Labour, shouted from a platform, " I am for hanging the Kaiser."

On December 6, the Prime Minister issued a statement of policy and aims in which he stated, with significant emphasis on the word *European*, that " All the European Allies have accepted the principle that the Central Powers must pay the cost of the war up to the limit of their capacity."

But it was now little more than a week to Polling Day, and still he had not said enough to satisfy the appetites of the moment. On December 8, *The Times*, providing as usual a cloak of ostensible decorum for the lesser restraint of its associates, declared in a leader entitled " Making Germany Pay," that " the public mind was still bewildered by the Prime Minister's various statements." " There is too much suspicion," they added, " of influences concerned to let the Germans off lightly, whereas the only possible motive in determining their capacity to pay must be the interests of the Allies." " It is the candidate who deals with the issues of to-day," wrote their Political Correspondent, " who adopts Mr. Barnes' phrase about ' hanging the Kaiser ' and plumps for the payment of the cost of the war by Germany, who rouses his audience and strikes the notes to which they are most responsive."

On December 9, at the Queen's Hall, the Prime Minister avoided the subject. But from now on, the debauchery of thought and speech progressed hour by hour. The grossest spectacle was provided by Sir Eric Geddes in the Guildhall at Cambridge. An earlier speech in which, in a moment of injudicious candour, he had cast doubts on the possibility of extracting from Germany the whole cost of the war had been the object of serious suspicion, and he had therefore a reputation to regain. " We will get out of her all you can squeeze out of a lemon and a bit more," the penitent shouted, " I will squeeze her until you can hear the pips squeak "; his policy was to take every bit of property belonging to Germans in neutral and Allied countries, and all her gold and silver and her jewels, and the contents of her picture-galleries and libraries, to sell the proceeds for the Allies' benefit. " I would strip Germany," he cried, " as she has stripped Belgium."

By December 11 the Prime Minister had capitulated. His Final Manifesto of Six Points issued on that day to the electorate furnishes a melancholy comparison with his programme of three weeks earlier. I quote it in full:

" 1. Trial of the Kaiser.
   2. Punishment of those responsible for atrocities.
   3. Fullest indemnities from Germany.
   4. Britain for the British, socially and industrially.
   5. Rehabilitation of those broken in the war.
   6. A happier country for all."

Here is food for the cynic. To this concoction of greed and sentiment, prejudice and deception, three weeks of the platform had reduced the powerful governors of England, who but a little while before had spoken not ignobly of Disarmament and a League of Nations and of a just and lasting peace which should establish the foundations of a new Europe. . . .

Apart from other aspects of the transaction, I believe that the campaign for securing out of Germany the general costs of the war was one of the most serious acts of political unwisdom for which our statesmen have ever been responsible. To what a different future Europe might have looked forward if either Mr. Lloyd George or Mr. Wilson had apprehended that the most serious of the problems which claimed their attention were not political or territorial but financial and economic, and that the perils of the future lay not in frontiers or sovereignties but in food, coal, and transport. Neither of them paid adequate attention to these problems at any stage of the Conference. But in any event the atmosphere for the wise and reasonable consideration of them was hopelessly befogged by the commitments of the British delegation on the question of Indemnities. The hopes to which the Prime Minister had given rise not only compelled him to advocate an unjust and unworkable economic basis to the Treaty with Germany, but set him at variance with the President, and on the other hand with competing interests to those of France and Belgium. The clearer it became that but little could be expected from Germany, the more necessary it was to exercise patriotic greed and " sacred egotism " and snatch the bone from the juster claims and greater need of France or the well-founded expectations of Belgium. Yet the financial problems which were about to exercise Europe could not be solved by greed. The possibility of *their* cure lay in magnanimity. . . .

I see few signs of sudden or dramatic developments anywhere. Riots and revolutions there may be, but not such, at present, as to have fundamental significance. Against political tyranny and injustice Revolution is a weapon. But what counsels of hope can Revolution offer to sufferers from economic privation, which does not arise out of the injustices of distribution but is general ? The only safeguard against revolution in Central Europe is indeed the fact that, even to the minds of men who are desperate, Revolution offers no prospect of improvement whatever. There may, therefore, be ahead of us a long, silent process of semi-starvation, and of a gradual, steady lowering of the standards of life and comfort. The bankruptcy and decay of Europe, if we allow it to proceed, will affect every one in the long-run, but perhaps not in a way that is striking or immediate.

This has one fortunate side. We may still have time to reconsider our course and to view the world with new eyes. For the immediate future events are taking charge, and the near destiny of Europe is no longer in the hands of any man. The events of the coming year will not be shaped by the deliberate acts of statesmen, but by the hidden currents, flowing continually beneath the surface of political history, of which no one can predict the outcome. In one way only can we influence these hidden currents—by setting in motion those forces of instruction and imagination which change *opinion*. The assertion of truth, the unveiling of illusion, the dissipation of hate, the enlargement and instruction of man's hearts and minds, must be the means.

In this autumn of 1919, in which I write, we are at the dead season of our fortunes. The reaction from the exertions, the fears, and the sufferings of the past five years is at its height. Our power of feeling or caring beyond the immediate questions of our own material well-being is temporarily eclipsed. The greatest events outside our own direct experience and the most dreadful anticipations cannot move us.

> In each human heart terror survives
> The ruin it has gorged: the loftiest fear
> All that they would disdain to think were true:
> Hypocrisy and custom make their minds
> The fanes of many a worship, now outworn.
> They dare not devise good for man's estate,
> And yet they know not that they do not dare.
> The good want power but to weep barren tears.
> The powerful goodness want: worse need for them.
> The wise want love; and those who love want wisdom;
> And all best things are thus confused to ill.
> Many are strong and rich, and would be just,
> But live among their suffering fellow-men
> As if none felt: they know not what they do.

We have been moved already beyond endurance, and need rest. Never in the lifetime of men now living has the universal element in the soul of man burnt so dimly.

For these reasons the true voice of the new generation has not yet spoken, and silent opinion is not yet formed. To the formation of the general opinion of the future I dedicate this book.

J. M. Keynes, *The Economic Consequences of the Peace* (London 1919), pp. 2–4, 127–32, 134–5, 277–9.

PART IX

BETWEEN THE WARS, 1919–1939

IN 1924–5 various proposals were made for increasing international security within the framework of the League of Nations. Two proposals originating at Geneva—the Draft Treaty of Mutual Assistance and the Geneva Protocol—were considered and rejected, and it was a proposal of a more limited kind that was finally adopted as the Treaty of Locarno in October 1925.

For the most part the Labour Party supported the idea of a general settlement involving an unlimited guarantee to support collective action against an aggressor who refused to submit to arbitration, while the Conservative Party, whose Foreign Secretary Austen Chamberlain was largely responsible for the Locarno agreement, preferred specific commitments in a limited area. It was the old controversy of limited or unlimited intervention by Britain in Continental affairs.

The next extract is from a speech by Arthur Henderson, one of the authors, under the Labour Government of 1924, of the Geneva Protocol. The Conservative Foreign Secretary had recently announced at Geneva that the British Government was unable to accept the Protocol and Henderson is making a last attempt to defend it. Later in the debate, Chamberlain announced the first suggestion from Germany for a five-power mutual guarantee, which later in the year was to be achieved at Locarno.

The extracts which follow Henderson's speech deal with Locarno itself and show Chamberlain's own view of the agreements, while the extract from *The Times* illustrates the mood in which the agreements were received. The leading article quoted appeared on 19th November—on the morning after the House of Commons by a large majority had voted the ratification of the Treaty.

Under the Treaty, Great Britain and Italy guaranteed the existing Franco-German and Belgian-German frontiers and promised to come to the assistance of France and Belgium if either were attacked by Germany, and of Germany if attacked by France and Belgium. But see Nos. 58 and 59 below.

53: ARTHUR HENDERSON. Speech in House of Commons

24 March 1925

THE Government, in my opinion, have taken a very serious step indeed in declaring against the policy embodied in the Protocol and by encouraging a return to the discredited and dangerous policy of separate and limited alliances and undertakings. That is what the proposal which has emanated from the Government in favour of special arrangements in order to meet special needs really amounts to. No other construction can be placed upon the speech delivered by the right hon. Gentleman at the Council of the League, coupled with the latest proposal of the five-power pact made by the German Government. . . .

What, may I ask, is the purpose of the Protocol? The purpose is defined in the closing words of the Resolution proposed by the then British Prime Minister,[1] and seconded by the French Prime Minister.[2] The words are: " It is to settle by pacific means all disputes which may arise between States." The Protocol, therefore, embodies a system of arbitration which no international dispute, whether juridical or political, can escape. It lays down as a foundation condition of international intercourse that all disputes

[1] Ramsay Macdonald.
[2] Edouard Herriot.

shall be settled by pacific methods. It defines and prescribes the sanctions which may be applied against any State which fails to observe its obligations. It cites the criteria for deciding which is a covenant-breaking State. The Protocol recognizes the fact that as there can be no disarmament without security and arbitration, so there can be no security or arbitration without disarmament. History demonstrates that armaments of themselves do not prevent war; on the contrary, they enormously increase the danger of war. When the mad race and competition in armaments creates an atmosphere of suspicion, jealousy and antagonism, war at last becomes inevitable.

Whatever may be the faults or deficiencies of the Protocol, and however much Members of this House may consider that the Protocol requires revision, its authors can claim that it does recognize, however much may be said to the contrary, that the first essential is to get rid of war as an instrument of policy. When we took the course we did we realized that militarist mentality had dominated the minds of the people of the respective nations so long that it would not be an easy task to transform the spirit that has operated in the minds of the nations, nor would it be easy to unbuild the powerful military machines of the world. To do that successfully, we must, at least, provide satisfactory means whereby international disputes of every kind and description can be peaceably dealt with and, if possible, settled.

Arbitration, obligatory and universal, in our judgment was the only alternative method to the appeal to force. True, that represents a departure from the old atmosphere of hatred and suspicion. The right hon. Gentleman said at Geneva: " Brute force is what the

nations fear, and only brute force can give security."
To deliver the nations from that false, dangerous and
discredited doctrine is the aim of the Protocol. . . .

The great object of the Protocol is the prohibition of
aggressive war, which it seeks to achieve in this way,
regarding aggressive war as an international crime.
The Protocol provides the means whereby the risk of
international conflict may be greatly diminished as a
result of the settlement of international disputes by
legal, peaceable and constitutional means. Surely, it
follows that if more comprehensive and, as I think,
more effective machinery for dealing with disputes is
provided, so, naturally, we expect the disputes to be
less dangerous and not more dangerous. Yet in spite
of this provision for the fuller application of the principle of arbitration, it has been objected to the
Protocol that it actually increases the danger of war.
That I cannot admit for I want to make it absolutely
clear that the Protocol creates no new obligation in this
respect. What the Protocol does, is to provide the
nations with the very means which we hoped all peace-
loving nations would naturally use to the full in order
to avoid war. It was not a theoretical admiration for
the principle of arbitration which animated the
framers of the Protocol, but the practical and urgent
need of seeking to organize the world for peace. . . .

Of course, if you omit the provisions for arbitration
and emphasize those defining the sanctions, you may
justify that charge, but you are misrepresenting the
purpose of the Protocol. We hoped that if the nations
used arbitration there would be no need for sanctions,
and we believe that most nations would use arbitration
if they accepted the Covenant. In view of the criticism
to which the Protocol has been subjected on this point,

I cannot emphasise too strongly the fact that the Protocol is only supplementary to the Covenant. It is not a new and independent instrument. The British Delegation made this position clear at Geneva, especially in their responsibility for accepting the sanctions. May I quote some words which I ventured to use at Geneva ? " We are remaining within the terms of the Covenant. We are undertaking no new obligation. We do not see how any power which has signed the Covenant, and which intends to carry out honourably the pledges it has given, can hesitate to subscribe to Article 11 of the Protocol. Surely ' loyal and effective co-operation ' in support of the Covenant is what may confidently be expected from every member of the League of Nations." And I also said: " What we wish to proclaim to the world is that we are determined to join hands and assist each other loyally and effectively in punishing the aggressor." This, we considered, would be pooled security, whereby the might of nations would become the servant of international justice. Further, apart from arbitration—which is, I admit, the foundation of the Protocol—we make provision for the reduction of armaments.

Hansard, Fifth Series, Vol. CLXXXII, pp. 291-2, 293-5, 295-6.

54: AUSTEN CHAMBERLAIN on the Locarno Treaties

1925

(a) . . . I am firmly convinced that the true line of progress is to proceed from the particular to the general, and not, as has hitherto been embodied in Covenant and Protocol, to reverse the process and attempt to eliminate the particular by the general. A form of guarantee which is so general that we undertake exactly the same obligations in defence, shall I say of the Polish Corridor (for which no British Government ever will or ever can risk the bones of a British grenadier) as we extend to these international arrangements or conditions on which, as our history shows, our national existence depends, is a guarantee so wide and general that it carries no conviction whatever and gives no sense of security to those who are concerned in our action.

> Letter to Lord Crewe, 16 February 1925, printed in Sir Charles Petrie, Bt., *The Life and Letters of the Right Hon. Sir Austen Chamberlain, K.G., P.C., M.P.*, Vol. II (London 1940), p. 258.

(b) I believe that a great work of peace has been done. I believe it above all because of the spirit in which it was done and the spirit which it has engendered. It would not have been done unless all the governments, and I will add all the nations, had felt the need to start a new and better chapter of international relations; but it would not have been done unless this country was prepared to take her share in guaranteeing the settlements so come to. . . .

We who live close to the Continent, we, who cannot disassociate ourselves from what passes there, whose safety, whose peace and the security of whose shores are manifestly bound up with the peace and security of the Continent, and, above all, of the Western nations, must make our decision; and we ask the House to approve the ratification of the Treaty of Locarno in the belief that by that treaty we are averting danger from our own country and from Europe, that we are safeguarding peace, and that we are laying the foundations of reconciliation and friendship with the enemies of a few years ago.

In the House of Commons, 18 November 1925, *Hansard*, Fifth Series, Vol. CLXXXVIII, pp. 431–2.

55: LEADING ARTICLE IN *THE TIMES*. The Locarno Debate

19 November 1925

GREAT BRITAIN has made it possible for the chief nations of Europe to conclude, seven years after the termination of the greatest war in history, the Locarno Treaty of Peace. If our own country had not participated in the guarantee of the security of the Western frontiers, it would have been very difficult for the Continental peoples to take the decisive step from the suspicious spirit of war to the temper that renders possible their pacific co-operation in common tasks. Commitments to the war spirit were entrenched in all the formulas of international intercourse. They necessarily determined the actions and the policies of Governments during a long and agitated period of post-war history. . . . To the secular controversy between France and Germany, aggravated to an alarming degree by the events of the last war, an end has to be put somehow. The presuppositions of this controversy and the bitter prejudices which they have provoked, and which have been sanctioned by legal forms and governmental policies, could not have been removed unless Great Britain had lent her aid at this critical moment in the changing tempo of the Continental peoples. It is just because Great Britain has vital interests, both on the Continent of Europe and in every part of the wide world that depends on Europe and on which Europe depends, that her action was of historical importance. Hesitation or failure on the part of our country at such a time would have left Europe and the world at a loss. The British Government took the right decision, agreed to guarantee security in the controversial area, was compelled, in virtue of this decision, to take a very active part in the negotiations of the Continental peoples for new forms, new premises, and new bases for friendly association in the works of peace, and thus found itself in the van of a world movement away from war towards the constructive peace that all the peoples desired. The point is that the European peoples could not have risen above the rut of war without Great Britain. It should be a source of pride and fresh confidence to our own sorely tried people that British intervention in the affairs of Europe has made peace in a large area of the continent to which we are attached something like a real possibility at last.

Yesterday's debate in the House of Commons on the Locarno Treaty was of exceptional importance. For one thing it provided a test of public opinion. . . . It had been preceded by a vague, hardly definable, but very powerful expression of British and European sentiment. Mr. Macdonald spoke yesterday of his own experience during a recent journey in Europe. He talked of a movement of " mass psychology "; during his journey he spoke of the Locarno Treaty as a response to " the soul of the people yearning for peace". It would indeed have been incongruous and inept if the British Parliament, or any important section of British opinion represented in the House, had repudiated an achievement in which the action of the British Government was the really decisive factor. There was no genuine divergence of views on essentials yesterday. The introduction of amendments and corrections, the somewhat artificial attempts to give a party colouring to a national sentiment, only served in the end to emphasize the strong feeling of all sorts and conditions of people that the right thing had been done at Locarno, and that for once a British Government had done something of which the whole nation could deeply and thoroughly approve. . . .

The Times, Thursday 19 November 1925.

56: AUSTEN CHAMBERLAIN. *Great Britain as a European Power*

From a paper read to the Royal Institute of International Affairs
4 February 1930

Sir Austen Chamberlain ceased to be Foreign Secretary on the fall of the Conservative ministry in 1929. The following reflections on the position of Britain in relation to Europe are printed as showing the growing importance of the world outside Europe in the shaping of British policy.

... Two circumstances have in recent years profoundly altered the condition of the problem. The first in point of time is the development of the means of rapid communication both of ideas and persons. Broadly speaking, no part of the world is now isolated either physically or morally from the rest, whether for the purposes of peaceful trade or international contention. Distance no longer spells detachment; abstention no longer secures immunity. The world has narrowed; the interests of all nations have become inextricably intertwined, and Britain, the nerve-centre of a world-wide Empire, feels and reacts to every electric disturbance, no matter how distant its source.

This interdependence of the nations is a fact which must increasingly affect the whole world. It is not

U

merely a sense of the appalling horrors of modern war which has driven the world to seek protection from it in the League of Nations; it is the growing perception that our interests are so interwoven that the victors suffer only less than the vanquished, and that even the neutral is involved in the common disaster to mankind. Nor is that all. The new communications carry the ideas of the West even more swiftly than its armies. East and West have met, and the clash has already confronted us with some of the most difficult and pressing problems of the day. The political ideas, still more perhaps the political catchwords, of Western civilization, uprooted from the soil from which they sprung, have been carried to alien lands where they are producing a strange and dangerous growth. The danger affects us more than most, for we stand as the symbol and type of Western civilization acclimatized among Eastern peoples, and we more than others need to seek a safe outlet for the ferment of the new wine which we have poured into the old bottles.

But this change, though it affects us more than others, does not affect us alone, and it may be thought to call for an adjustment of our policy rather than for any fundamental alteration in its objects. A different problem and one peculiar to ourselves is raised by the constitutional development of the British Empire. The balance of the British Empire has shifted. Great Britain, from being as it were sole Minister of Foreign Affairs, sole mouthpiece of the Empire in the councils of the world, is now only one among many voices, *primus inter pares* it may be, but no longer alone. The self-governing Dominions rule their own destinies, have their own representatives in foreign capitals, declare their own policy if they will, and are bound by no engagement to which they have not given their explicit consent. We are partners in a new experiment in government to which neither our own history nor the example of other Empires, ancient or modern, afford a parallel. And observe that it is not the result of any settled purpose or any carefully prepared plan. Wide as were the divergencies of purpose and prophecy in regard to the future of the British Empire in the nineteenth century, you will not find this solution advocated or foreseen by those who discussed imperial problems; in so far as it is the result of policy, it is the accident of omissions rather than the product of any settled purpose or clearly conceived ideas.

It is obvious that this new distribution of executive power in the Empire must profoundly affect the conduct of foreign affairs. It requires for its successful operation the daily interchange of information and, in all grave issues, prior consultation and pre-arranged co-operation. It renders rapid decision far more difficult, and may tend to that extent to deprive us of initiative and lessen our influence in the world, and it certainly necessitates a development of the means at present existing for bringing into harmony the views and interests of the widely scattered nations of the British Commonwealth.

But it may be asked, Has it not done more than this? Do not the increased importance, the growing strength, both political and economic, and the new freedom of the Dominions require not merely new methods and new machinery for the conduct of our foreign relations, but a wholly different orientation of our foreign policy itself, and in particular, now that so much of the authority and power of the Empire is situated in other continents, must we not completely

revise our attitude to Europe and its problems? I
have not found this idea anywhere very clearly expressed, but unless I am mistaken it underlies and
perhaps unconsciously colours a good many contemporary utterances. Thus in the sphere of trade—
and no one will deny the influence which the interests
of trade have often exercised on our foreign policy in
the past—we begin to hear talk of the United States
of America, the United States of Europe and the
British Empire as of three comparable but contrasting
entities; and so too in the political sphere when, in
the course of speeches made in Canada, I spoke of the
unique position and influence which the Empire might
hold in the world, linked as its fortunes are by these
islands to those of the continent of Europe yet detached from Europe by the Dominions, I was re-
proached by an English critic with being false to the
teaching of my father and jeopardizing imperial unity.

I need not stop to correct this gross misrepresenta-
tion of my father's views in an audience which is
familiar with the course of Anglo-German relations
towards the close of the last century and in the early
years of the present one.[1] He was one of the first to
recognize that in the world in which we live, isolation
must deprive us of our proper influence in shaping the
course of events and might easily endanger our safety.
With Germany unfriendly, France embittered, Italy
uncertain and Russia hostile, we were indeed isolated,
and even though the loyalty and support of the Colonies
made that isolation splendid it did not render it safe.

In truth even then we were isolated only in the sense
that we had no friends. We were isolated but not
insulated, and if the continental Powers could have

[1] cf., Nos. 38 and 39 above.

composed even temporarily the deeper quarrels which divided them, it would have fared ill with us. The fact is that we never have been able to free ourselves from the conditions which geography has set for us, and if that same geographical position has been the origin of our colonizing enterprise and world-wide empire, it has not less clearly determined that we cannot separate our fortunes from those of Europe. Again and again you find the notion that our interference in continental affairs should be as infrequent as possible, stated either as an object of policy or as a fact, but the very men who have proclaimed it have been the first to illustrate its limitations. As often, it is Disraeli who gives to the idea its most philosophic expression, and in his own language explains it by the beginnings of that imperial growth whose development is the most striking factor of to-day. "The abstention of England," he said in 1866, "from any unnecessary interference in the affairs of Europe is the consequence, not of her decline of power, but of her increased strength. England is no longer a mere European Power; she is the metropolis of a great maritime empire, extending to the boundaries of the furthest ocean. It is not because England has taken refuge in a state of apathy that she now almost systematically declines to interfere in the affairs of the continent of Europe. England is as ready and willing to interfere as in old days when the necessity of her position requires it. There is no Power, indeed, that interferes more than England. . . . On the contrary, she has a greater sphere of action than any European Power, and she has duties devolving upon her on a much larger scale. Not that we can ever look with indifference upon what takes place on the Continent. We are interested in the peace and prosperity of Europe, and I do not say that there may not be occasions on which it may be the duty of England to interfere in European wars."

And a few years later, in 1869, his great rival, Mr. Gladstone, concluded a survey of the principles of British foreign policy in the words: " I do not believe that England ever will or can be unfaithful to her great tradition, or can forswear her interest in the common transactions and the general interests of Europe," though he very wisely added, " her credit and her power form a fund which, in order that they may be made the most of, should be thriftily used." Thus on the one hand we have Disraeli, the later exponent of a spirited foreign policy, consciously balancing the growth of our imperial interests against a lessened participation in European affairs, and on the other Mr. Gladstone, who would never willingly have embarked on such enterprises as fed the imagination of Disraeli, definitely repudiating the idea that we can ignore or neglect our European interests and duties.

What, then, has occurred since their time to alter the fundamental conceptions of British policy or to reverse their judgment ? If our power is now shared with the Dominions, their interests and safety are inseparably connected with our own. If they lie farther removed from the quarrels, the suspicions and the jealousies of the old Europe, yet the world has narrowed, distances have lessened, and the interests of all parts have become more closely involved one with another. Canning boasted that he called a new world into existence to redress the balance of the old, and any disturbance of the old world must now affect the balance of the new.

Nor is it only this geographical contraction of the

world, if I may be permitted such a phrase, or the greater intricacy of modern finance and trade which forbid Great Britain and her sister nations to seek security in isolation. The experience of 1914 is there to teach us how great a matter a little fire kindleth, and how desperately the affairs of another country may affect our own existence. In the endeavour to prevent a repetition of that calamity, we and the Dominions have become members of the League of Nations. We have thus committed ourselves more deeply than ever before to active participation in the affairs of the Continent, and the Dominions have become, by their own act and not merely by their association with Great Britain, as directly if not as intimately involved as ourselves. Far from lessening their concern with the affairs of the old world, the growth of their power and the attainment of their autonomy has resulted in their becoming principals in engagements and responsibilities to which before they were only vicariously bound.

Nothing, therefore, has occurred to release us from the necessity of maintaining a watchful interest in continental affairs. On the contrary, positive engagements now reinforce and extend our old interests, and in those positive engagements arising from the Covenant the share of the Dominions is the same as our own. If, then, any change is required in our attitude and policy towards Europe, it cannot be found in abstention from European activities; it must be sought, if at all, in a revision of our objects and a change in the methods by which we pursue them. The necessity for a change of method results so clearly not only from the constitutional growth of the Empire but also from the signature of the Covenant, reinforced as it now is by the Peace Pact,[1] that I need not dwell upon it. We must work wherever possible with and through the League. Our policy and the means by which we pursue it must be such as we can defend and justify before that august assembly of nations. Our interest in our neighbours must be more active, our co-operation with them more constant and complete; but is there any reason to suppose that our fundamental purpose must be changed and that the rules which determined our action in the past no longer apply. . . ?

[1] The " Kellogg Pact " of 1928, renouncing war " as an instrument of national policy."

Journal of the Royal Institute of International Affairs, Vol. IX, No. 2 (London, March 1930), pp. 181–5.

57: VISCOUNT CECIL. *The Peace Ballot*

In the later part of 1934, the League of Nations Union, as part of its campaign to maintain support for the idea of " collective security " through the League of Nations, circulated a questionnaire which was answered by 11,559,165 people. The questions were:

1. Should Britain remain a member of the League of Nations ?
2. Are you in favour of an all-round reduction in armaments by international agreement ?
3. Are you in favour of an all-round abolition of national military and naval aircraft by international agreement ?
4. Should the manufacture and sale of armaments for private profit be prohibited by international agreement ?
5. Do you consider that, if a nation insists on attacking another, the other nations should combine to compel it to stop by
   (a) Economic and non-military measures ?
   (b) If necessary, military measures ?

Over 11 million voters answered " Yes " to Question 1, over 10 million to questions 2, 4 and 5 (a), and nearly as many to Question 3. 6,784,368 answered " Yes " to Question 5 (b) and 2,351,981 " No ".

The results were published in a pamphlet to which the following Conclusion was written by Viscount Cecil, for long the best known exponent of League of Nations ideals, and a man who had played a great part in its foundation.

THE Ballot is over. More than eleven millions of our fellow-countrymen have declared their opinions on the broad issue of Peace and Disarmament through the League of Nations, and on the subsidiary points raised by the questions put to them. Their answer has been plain and decisive. . . .

What, then, is to be the final outcome of all the immense labour and considerable sums of money which have been so freely given to attain this striking result ? To answer that question, we must look back at the objects with which the Ballot was started more than a year ago.

At that time, certain things were clear. The situation in Europe had become very bad and was rapidly getting worse. The world was moving towards war. The disastrous events in the Far East had shaken the whole system of organized peace—a militarist nation, ignoring its international engagements, had seized vast provinces belonging to a neighbour, and had successfully defied the protests of Geneva.

Several countries in Europe had accepted dictatorships which openly preached force as the right method for settling international relations. Two great countries had given notice of withdrawal from the League. Economic nationalism, the product of the grave commercial and financial world crisis, had helped to revive the old doctrines of isolation and racialism reminiscent of the worst medieval times. Europe appeared to be drifting back into the tribalism from which it had been rescued by Christian civilization.

Inevitably, this tendency had seriously weakened the League of Nations. That institution rests upon the conception that the interests of each nation will be best served by the well-being of all, and that nationalism must not be allowed to infringe this principle. Hence the growth of tribalism had brought about a revival of the fashion, prevalent in the early days of the League, to sneer at and belittle Geneva; and to be indifferent, if not actually hostile, to international Disarmament.

And yet to many of us it appeared that the only hope for the future was in the League. We regarded it, however imperfect it might be, as in the direct line of Christian progress. We held that a policy of national isolation was both futile and immoral; and that a return to the old ideas of military preparation and alliances as the guarantee of peace could only lead to another war even more desolating than that of 1914. We believed, therefore, that it was urgent to reverse the disintegrating movement in progress, and to restore as far as possible the prestige and authority of the League of Nations.

Obviously, as private citizens in a single member of the European community, our opportunities to help were limited. We could not direct the policy of our country, much less that of Europe. But we were convinced that the British peoples had unrivalled influence in the councils of the nations; and that, if the British Government could be encouraged to resume its leadership at Geneva, much could still be done to arrest the threatened relapse into international anarchy.

Our first object, therefore, was to assure the Administration that, in the support of the collective system, they had behind them the overwhelming approval of the people of the United Kingdom. We were confident of the existence of that approval, and we hoped that by the Ballot we should be able to make it articulate.

The result has exceeded our most sanguine expectations. The timid and the doubters have been shown to be mistaken. Once again the British people have responded splendidly to a frank appeal for their assistance.

Can we say that British policy has been in any degree assisted by our efforts ? I think we certainly can. Since the Ballot was started, there can be no doubt that a great change has come over the tone of public statements about the League. Up to a year ago official references to the League were rare and, when they did occur, they were politely sceptical. They reminded me of the way in which M. Clemenceau always began his conversations on the subject. " I like the League," he would say, " I like the League—but I do not believe in it."

Now that tone has almost vanished. When it made its reappearance in the recent White Paper on Defence,[1] it was greeted with such widespread disapproval that I hope we have seen the last of it. Certainly most ministerial utterances on the subject are of a very different character.

When the Lord Privy Seal[2] recently professed his conviction that reliance on the League was our only hope, his was no longer the voice of one crying in the ministerial wilderness, but rather a clear and vigorous repetition of the now usual official praise of the collective system.

Nor is the change confined to speeches. The intervention in the Saar,[3] the action on the Serbo-Hungarian dispute over the responsibility for the assassination of King Alexander,[4] the insistence on a peaceful settlement of the Abyssinian difficulty are all welcome instances of a vigorous use of the League machinery to solve international problems.

[1] Cmd. 4827, published 4 March 1935.
[2] Mr. Anthony Eden.
[3] The plebiscite in the Saar, which decided its return to Germany, was organized by the League, and held on 13 January 1935.
[4] 9 October 1934.

It is no doubt difficult to be sure that these signs of revived reliance on the League have any connection with the Ballot. *Post hoc* is not always *propter hoc*. But I am myself well assured that the Ballot has played a valuable part in this revival, and none of us have ever claimed that it could do more.

It would, however, be a grave mistake to think that all is now well. On the contrary, recent events in Europe are in the highest degree disquieting. They need not be set out here. It is enough to say that every agency for peace must be fully employed if we are to get back to even such a position in Europe as the League occupied in 1931. We have begun well. But it is only a beginning.

Our first business is to bring home to influential quarters full knowledge of what has actually been achieved. I hope therefore that, by the time these words are read, we shall have resolved to bring formally before the Government the results of the Ballot. That should be done by an influential deputation to the Prime Minister or Foreign Secretary.

But that is not enough. Ministers can do no more than Parliament approves. We should therefore bring the National Declaration to the notice of every Member of Parliament. The machinery created all over the country for the Ballot must not be allowed to disappear. In some form or other it should be kept in being in every constituency.

As a first step, an interview should be sought through its means with each Member of Parliament, in order to present to him the result of the Ballot not only in his own constituency but throughout the country.

Nor must we forget that a second object of the Ballot was to convey to foreign countries the assurance that the British people stood firmly behind the League. If the Continent could be sure of that, it would be a great appeasement of the anxiety, almost amounting to panic, with which recent developments are there regarded.

That is why I personally have attached so much importance to the answers to both branches of Question 5. In recent years too many people, some of them occupying influential positions, have been ready to suggest that, contrary to all the best traditions of their history, the British people would not be ready to fulfil their obligations under the Covenant; that they would never be ready to risk their money, and still less their lives, in the repression of lawless breaches of international peace. It is satisfactory to know that there is no justification for such a slander on our people. By immense majorities, they have declared themselves ready to restrain an aggressor by economic action and, with more reluctance and by smaller but still important majorities, to follow this up, if it should prove essential, by military measures.

Not less important has been the answer to Question 3. All-round abolition of national naval and military aircraft, which has been supported in eighty-five per cent of these answers, is, I am convinced, the way of true security for the world against the greatest of man-made perils. No doubt there are difficulties. But, if the whole influence of the British Empire is used to secure this policy, I believe it will be successful. Control or internationalization of civil aviation will be essential, and on this our Government should put forward a practical scheme forthwith. Should it turn out to be impossible, in the situation that has now developed, to secure agreement at once upon all-round

abolition, we ought next to try for abolition of all
"bombing" planes and the prohibition of *all* bombing.
Our object should be to reduce the danger of war,
especially the danger of sudden attack—not to attempt
to make rules for the polite conduct of war.

I trust that adequate steps will be taken to bring
these very satisfactory results before the notice of the
people of Europe, and that they will be urged to furnish proof that their fellow-countrymen are as earnest
in the pursuit of peace as we are ourselves.

I have just said that a considerable minority were
averse from enforcing peace by military action. There
was also an appreciable minority who did not favour
the abolition of air warfare. I cannot help feeling that
the hesitation on both points is largely due to misunderstanding. No doubt there is a certain school of
opinion worthy of the utmost respect who conscien-
tiously object to the use of force for any purpose what-
soever, even to protect the weak from oppression by
the strong. But their numbers would scarcely account
for the size of the minority on Question 5b and would
certainly not explain at all the action of those who
voted (on Question 3) against the suppression of air
warfare. In each case, the explanation of the greater
part of these negative votes is more likely to have been
a misapprehension of the argument on the opposite
side.

In other words, though the third object of the
Ballot—the education of the people—has been in great
measure attained by it, much still remains to be done
in this direction. For this purpose, it would not be
enough to maintain a nucleus of Declaration machinery which I have already said would be in certain
other ways desirable. Such machinery would not be

appropriate for the continuance of an educational campaign. But the peace Societies, and particularly the League of Nations Union, are well suited for educational work. Much has already been done by the Union in this direction, and its capacity for teaching is only limited by the extent of its membership. I hope very much, therefore, that one of the results of the Ballot may be a large increase in the membership of the League of Nations Union. Nothing would more effectively drive home the lessons of the Ballot.

Here, then, is the programme of immediate action to carry on the work so splendidly begun. Let us " tell the world," including the Government, Parliament, and foreign opinion, what the Ballot has revealed to be the opinion of the British people; and let us strengthen and complete knowledge of these topics by writing and speaking, by the platform and the Press, and above all by enrolling in permanent societies large numbers of those who have shown by their votes that they are deeply interested in these questions.

In that way we may hope to make support for Peace and Disarmament through the League as axiomatic in our public life as other elementary doctrines of political and international morality.

From *The Peace Ballot* (London 1935), pp. 59-64.

On Saturday, March 7th 1936, Hitler denounced the Locarno Agreement on the grounds that the Franco-Soviet Pact of 1935 was incompatible with it—and occupied the zone of the Rhineland demilitarized by the Treaty of Versailles. At the same time he made proposals for a new general settlement to include a twenty-five-year non-aggression pact in the west, trilateral pacts with Poland and Czechoslovakia and an air pact. The leading article in *The Times* of March 9th reflects the confusion caused in British public opinion by these events (just as it had reflected the enthusiasm aroused by the Locarno Treaty in 1925: see No. 55 above).

No action except to protest was taken by the French and British governments.

As a result of this move of Hitler's, the structure built by the Treaties of Versailles and Locarno collapsed: its place was taken by attempts to reach direct agreements with Germany and Italy. This policy of " appeasement " came to be particularly associated with Mr. Neville Chamberlain, who succeeded Baldwin as Prime Minister in May 1937. It was a policy that reached its climax at the Munich conference in September 1938.

58: LEADING ARTICLE IN *THE TIMES*—A Chance to Rebuild

9 March 1936

HERR HITLER'S invasion of the Rhineland is a challenge, abrupt in form and deliberate in fact, to the voluntary agreement which has maintained the inviolability of the eastern frontiers of France and Belgium for the last eleven years. The Locarno Treaty,

X   305

which embodied this understanding, was designed to inaugurate a process. Locarno was intended to call mutual good faith and confidence into play among the Signatories. Certain penal and discriminatory clauses in the main Peace Treaties preserved the mood of war-bitterness and war-exhaustion in which they were drafted, maintained an unstable equilibrium, and threatened the durability of the settlement as a whole. They were to yield to negotiation and consent, and to disappear, leaving the peace of Europe refounded upon something more lasting than a preponderance of force. The Locarno agreement was in some ways ahead of its time. So much so that, whatever the reasons in detail, it was never in fact allowed to create the conditions requisite to that frank understanding between France and Germany which was and is the first essential of European stability. But the agreement in another respect was not ahead of its time. It embodied the clauses of the Versailles Treaty which imposed demilitarization upon the German side only of the Franco-German frontier. Thus, having failed as the starting point of a process of appeasement it survived only in German eyes as an additional guarantee of one of the " inequalities " in which the Nazi movement of resurgence and revolt had its birth. In the view, not of Nazidom alone, but of all Germans, the sacrifice offered in Germany's free acceptance of the " inequality " had proved vain.

Herr Hitler's action thus strikes the Locarno arrangement in its weakest joint. For some time past it has been widely admitted both in France and in this country that discriminatory demilitarization in the Rhineland was not destined to endure for ever. How it might end was less certain. It has now been ended by an act which . . . is aimed not so much at the intentions of Locarno as at the particular servitude which it borrowed from the Versailles Treaty. It is none the less plainly the breach of a Treaty freely negotiated and constantly reaffirmed. The more sensationally minded have described it also during the week-end as an act of " aggression." If it be that as well, there is still a distinction to be drawn between the march of detachments of German troops, sent to occupy territory indisputably under German sovereignty, and an act which carries fire and sword into a neighbour's territory. Anger and panic would, at the least, be over-hasty interpreters of the event. No one in this country can or will wish to dispute that the engagements of Locarno have been grossly violated and that the obligations of the guarantor may now be invoked. With these facts taken for granted, it becomes the task of the government and the guaranteed Powers in council to examine jointly and dispassionately the whole meaning of the move which confronts them. . . .

Herr Hitler has endeavoured to give to his default, flagrant and indefensible in itself, a constructive political implication. A breach of a treaty is not to be condoned or explained away. But those who are called to sit in judgment upon it will fall short of what is due to their peoples if they fail to test it not only by the text of the treaty but also by its consequences. What is the right advantage to be wrung from it ? Is this but the latest and worst blow to the sanctity of international law ? Will the ends for which treaties exist be vindicated here solely by the machinery of penalty and enforcement. . . ?

There are glaring gaps [in the settlement proposed by Hitler] to be filled, deep obscurities to be examined.

But the questions for statesmanship are whether the Locarno Treaty is to be made the means or the bar to the explanation of this offer, whether Europe will be safer and its economic recovery nearer according as the Locarno Powers agree to examine or determine to reject it. The offer, let it be observed, is made subject to no condition that can be ruled out as arbitrary or inadmissible. . . .

British opinion will be nearly unanimous in its desire to turn an untoward proceeding to account and, far from weakening the regime of treaties, to seize the opportunity of hardening and strengthening the collective system which opens with the Geneva offer of re-entry. What upholds the League secures French no less than British interests. More than that. Where French security is at stake the two are found to coincide. It is one of the self-evident facts of Europe, over and above specific undertakings, that any threat to French or Belgian territory engages Britain. If this was not clear formerly, it is clear to the great majority in this island now, though the truth was already explicit in the Locarno Treaty itself. The whole meaning of collective security has gained in clarity through experience. The lead which this country has given has enabled the collective system, incompletely manned as it is, to show a vigour which has discomfited its enemies and some of its former friends. But for recent British determination in support of the League is it conceivable that such an offer as that which Herr Hitler has made would now lie upon the table? France and Britain alike have reason for indignation and food for suspicions. But, since neither stands alone, they have the more power, even while they are forced into an admitted offence against the law of Europe, to take a steady measure of the undertakings which Germany has offered in extenuation. The old structure of European peace, one-sided and unbalanced, is nearly in ruins. It is the moment, not to despair, but to rebuild.

The Times, Monday 9 March 1936.

59: DEBATE IN HOUSE OF COMMONS

26 March 1936

THE SECRETARY OF STATE FOR FOREIGN AFFAIRS (MR. EDEN): We must distinguish between what may be national sentiment and what are, for good or ill, our national obligations. Likely enough, there may be many people in this country who say to themselves now, " In our judgment the territories of France and Germany should be treated on exactly equal terms." It may be that people feel that, but those are not the terms of the Treaty of Locarno. . . .

There are some who may regard us as freely and fortunately placed at this anxious moment in European affairs, some who regard us as arbiters with a fortunate destiny. But we are not arbiters in this business; that is not so. We are guarantors of this Treaty, and as guarantors, for good or ill—I am not arguing that— we have certain commitments and they are very definite. I will draw the attention of the House to Article 4 of the Locarno Treaty. It runs as follows: " If one of the high contracting parties alleges that a violation of Article 2 of the present Treaty or a breach of Articles 42 or 43 of the Treaty of Versailles has been or is being committed, it shall bring the question at once before the Council of the League of Nations."

That has been done——

" As soon as the Council of the League of Nations

is satisfied that such violation or breach has been committed, it will notify its findings without delay to the Powers signatory of the present Treaty, who severally agree that in such case they will each of them come immediately to the assistance of the Power against whom the act complained of is directed."

Those words are clear. It cannot be said in the light of them, that we are uncommitted and free arbiters. Our position is far different, and I want in all bluntness to make this plain to the House—I am not prepared to be the first British Foreign Secretary to go back on a British signature. And yet our object throughout this difficult period has been to seek a peaceful and agreed solution. I consider that we are bound to do so by Article 7 of the Locarno Treaty itself, which states:

The present Treaty, which . . . is in conformity with the Covenant of the League of Nations, shall not be interpreted as restricting the duty of the League to take whatever action may be deemed wise and effectual to safeguard the peace of the world."

It is in the spirit of that Article that we have sought conciliation and attempted to bring about an agreement and understanding, and to do that without impairing confidence in our good faith or in our determination to carry out the obligations to which we have set our name. I do not pretend that our task would not have been easier had we been entirely free. That does not arise. We have entered upon our task with the weight of these commitments heavy upon us. . . .

We neither denied the gravity of the breach of the Treaty which had been committed nor the consequences to Europe, but we thought it our imperative duty to seek by negotiation to restore confidence. That being our objective from the very first hour of this critical fortnight, we have sought throughout to re-build. But—we must face this fact—it is not possible to rebuild unless your foundations can be well and truly laid, and your foundations cannot be well and truly laid if some of those engaged in the task believe that the building will ultimately share the fate of its predecessor. It has been our task to create an atmosphere of confidence in which these negotiations could take place. . . .

I want to say one word to those who would argue that it is our duty at this time to keep free from all entanglements in Europe. With respect, I wonder whether those who say that are quite clear about what they mean. If they mean we must turn a blind eye to all that happens in Europe, I say that is to take no account at all of realities. We have never been able in all our history to disassociate ourselves from events in the Low Countries, neither in the time of Queen Elizabeth, nor in the time of Marlborough, nor in the time of Napoleon, and still less at the present day, when modern developments of science have brought a striking force so much nearer to our shores. It is a vital interest of this country that the integrity of France and Belgium should be maintained and that no hostile force should cross their frontiers. The truth is . . . there was nothing very new in Locarno. . . . It was a new label, but it was an old fact and that fact has been the underlying purpose of British foreign policy throughout history. . . . What Locarno did was to carry a stage further commitments which we already bore under the Covenant in respect of a much wider area. . . .

But it may be that those who urge that we should disentangle ourselves from Europe have something in mind rather different, or very different from what I have just described. They may be thinking of another situation when, owing to obligations elsewhere, our neighbours may become involved in conflict and may call for help in a quarrel that is not ours. That I believe to be a general apprehension. The people of this country are determined that that shall not happen, and that is the view of the Government. We agree with it entirely. Our obligations are world-wide obligations, are the obligations of the Covenant, and we stand firm in support of them, but we do not add, nor will we add, one jot to those obligations, except in the area already covered by the Locarno Treaty. . . .

Our objectives in all this are threefold—first to avert the danger of war, second to create conditions in which negotiations can take place and third, to bring about the success of those negotiations so that they may strengthen collective security, further Germany's return to the League and, in a happier atmosphere, allow those larger negotiations on economic matters and on matters of armaments which are indispensable to the appeasement of Europe to take place. I assure the House that it is the appeasement of Europe as a whole that we have constantly before us. . . .

We are, I believe, only at the beginning of a period which must be, at best, one of most critical international negotiations. . . . I do not intend to approach the problem of the immediate future with the idea of being bound to the divergent policies of either France or Germany. Our policy is the Covenant and membership of the League. We know our obligations and are prepared to fulfil them. . . .

I say, first, to the British public: We cannot secure

peace unless you are prepared frankly to recognize the real perplexities of the present international situation. We cannot ensure peace if you refuse to take upon yourselves obligations to assist us at this time. We cannot ensure peace, unless, in this country and elsewhere, we divest ourselves of prejudices about this or that foreign nation and unless in this country we can divest ourselves of prejudices about our own politicians. It is fantastic to suggest that we are bound to the chariot wheels of this or that foreign country. I would like to say to France, that we cannot ensure peace unless the French government is prepared to approach with an open mind, the problems which still separate it from Germany. I would like to say to Germany: How can we hope to enter on negotiations with any prospect of success, unless you are prepared to do something to allay the anxieties in Europe which you have created. . . ?

I believe that the purpose for which I am working . . . is one which is shared by the great majority of the men and women of this country. It is to maintain peace, to strengthen the League, to uphold the sanctity of treaties, and above all to seek, without respite, to fashion from the troubled present a future which may be freed from the haunting fears that shadow our own time.

Hansard, Fifth Series, Vol. CCCX, pp. 1435–49.

MR. CHURCHILL: When we think of the great power and influence which this country exercises we cannot look back with much pleasure on our foreign policy in the last five years. They certainly have been very disastrous years. God forbid that I should lay on the Government of my own country the charge of sole responsibility for the evils which have come upon the world in that period. I would not do such a thing, but certainly in that period we have seen the most depressing and alarming change in the outlook of mankind which has ever taken place in so short a period. Five years ago all felt safe, five years ago all were looking forward to peace, to a period in which mankind would rejoice in the treasures which science can spread to all classes if the conditions of peace and justice prevail. Five years ago to talk of war would have been regarded not only as a folly and a crime but almost as a sign of lunacy. The difference in our position now! We find ourselves compelled once again to face the hateful problems and ordeals which those of us who worked and toiled in the last great struggle hoped were gone for ever.

Some responsibility rests upon the conduct of our own affairs. I do not think that it is very easy to set out over those years the various successive acts of policy and utterances of various British Foreign Secretaries and connect them into one harmonious theme. We have very much baffled the Continent of Europe at times, and we have erred also, I think, in trying to gain the sympathy of sections of our public, seeking to gain transient applause by putting forward platitudes, by putting forward hopes which no one really felt could be realized. In this period we have undoubtedly disturbed the confidence of Europe— from the highest motives. Undoubtedly nothing was more honourable than the disarmament which Britain practised on herself, nothing was more idealistic than

315

the counsels which we gave to others, differently situated. Even upon this question of sanctions we have taken the lead. A very great responsibility rests upon us in that matter.

I feel that in this island—where we are still blessed by being surrounded by a strip of salt water, in spite of the alterations which later developments have made in our situation—we ought to be very careful that in our interventions in the foreign sphere we understand fully the consequences they may bring to those who live upon the Continent and the feelings which they may create there, in contrast with the sentiments they may arouse in us. I do trust that the Government will not seek to win the easy applause of public opinion, but will confront the nation steadily and robustly with the realities of the situation, knowing the comprehension which the nation will give in return to those who deal with it faithfully. . . .

There are, of course, two practical foreign policies for our country. The first is an alliance between Great Britain and France, the two surviving liberal democracies of the West, who, strongly armed, rich, powerful, with the seas at their disposal, with great air forces and great armies, would stand with their backs to the ocean and allow the explosion which may come in Europe to blast its way eastward or southward. That is a practical foreign policy, but I do hope that we shall not resign ourselves to that, without first an earnest effort to persevere in the other policy, namely, the establishment of real collective security under the League of Nations and of the reign of law and respect for international law throughout Europe. I venture to make a suggestion which I feel will not be entirely repugnant to those who sit opposite, namely, that, apart from this particular emergency and apart from the measures which the Foreign Secretary has taken, we should endeavour now with great resolution to establish effective collective security. In my view, all the nations and States that are alarmed at the growth of German armaments ought to combine for mutual aid, in pacts of mutual assistance, approved by the League of Nations and in accordance with the Covenant of the League. . . .

I am looking for peace. I am looking for a way to stop war, but you will not stop it by pious sentiments and appeals. You will stop it only by making practical arrangements.

The whole history of the world is summed up in the fact that when nations are strong they are not always just, and when they wish to be just they are often no longer strong. I desire to see the collective forces of the world invested with overwhelming power. If you are going to run this thing on a narrow margin and to depend on a very slight margin, one way or the other, you are going to have war. But if you get five or ten on one side, all bound rigorously by the Covenant and the conventions which they own, then, in my opinion you have an opportunity of making a settlement which will heal the wounds of the world. Let us have this blessed union of power and justice: " Agree with thine adversary quickly while thou art in the way with him." Let us free the world from the approach of a catastrophe, carrying with it calamity and tribulation beyond the tongue of man to tell.

Ibid., pp. 1523-30.

MR. ATTLEE: The Locarno agreement was introduced

after the Protocol had been rejected, and I think that
you could trace a good many of our post-war difficulties to that fact, because you had there an attempt to
evade the main League position and to limit liability,
which inevitably lead to some kind of alliance. . . .
There are talks at the present time that Italy must
come in for this purpose and stand against Germany.
That is not the League principle; that is the old principle of alliances, the old balancing one way and
another. I thought that the right hon. Gentleman the
Member for West Birmingham (Sir A. Chamberlain)
indicated very clearly that point of view with regard
to collective security. He talked about Belgium and
Holland and the historic position of the Low Countries, and how this country had always insisted that no
Power should get control over those countries that lie
so near our shores.

That is historically true, but he was not talking
League language there; he was talking the language of
national defence. The real League position does not
differentiate between frontiers. It does not say that
this country is more interested in the frontiers of
Holland and Belgium, because of the historic position,
than in the frontiers of Czechoslovakia or the frontiers
of Poland. The League position is that we are out to
defend the rule of law and not particular territories. . . .

Some people talk of collective security very much
as Lord Chesterfield talked of religion in the famous
letter to his son. It is only a collateral security. People
are thinking all the time in terms of national defence.
We say that you should seek your full security through
the League. We do not think that we should say that
we are going to make ourselves strong for defence and
then as collateral security have the League in the

background. We want to see the League developed so that you will get a real reduction of armaments, so that no nation will feel that it can stand by its own armaments, but all will have to depend on collective security. I noticed what I thought was a disturbing note in the speech of the Foreign Secretary in that he talked exclusively of agreements in the West. You cannot divide peace in Europe. You must have one peace running right through. I think we ought to give up altogether the old traditional doctrine of the balance of power, that balance of armed strength which we used to support for so many years, when we always joined against anyone who was likely to get power on the continent of Europe. That is obsolete now. The way to get peace is not through the balance of power but through the League. . . .

Ibid. pp. 1534–5

60: NEVILLE CHAMBERLAIN. Letter to Mrs. Morton Prince, Boston, Massachusetts

16 January 1938

. . . I am just now in closer relations with the American Government than has been the case within my recollection. I have made more than one attempt, while I have been Prime Minister, to draw them even closer still and I have had more than one disappointment. But I fully recognize that goodwill on the part of the U.S. Government is not wanting, the trouble is that public opinion in a good part of the States still believes it possible for America to stand outside Europe and watch it disintegrate, without being materially affected herself.

I can well understand that frame of mind, and the fate of Spain and China does not invite any country to risk being involved in such miseries if she can avoid it. Indeed, we have a similar school of thought here. . . . Yet, though many people are haunted by a constantly recurring fear of war, we are too close to the danger spots for any but a few cranks to hope that we could remain safe in isolation. We are a very rich and very vulnerable Empire, and there are plenty of poor adventurers not very far away who look on us with hungry eyes.

In spite of my disappointment, I intend to keep on doing everything I can to promote Anglo-American understanding and co-operation. Not because I want or expect America to pull our chestnuts out of the fire for us; in any co-operation we shall always do our part, and perhaps more than our share. But I believe that Americans and British want the same fundamental things in the world, peace, liberty, order, respect for international obligations, freedom for every country to devote all its resources to the improvement of the conditions of its own people, instead of being forced to pile armaments on its own back 'til it comes near breaking. I believe that these things must be wanted too by Germans, Italians, Russians, and Japanese. But those people are in the grip of their governments, and in some cases the Governments are so constituted that they must maintain their prestige or die. They cannot afford to admit a mistake, their power is so great that they are tempted to use it to increase their prestige without regard to ultimate consequences. They pay no heed to reason, but there is one argument to which they will always give attention, and that is force. U.S.A. and U.K. in combination represent a force so overwhelming that the mere hint of the possibility of its use is sufficient to make the most powerful of dictators pause, and that is why I believe that co-operation between our two countries is the greatest instrument in the world for the preservation of peace, and the attainment of those objects of which I spoke just now.

Unhappily France keeps pulling her own house down about her ears. We are on excellent terms with her. With the Chautemps government which has just fallen we found ourselves in general agreement about all aims and objects. But France's weakness is a public danger just when she ought to be a source of strength and confidence, and as a friend she has two faults which destroy half her value. She never can keep a secret for more than half an hour, nor a government for more than nine months!

Meanwhile, as a realist, I must do what I can to make this country safe. The calm, the good sense, and the courage of the English people are amazing. They are never rattled, and they seem by some instinct to sift the situation and pick out the salient points. They are perfectly aware that, until we are fully rearmed, our position must be one of great anxiety. They realize that we are in no position to enter light-heartedly upon war with such a formidable power as Germany, much less if Germany were aided by Italian attacks on our Mediterranean possessions and communications. They know that France, though her army is strong, is desperately weak in some vital spots, and they are always alarmed lest out of loyalty to her we should be led into a quarrel over causes which are of little interest to us, and for which she could not give us decisive aid.

Therefore our people see that in the absence of any powerful ally, and until our armaments are completed, we must adjust our foreign policy to our circumstances, and even bear with patience and good humor actions which we should like to treat in very different fashion. I do not myself take too pessimistic a view of the situation. The dictators are too often regarded as though they were entirely inhuman. I believe this idea to be quite erroneous. It is indeed the human side of the dictators that makes them dangerous, but on the other hand, it is the side on which they can be approached with the greatest hope of successful issue.

I am about to enter upon a fresh attempt to reach a

reasonable understanding with both Germany and Italy, and I am by no means unhopeful of getting results. I have an idea that when we have done a certain amount spade-work here we may want help from U.S.A. It may well be that a point will be reached when we shall be within sight of agreement, and yet just unable to grasp it without a helping hand. In such an event a friendly and sympathetic President might be able to give just the fresh stimulus we required, and I feel sure that the American people would feel proud if they could be brought in to share in the final establishment of peace.

Printed in Keith Feiling, *The Life of Neville Chamberlain* (London 1946), pp. 322–4.

61: NEVILLE CHAMBERLAIN. Speech to Birmingham Unionist Association, Town Hall, Birmingham

8 April 1938

. . . No one who has watched the growing expenditure on armaments can doubt that the Chancellor of the Exchequer has before him a difficult and unenviable task, and no one questions, I think, the determination of this people to see this business of rearmament through, recognizing as we must that it is our best security against war, that of all sacrifices none is so terrible as those of war. You may have read that at the beginning of this week we had in the House of Commons a debate, a rather lively debate, on foreign affairs. That was only the last of a whole series of debates on that subject, and, although we are told nowadays that people do not read of what goes on in the House of Commons, I cannot help thinking that the general outlines of the Government's foreign policy are fairly freely read.

We are bound by certain treaties, entered into with general approval, to go to the assistance of France and of Belgium in the event of unprovoked aggression against either of those two countries. But we have declined to commit ourselves to a similar undertaking in respect of other countries farther away, in which our vital interests are not concerned to the same extent, and which might be involved in war under conditions

over which we would have no control. Now it is quite
true that in these days no one can say where or when
a war will end once it has begun, or what Governments may ultimately be entangled in a dispute which
originally might have been confined to some remote
corner of Europe. But at least we ought to reserve to
ourselves the right to say whether we consider it necessary to enter into such a war or not, and we ought not
to hand over to others the determination of our action
when it might involve such tremendous consequences
to ourselves.

Sometimes we are told that if only we took a bolder
course, if we were to lay down here and now precisely
the circumstances in which we would or would not
go to war, we should give such a warning to the world
that there would in fact be no war. That would be a
gamble, and it would be a gamble not with money, but
with the lives of men, women and children of our own
race and blood. I am not prepared to enter into a
gamble of that kind, and though the stern necessity
for war may arise in the future, as it has arisen in the
past, I would not give the word for it unless I were
absolutely convinced that in no other way could we
preserve our liberty.

Then there are other critics who say they cannot
understand what the policy of His Majesty's Government is, and they conclude therefore that there can be
no policy. You may remember what Johnson said to
a man who said he could not understand his reason-
ing: " Sir, I can give you a reason, but I cannot give
you understanding." Our policy has been stated often
enough and clearly enough, but nevertheless, I will
state it again to-night. But before I come to that, I
would like to say to you what our policy is not.

Our policy is not one of dividing Europe into two opposing *blocs* of countries, each arming against the other amidst a growing flood of ill-will on both sides, which can only end in war. That seems to us to be a policy which is dangerous and stupid. You may say we may not approve of dictatorships. I think, perhaps, most of us in this room do not approve of them, but there they are. You cannot remove them. We have to live with them, and to us in the Government it seems that, while we must continue to arm until we can get a general agreement to disarm, it is only common sense that in the meantime we should try to establish friendly relations with any country that is willing to be friends with us. We should take any and every opportunity to try to remove any genuine and legitimate grievances that may exist.

During the recent weeks we have been engaging in conversations for this purpose with the Italian Government, with the result that a whole cloud of suspicions and misunderstandings has been blown away. There is to-day a good prospect of restoring those old friendly relations which, until they were recently broken, had lasted so long that they had become almost traditional between our two countries.

Anyone would think that such a happy change as that, such a lightening of the tension, such a prospect of getting rid of a state of feeling which was becoming a menace both to Italy and ourselves, would have been welcomed everywhere, and yet the whole of the Opposition, the Socialists and Liberals, with the notable exception of the veteran George Lansbury and George's friends who have the courage to express their approval, have denounced these conversations with the utmost bitterness. They have painted the most

fantastic pictures of the subjects which we are supposed to be discussing. They have talked about vast
loans, about surrenders to dictators, about the gulli-
bility of the Prime Minister in believing a single word
that was said to him, and even declare that they
believe we were going to sacrifice the British Empire
itself in a panic.

I only ask you to have a little patience, to wait a
little longer—and I do not think it will be very much
longer—before our agreement with Italy is concluded
and published, and then, if you are not of my opinion,
if you do not believe that it is not the Prime Minister
who has been fooled, but the Socialists and Liberals
who have fooled themselves, I will be prepared to eat
my hat.

So, believe me, the Government have a very clear
and definite foreign policy, which they keep always
before them, and which they continue to pursue by
various methods according to the circumstances of the
time. The object of that policy is to maintain peace
and to give confidence to the people, if that be possible,
that peace will be maintained, so that they may all go
about their occupations free from a sense of menace
lurking always in the background.

Our policy is based upon two conceptions. The
first is this: That, if you want to secure a peace which
can be relied upon to last, you have got to set about it.
You have got to inform yourself what are the difficulties, where are the danger spots, what are the reasons
for any likely or possible disturbance of the peace; and,
when you have found that out, you must exert yourself to find the remedy.

The second conception is this: In any armed world
you must be armed yourself. You must see to it that

your preparations, or defensive and offensive forces, are so organized and built up that nobody will be tempted to attack you, but that, on the contrary, when your voice is raised for peace, it will be listened to with respect. These, then, are the two pillars of our foreign policy—to seek peace by friendly discussion and negotiation, and to build up our armed forces to a level which is proportionate to our responsibilities and to the part we desire to play in preserving peace. . . .

Printed in Neville Chamberlain, *The Struggle for Peace* (London), pp. 170–3.

62: NEVILLE CHAMBERLAIN. Speech at National Government Rally, Broughton House, Kettering

22 July 1938

. . . It is a striking fact and a tragic one that at the present time foreign affairs are dominating the minds of the people of this country almost to the exclusion of subjects which in ordinary times would have occupied their whole attention. Indeed, we are not alone in that respect; for I think all the peoples of the world are asking themselves this same question: " Are we to be allowed to live our lives in peace or are we to be plunged against our will into war ? "

When I look round the world I must say I am appalled at the prospects. War, accompanied by horrible barbarities, inflicted either wittingly or unwittingly upon civilian populations, is going on to-day in China and much nearer to us in Spain. Almost every week we hear rumours of war on this question or on that in other parts of the world, and all the principal nations are spending their precious savings on devising and manufacturing the most efficient instruments for the destruction of one another. I wonder whether, since the world began, has it ever seen such a spectacle of human madness and folly ?

During the last twenty years we and our allies and associates have been telling ourselves that we won the Great War. There have been disputes about the man

329

who won the war and even about the country that won the war, but nobody has ever doubted that we were the winners.

Well, we fought to preserve this free democracy from foreign domination and dictation, and to maintain the rule of order and law rather than the rule of force. Certainly we succeeded in preserving our freedom, and if our liberties were in danger again, and if we were sure that there was no other way of preserving them except by war, we would fight again. But think for a moment what the use of force involves us in.

When I think of those four terrible years and I think of the 7,000,000 of young men who were cut off in their prime, the 13,000,000 who were maimed and mutilated, the misery and the suffering of the mothers and the fathers, the sons and the daughters, and the relatives and the friends of those who were killed, and the wounded, then I am bound to say again what I have said before, and what I say now, not only to you, but to all the world—in war, whichever side may call itself the victor, there are no winners, but all are losers.

It is those thoughts which have made me feel that it was my prime duty to strain every nerve to avoid a repetition of the Great War in Europe. And I cannot believe that anyone who is not blinded by party prejudice, anyone who thinks what another war would mean, can fail to agree with me and to desire that I should continue my efforts.

Ever since the beginning of the war in Spain my colleagues and I realized the inherent danger in the situation, that it might lead to war in Europe; and it was because of that consideration, that in conjunction with the Government of France, we decided very early upon a policy of non-intervention with the express purpose of confining the civil war to Spain and preventing it from becoming a general conflagration. We have had endless difficulties in that policy, but in spite of them all, in spite of the sneers and jeers of the Oppositions, we have succeeded in our main objects. We have kept other countries out of the war, and today, at long last, the British plan for the withdrawal of foreign volunteers from Spain has been accepted, and we are hopeful that it will not now be long before they leave that country to Spaniards.

The situation has been complicated by the bombing by General Franco's aeroplanes of British ships entering the zone of hostilities in Spanish ports, and the Government have been fiercely denounced by those great patriots who sit opposite to us in the House of Commons for allowing the British flag to be insulted, and particularly for allowing British property to be destroyed. There is nothing like your Socialists for standing up for British property. Well not a long time ago we gave a warning to British shipowners that, while we were intending to give them full protection so long as their ships were on the high seas, we could not undertake to protect them after they had entered territorial waters in the zone of fighting, and we said that, because, after very carefully examining all the possible means of giving them protection, we were satisfied that we could not do so without at any rate a very considerable risk of being ourselves involved in the war.

Well, now, the risks which are run by these ships literally mean that the rate of freight which has to be paid is very high, and shipowners are getting as much as four and five times the ordinary rates of freight for voyages to these ports. We have given this warning.

If, in spite of it and for the sake of making these profits, these shipowners still send their ships to these waters and then get bombed, is it reasonable that we should be asked to take action which might presently involve not only them but you in the horrors of war which I have been trying to describe, and you are not getting any profits at all . . . ?

Ibid., pp. 237–40.

In the period after the annexation of Austria in March 1938, Chamberlain tried to find a peaceful solution of the quarrel between Germany and Czechoslovakia. After the failure of his personal meetings with Hitler at Berchtesgaden (15th September) and Godesberg (22nd-23rd September) war seemed in sight, and on 27th September Chamberlain broadcast on the reasons for which he would be prepared to go to war. However, the Conference at Munich on 29th September between Hitler, Mussolini, Chamberlain and Daladier enabled Hitler's wishes to be met without resorting to war.

Mr. Duff Cooper resigned after the Munich agreement and his explanation preceded the debate on the Munich Agreement in the House of Commons on 3rd October, in which he and Mr. Churchill joined with most of the Labour Party in attacking Chamberlain's policy.

63: NEVILLE CHAMBERLAIN. Broadcast Address

27 September 1938

. . . How horrible, fantastic, incredible it is that we should be digging trenches and trying on gas-masks here because of a quarrel in a far-away country between people of whom we know nothing. . . .

However much we may sympathize with a small nation confronted by a big and powerful neighbour, we cannot in all circumstances undertake to involve the whole British Empire in war simply on her account. If we have to fight it must be on larger issues than that. I am myself a man of peace to the depths of my soul. Armed conflict between nations is a nightmare to me;

but if I were convinced that any nation had made up its mind to dominate the world by fear of its force, I should feel that it must be resisted. Under such a domination life for people who believe in liberty would not be worth living; but war is a fearful thing, and we must be very clear, before we embark on it, that it is really the great issues that are at stake, and that the call to risk everything in their defence, when all the consequences are weighed, is irresistible.

Ibid., p. 275–6.

64: DEBATE IN THE HOUSE OF COMMONS

3-5 October 1938

MR. DUFF COOPER: The House will, I am sure, appreciate the peculiarly difficult circumstances in which I am speaking this afternoon. It is always a painful and delicate task for a Minister who has resigned to explain his reasons to the House of Commons, and my difficulties are increased this afternoon by the fact, of which I am well aware, that the majority of the House are most anxious to hear the Prime Minister and that I am standing between them and him. But I shall have, I am afraid, to ask for the patience of the House, because I have taken a very important, for me, and difficult decision, and I feel that I shall have to demand a certain amount of time in which to make plain to the House the reasons for which I have taken it.

At the last Cabinet meeting that I attended, last Friday evening, before I succeeded in finding my way to No. 10 Downing Street, I was caught up in the large crowd that were demonstrating their enthusiasm and were cheering, laughing, and singing; and there is no greater feeling of loneliness than to be in a crowd of happy, cheerful people and to feel that there is no occasion for oneself for gaiety or for cheering. That there was every cause for relief I was deeply aware, as much as anybody in this country, but that there was great cause for self-congratulation I was uncertain. Later, when I stood in the hall at Downing Street, again among enthusiastic throngs of friends and colleagues who were all as cheerful, happy, glad, and enthusiastic as the crowd in the street, and when I heard the Prime Minister from the window above saying that he had returned, like Lord Beaconsfield, with " peace with honour," claiming that it was peace for our time, once again I felt lonely and isolated; and when later, in the Cabinet room, all his other colleagues were able to present him with bouquets, it was an extremely painful and bitter moment for me that all that I could offer him was my resignation.

Before taking such a step as I have taken, on a question of international policy, a Minister must ask himself many questions, not the least important of which is this: Can my resignation at the present time do any material harm to His Majesty's Government; can it weaken our position; can it suggest to our critics that there is not a united front in Great Britain ? Now I would not have flattered myself that my resignation was of great importance, and I did feel confident that so small a blow could easily be borne at the present time, when I think that the Prime Minister is more popular than he has ever been at any period; but had I had any doubts with regard to that facet of the problem, they would have been set at rest, I must say, by the way in which my resignation was accepted, not, I think, with reluctance, but really with relief.

I have always been a student of foreign politics. I have served 10 years in the Foreign Office, and I have studied the history of this and of other countries, and I have always believed that one of the most important principles in foreign policy and the conduct of

336

foreign policy should be to make your policy plain to other countries, to let them know where you stand and what in certain circumstances you are prepared to do. I remember so well in 1914 meeting a friend, just after the declaration of war, who had come back from the British Embassy in Berlin, and asking him whether it was the case, as I had seen it reported in the papers, that the Berlin crowd had behaved very badly and had smashed all the windows of the Embassy, and that the military had had to be called out in order to protect them. I remember my friend telling me that, in his opinion and in that of the majority of the staff, the Berlin crowd were not to blame, that the members of the British Embassy staff had great sympathy with the feelings of the populace, because, they said, " These people have never thought that there was a chance of our coming into the war." They were assured by their Government—and the Government themselves perhaps believed it—that Britain would remain neutral, and therefore it came to them as a shock when, having already been engaged with other enemies, as they were, they found that Great Britain had turned against them.

I thought then, and I have always felt, that in any other international crisis that should occur our first duty was to make it plain exactly where we stood and what we would do. I believe that the great defect in our foreign policy during recent months and recent weeks has been that we have failed to do so. During the last four weeks we have been drifting, day by day, nearer into war with Germany, and we have never said, until the last moment, and then in most uncertain terms, that we were prepared to fight. We knew that information to the opposite effect was being poured into the ears of the head of the German State. He had been assured, reassured, and fortified in the opinion that in no case would Great Britain fight.

When Ministers met at the end of August on their return from a holiday there was an enormous accumulation of information from all parts of the world, the ordinary information from our diplomatic representatives, also secret, and less reliable information from other sources, information from Members of Parliament who had been travelling on the Continent and who had felt it their duty to write to their friends in the Cabinet and give them first-hand information which they had received from good sources. I myself had been travelling in Scandinavia and in the Baltic States, and with regard to all this information—Europe was very full of rumours at that time—it was quite extraordinary the unanimity with which it pointed to one conclusion and with which all sources suggested that there was one remedy. All information pointed to the fact that Germany was preparing for war at the end of September, and all recommendations agreed that the one way in which it could be prevented was by Great Britain making a firm stand and stating that she would be in that war, and would be upon the other side.

I had urged even earlier, after the rape of Austria, that Great Britain should make a firm declaration of what her foreign policy was, and then and later I was met with this, that the people of this country are not prepared to fight for Czechoslovakia. That is perfectly true, but I tried to represent another aspect of the situation, that it was not for Czechoslovakia that we should have to fight, that it was not for Czechoslovakia that we should have been fighting if we had gone to war last week. God knows how thankful we all are to have avoided it, but we also know that the people of this country were prepared for it—resolute, prepared, and grimly determined. It was not for Serbia that we fought in 1914. It was not even for Belgium, although it occasionally suited some people to say so. We were fighting then, as we should have been fighting last week, in order that one great Power should not be allowed, in disregard of treaty obligations, of the laws of nations and the decrees of morality to dominate by brutal force the Continent of Europe. For that principle we fought against Napoleon Bonaparte, and against Louis XIV of France and Philip II of Spain. For that principle we must ever be prepared to fight, for on the day when we are not prepared to fight for it we forfeit our Empire, our liberties and our independence.

I besought my colleagues not to see this problem always in terms of Czechoslovakia, not to review it always from the difficult strategic position of that small country, but rather to say to themselves, " A moment may come when, owing to the invasion of Czechoslovakia, a European war will begin, and when that moment comes we must take part in that war, we cannot keep out of it, and there is no doubt upon which side we shall fight. Let the world know that and it will give those who are prepared to disturb the peace reason to hold their hand." It is perfectly true that after the assault on Austria the Prime Minister made a speech in this House—an excellent speech with every word of which I was in complete agreement—and what he said then was repeated and supported by the Chancellor of the Exchequer at Lanark. It was, however, a guarded statement. It was a statement to the effect that if there were such a war it would be unwise for anybody to count upon the possibility of our staying out.

That was not the language which the dictators understand. Together with new methods and a new morality they have introduced also a new vocabulary into Europe. They have discarded the old diplomatic methods of correspondence. Is it not significant that during the whole of this crisis there has not been a German Ambassador in London and, so far as I am aware, the German Chargé d'Affaires has hardly visited the Foreign Office ? They talk a new language, the language of the headlines of the tabloid Press, and such guarded diplomatic and reserved utterances as were made by the Prime Minister and the Chancellor of the Exchequer mean nothing to the mentality of Herr Hitler or Signor Mussolini. I had hoped that it might be possible to make a statement to Herr Hitler before he made his speech at Nuremberg. On all sides we were being urged to do so by people in this country, by Members in this House, by Leaders of the Opposition, by the Press, by the heads of foreign States, even by Germans who were supporters of the régime and did not wish to see it plunged into a war which might destroy it. But we were always told that on no account must we irritate Herr Hitler; it was particularly dangerous to irritate him before he made a public speech, because if he were so irritated he might say some terrible things from which afterwards there would be no retreat. It seems to me that Herr Hitler never makes a speech save under the influence of considerable irritation, and the addition of one more irritant would not, I should have thought, have made a great difference, whereas the communication of a solemn fact would have produced a sobering effect.

After the chance of Nuremberg was missed I had hoped that the Prime Minister at his first interview with Herr Hitler at Berchtesgaden would make the position plain, but he did not do so. Again, at Godesberg I had hoped that that statement would be made in unequivocal language. Again I was disappointed. Hitler had another speech to make in Berlin. Again an opportunity occurred of telling him exactly where we stood before he made that speech, but again the opportunity was missed, and it was only after the speech that he was informed. He was informed through the mouth of a distinguished English civil servant[1] that in certain conditions we were prepared to fight. We know what the mentality or something of the mentality of that great dictator is. We know that a message delivered strictly according to instructions with at least three qualifying clauses was not likely to produce upon him on the morning after his great oration the effect that was desired. Honestly, I did not believe that he thought there was anything of importance in that message. It certainly produced no effect whatever upon him and we can hardly blame him.

Then came the last appeal from the Prime Minister on Wednesday morning. For the first time from the beginning to the end of the four weeks of negotiations Herr Hitler was prepared to yield an inch, an ell perhaps, but to yield some measure to the representations of Great Britain. But I would remind the House that the message from the Prime Minister was not the first news that he had received that morning. At dawn he had learned of the mobilization of the British Fleet.

[1] Sir Horace Wilson, who, with the British Ambassador in Berlin, visited Hitler on the morning of September 27th, the day after Hitler's speech in the *Sportpalast*.

It is impossible to know what are the motives of man and we shall probably never be satisfied as to which of these two sources of inspiration moved him most when he agreed to go to Munich, but we do know that never before had he given in and that then he did. I had been urging the mobilization of the Fleet for many days. I had thought that this was the kind of language which would be easier for Herr Hitler to understand than the guarded language of diplomacy or the conditional clauses of the Civil Service. I had urged that something in that direction might be done at the end of August and before the Prime Minister went to Berchtesgaden. I had suggested that it should accompany the mission of Sir Horace Wilson. I remember the Prime Minister stating it was the one thing that would ruin that mission, and I said it was the one thing that would lead it to success.

That is the deep difference between the Prime Minister and myself throughout these days. The Prime Minister has believed in addressing Herr Hitler through the language of sweet reasonableness. I have believed that he was more open to the language of the mailed fist. I am glad so many people think that sweet reasonableness has prevailed, but what actually did it accomplish? The Prime Minister went to Berchtesgaden with many proposals and alternatives to put before the Führer, prepared to argue and negotiate, as anybody would have gone to such a meeting. He was met by an ultimatum. So far as I am aware no suggestion of an alternative was ever put forward. Once the Prime Minister found himself in the atmosphere of Berchtesgaden and face to face with the personality of Hitler he knew perfectly well, being a good judge of men, that it would be a waste of time

342

to put forward any alternative suggestion. So he returned to us with those proposals, wrapped up in a cloak called " Self-determination," and laid them before the Cabinet. They meant the partition of a country, the cession of territory, they meant what, some weeks or days before, had been indignantly repudiated throughout the country.

After long deliberation the Cabinet decided to accept that ultimatum, and I was one of those who agreed in that decision. I felt all the difficulty of it; but I foresaw also the danger of refusal. I saw that if we were obliged to go to war it would be hard to have it said against us that we were fighting against the principle of self-determination, and I hoped that if a postponement could be reached by this compromise there was a possibility that the final disaster might be permanently avoided. It was not a pleasant task to impose upon the Government of Czechoslovakia so grievous a hurt to their country, no pleasant or easy task for those upon whose support the Government of Czechoslovakia had relied to have to come to her and say " You have got to give up all for which you were prepared to fight "; but, still, she accepted those terms. The Government of Czechoslovakia, filled with deep misgiving, and with great regret, accepted the harsh terms that were proposed to her.

That was all that we had got by sweet reasonableness at Berchtesgaden. Well, I did think that when a country had agreed to be partitioned, when the Government of a country had agreed to split up the ancient Kingdom of Bohemia, which has existed behind its original frontier for more than 1,000 years, that was the ultimate demand that would be made upon it, and that after everything which Herr Hitler had asked for in the first instance had been conceded he would be willing, and we should insist, that the method of transfer of those territories should be conducted in a normal, in a civilized manner, as such transfers have always been conducted in the past.

The Prime Minister made a second visit to Germany, and at Godesberg he was received with flags, bands, trumpets and all the panoply of Nazi parade; but he returned again with nothing but an ultimatum. Sweet reasonableness had won nothing except terms which a cruel and revengeful enemy would have dictated to a beaten foe after a long war. Crueller terms could hardly be devised than those of the Godesberg ultimatum. The moment I saw them I said to myself, " If these are accepted it will be the end of all decency in the conduct of public affairs in the world." We had a long and anxious discussion in the Cabinet with regard to the acceptance or rejection of those terms. It was decided to reject them, and that information, also, was conveyed to the German Government. Then we were face to face with an impossible position, and at the last moment—not quite the last moment, but what seemed the last moment—another effort was made, by the dispatch of an emissary to Herr Hitler with suggestions for a last appeal. That emissary's effort was in vain, and it was only, as the House knows, on that fateful Wednesday morning that the final change of policy was adopted. I believe that change of policy, as I have said, was due not to any argument that had been addressed to Herr Hitler—it has never been suggested that it was—but due to the fact that for the first moment he realized, when the Fleet was mobilized, that what his advisers had been assuring him of for weeks and months was untrue and that the

British people were prepared to fight in a great cause.

So, last of all, he came to Munich and terms, of which the House is now aware, were devised at Munich, and those were the terms upon which this transfer of territory is to be carried out. The Prime Minister will shortly be explaining to the House the particulars in which the Munich terms differ from the Godesberg ultimatum. There are great and important differences, and it is a great triumph for the Prime Minister that he was able to acquire them. I spent the greater part of Friday trying to persuade myself that those terms were good enough for me. I tried to swallow them—I did not want to do what I have done —but they stuck in my throat, because it seemed to me that although the modifications which the Prime Minister obtained were important and of great value— the House will realize how great the value is when the Prime Minister has developed them—that still there remained the fact that that country was to be invaded, and I had thought that after accepting the humiliation of partition she should have been spared the ignominy and the horror of invasion. If anybody doubts that she is now suffering from the full horror of invasion they have only to read an article published in the *Daily Telegraph* this morning, which will convince them. After all, when Naboth had agreed to give up his vineyard he should have been allowed to pack up his goods in peace and depart, but the German Government, having got their man down, were not to be deprived of the pleasure of kicking him. Invasion remained; even the date of invasion remained unaltered. The date laid down by Herr Hitler was not to be changed. There are five stages, but those stages are almost as rapid as an army can move. Invasion and

345

the date remained the same. Therefore, the works, fortifications, and guns on emplacements upon which that poor country had spent an enormous amount of its wealth were to be handed over intact. Just as the German was not to be deprived of the pleasure of kicking a man when he was down, so the army was not to be robbed of its loot. That was another term in the ultimatum which I found it impossible to accept. That was why I failed to bring myself to swallow the terms that were proposed—although I recognized the great service that the Prime Minister had performed in obtaining very material changes in them which would result in great benefit and a great lessening of the sufferings of the people of Czechoslovakia.

Then he brought home also from Munich something more than the terms to which we had agreed. At the last moment, at the farewell meeting, he signed with the Führer, a joint declaration. (An Hon. Member: "Secret.") I do not think there was anything secret about the declaration. The joint declaration has been published to the world. I saw no harm, no great harm and no very obvious harm, in the terms of that declaration, but I would suggest that for the Prime Minister of England to sign, without consulting with his colleagues and without, so far as I am aware, any reference to his Allies, obviously without any communication with the Dominions and without the assistance of any expert diplomatic advisers, such a declaration with the dictator of a great State, is not the way in which the foreign affairs of the British Empire should be conducted.

There is another aspect of this joint declaration. After all, what does it say? That Great Britain and Germany will not go to war in future and that every thing will be settled by negotiation. Was it ever our intention to go to war? Was it ever our intention not to settle things by communication and counsel? There is a danger. We must remember that this is not all that we are left with as the result of what has happened during the last few weeks. We are left, and we must all acknowledge it, with a loss of esteem on the part of countries that trusted us. We are left also with a tremendous commitment. For the first time in our history we have committed ourselves to defend a frontier in Central Europe.

Hansard, Fifth Series, Vol. CCCXXXIX, pp. 29–38.

THE PRIME MINISTER (MR. CHAMBERLAIN): When the House met last Wednesday, we were all under the shadow of a great and imminent menace. War, in a form more stark and terrible than ever before, seemed to be staring us in the face. Before I sat down, a message had come which gave us new hope that peace might yet be saved, and to-day, only a few days after, we all meet in joy and thankfulness that the prayers of millions have been answered, and a cloud of anxiety has been lifted from our hearts. Upon the Members of the Cabinet the strain of the responsibility of these last few weeks has been almost overwhelming. Some of us, I have no doubt, will carry the mark of it for the rest of our days. Necessarily, the weight fell heavier upon some shoulders than others. While all bore their part, I would like here and now to pay an especial tribute of gratitude and praise to the man upon whom fell the first brunt of those decisions which had to be taken day by day, almost hour by hour. The calmness, patience,

347

and wisdom of the Foreign Secretary[1], and his lofty conception of his duty, not only to this country but to all humanity, were an example to us all, and sustained us all through the trials through which we have been passing.

Before I come to describe the Agreement which was signed at Munich in the small hours of Friday morning last, I would like to remind the House of two things which I think it is very essential not to forget when those terms are being considered. The first is this: We did not go there to decide whether the predominantly German areas in the Sudetenland should be passed over to the German Reich. That had been decided already. Czechoslovakia had accepted the Anglo-French proposals. What we had to consider was the method, the conditions and the time of the transfer of the territory. The second point to remember is that time was one of the essential factors. All the elements were present on the spot for the outbreak of a conflict which might have precipitated the catastrophe. We had populations inflamed to a high degree; we had extremists on both sides ready to work up and provoke incidents; we had considerable quantities of arms which were by no means confined to regularly organized forces. Therefore, it was essential that we should quickly reach a conclusion, so that this painful and difficult operation of transfer might be carried out at the earliest possible moment and concluded as soon as was consistent with orderly procedure, in order that we might avoid the possibility of something that might have rendered all our attempts at peaceful solution useless. . . .

Before giving a verdict upon this arrangement, we

[1] Lord Halifax

should do well to avoid describing it as a personal or a national triumph for anyone. The real triumph is that it has shown that representatives of four great Powers can find it possible to agree on a way of carrying out a difficult and delicate operation by discussion instead of by force of arms, and thereby they have averted a catastrophe which would have ended civilization as we have known it. The relief that our escape from this great peril of war has, I think, everywhere been mingled in this country with a profound feeling of sympathy—(Hon. Members: "Shame.") I have nothing to be ashamed of. Let those who have, hang their heads. We must feel profound sympathy for a small and gallant nation in the hour of their national grief and loss. . . .

I pass from that subject, and I would like to say a few words in respect of the various other participants, besides ourselves, in the Munich Agreement. After everything has been said about the German Chancellor to-day and in the past, I do feel that the House ought to recognize the difficulty for a man in that position to take back such emphatic declarations as he has already made amidst the enthusiastic cheers of his supporters, and to recognize that in consenting, even though it were only at the last moment, to discuss with the representatives of other Powers those things which he had declared he had already decided once for all, was a real and substantial contribution on his part. With regard to Signor Mussolini, his contribution was certainly notable and perhaps decisive. It was on his suggestion that the final stages of mobilization were postponed for 24 hours to give us an opportunity of discussing the situation, and I wish to say that at the Conference itself both he and the Italian Foreign

349

Secretary, Count Ciano, were most helpful in the discussions. It was they who, very early in the proceedings, produced the Memorandum which M. Daladier and I were able to accept as a basis of discussion. I think that Europe and the world have reason to be grateful to the head of the Italian Government for his work in contributing to a peaceful solution.

M. Daladier had in some respects the most difficult task of all four of us, because of the special relations uniting his country and Czechoslovakia, and I should like to say that his courage, his readiness to take responsibility, his pertinacity and his unfailing good humour were invaluable throughout the whole of our discussions. There is one other Power which was not represented at the Conference and which nevertheless we felt to be exercising a constantly increasing influence. I refer, of course, to the United States of America. Those messages of President Roosevelt, so firmly and yet so persuasively framed, showed how the voice of the most powerful nation in the world could make itself heard across 3,000 miles of ocean and sway the minds of men in Europe.

In my view the strongest force of all, one which grew and took fresh shapes and forms every day was the force not of any one individual, but was that unmistakable sense of unanimity among the peoples of the world that war somehow must be averted. The peoples of the British Empire were at one with those of Germany, of France and of Italy, and their anxiety, their intense desire for peace, pervaded the whole atmosphere of the conference, and I believe that that, and not threats, made possible the concessions that were made. I know the House will want to hear what I am sure it does not doubt, that throughout these discussions the Dominions, the Governments of the Dominions, have been kept in the closest touch with the march of events by telegraph and by personal contact, and I would like to say how greatly I was encouraged on each of the journeys I made to Germany by the knowledge that I went with the good wishes of the Governments of the Dominions. They shared all our anxieties and all our hopes. They rejoiced with us that peace was preserved, and with us they look forward to further efforts to consolidate what has been done.

Ever since I assumed my present office my main purpose has been to work for the removal of those suspicions and those animosities which have so long poisoned the air. The path which leads to appeasement is long and bristles with obstacles. The question of Czechoslovakia is the latest and perhaps the most dangerous. Now that we have got past it, I feel that it may be possible to make further progress along the road to sanity.

My right hon. Friend has alluded in somewhat bitter terms to my conversation last Friday morning with Herr Hitler. I do not know why that conversation should give rise to suspicion, still less to criticism. I entered into no pact. I made no new commitments. There is no secret understanding. Our conversation was hostile to no other nation. The objects of that conversation, for which I asked, was to try to extend a little further the personal contact which I had established with Herr Hitler and which I believe to be essential in modern diplomacy. We had a friendly and entirely non-committal conversation, carried on, on my part, largely with a view to seeing whether there could be points in common between the head of a democratic Government and the ruler of a totalitarian State. We see the result in the declaration which has been published, in which my right hon. Friend finds so much ground for suspicion. What does it say?

There are three paragraphs. The first says that we agree

> "in recognizing that the question of Anglo-German relations is of the first importance for the two countries and for Europe."

Does anyone deny that? The second is an expression of opinion only. It says that:

> "We regard the agreement signed last night and the Anglo-German Naval Agreement as symbolic of the desire of the two peoples never to go to war with one another again."

Once more I ask, does anyone doubt that that is the desire of the two peoples? What is the last paragraph?

> "We are resolved that the method of consultation shall be the method adopted to deal with any other questions that may concern our two countries, and we are determined to continue our efforts to remove possible sources of difference and thus to contribute to assure the peace of Europe."

Who will stand up and condemn that sentence?

I believe there are many who will feel with me that such a declaration, signed by the German Chancellor and myself, is something more than a pious expression of opinion. In our relations with other countries everything depends upon there being sincerity and good will on both sides. I believe that there is sincerity and good will on both sides in this declaration. That is why to me its significance goes far beyond its actual words. If there is one lesson which we should learn from the events of these last weeks it is this, that lasting peace is not to be obtained by sitting still and waiting for it to come. It requires active, positive efforts to achieve it. No doubt I shall have plenty of critics who will say that I am guilty of facile optimism, and that I should disbelieve every word that is uttered by rulers of other great States in Europe. I am too much of a realist to believe that we are going to achieve our paradise in a day. We have only laid the foundations of peace. The superstructure is not even begun.

For a long period now we have been engaged in this country in a great programme of rearmament, which is daily increasing in pace and in volume. Let no one think that because we have signed this agreement between these four Powers at Munich we can afford to relax our efforts in regard to that programme at this moment. Disarmament on the part of this country can never be unilateral again. We have tried that once, and we very nearly brought ourselves to disaster. If disarmament is to come it must come by steps, and it must come by the agreement and the active co-operation of other countries. Until we know that we have obtained that co-operation and until we have agreed upon the actual steps to be taken, we here must remain on guard.

When, only a little while ago, we had to call upon the people of this country to begin to take those steps which would be necessary if the emergency should come upon us, we saw the magnificent spirit that was displayed. The Naval Reservists, the Territorial Army, the Auxiliary Air Force, the Observers' Corps, obeyed the summons to mobilize very readily. We must remember that most of these men gave up their peace time work at a moment's notice to serve their country. We should like to thank them. We should like to thank also the employers who accepted the inevitable inconvenience of mobilization. I know that they will show the same spirit of patriotic co-operation in taking back all their former employees when they are demobilized. I know that, although the crisis has passed, they will feel proud that they are employing men upon whom the State can rely if a crisis should return.

While we must renew our determination to fill up the deficiencies that yet remain in our armaments and in our defensive precautions, so that we may be ready to defend ourselves and make our diplomacy effective —(Interruption)—yes I am a realist—nevertheless I say with an equal sense of reality that I do see fresh opportunities of approaching this subject of disarmament opening up before us, and I believe that they are at least as hopeful to-day as they have been at any previous time. It is to such tasks—the winning back of confidence, the gradual removal of hostility between nations until they feel that they can safely discard their weapons, one by one, that I would wish to devote what energy and time may be left to me before I hand over my office to younger men.

MR. CHURCHILL: . . . I will, therefore, begin by saying the most unpopular and most unwelcome thing. I will begin by saying what everybody would like to ignore or forget but which must nevertheless be stated, namely, that we have sustained a total and unmitigated defeat, and that France has suffered even more than we have.

VISCOUNTESS ASTOR: Nonsense.

MR. CHURCHILL: When the Noble Lady cries " Nonsense," she could not have heard the Chancellor of the Exchequer admit in his illuminating and comprehensive speech just now that Herr Hitler had gained in this particular leap forward in substance all he set out to gain. The utmost my right hon. Friend the Prime Minister has been able to secure by all his immense exertions, by all the great efforts and mobilization which took place in this country, and by all the anguish and strain through which we have passed in this country, the utmost he has been able to gain— (HON. MEMBERS: " Is peace."). I thought I might be allowed to make that point in its due place, and I propose to deal with it. The utmost he has been able to gain for Czechoslovakia and in the matters which were in dispute has been that the German dictator, instead of snatching his victuals from the table, has been content to have them served to him course by course. . . .

We are asked to vote for this Motion which has been put upon the Paper, and it is certainly a Motion couched in very uncontroversial terms, as, indeed, is the Amendment moved from the Opposition side.[1] I cannot myself express my agreement with the steps which have been taken, and as the Chancellor of the Exchequer has put his side of the case with so much

[1] At the opening of the debate on October 5th, the Chancellor of the Exchequer (Sir J. Simon) had moved: " That this House approves the policy of His Majesty's Government by which war was averted in the recent crisis and supports their efforts to secure a lasting peace." The opposition amendment ran: " That this House, while profoundly relieved that war has been averted for the time being, cannot approve a policy which has led to the sacrifice of Czechoslovakia under threat of armed force and to the humiliation of our country and its exposure to grave dangers; and realizing the intense desire of all peoples for lasting peace, demands an active support of the method of collective security through the League of Nations and the immediate initiation by His Majesty's Government of proposals for the summoning of a world conference to consider the removal of economic and political grievances which imperil peace." The Government motion was carried on October 6th by 366 votes to 144.

AA*

ability I will attempt, if I may be permitted, to put the case from a different 'angle. I have always held the view that the maintenance of peace depends upon the accumulation of deterrents against the aggressor, coupled with a sincere effort to redress grievances. Herr Hitler's victory, like so many of the famous struggles that have governed the fate of the world, was won upon the narrowest of margins. After the seizure of Austria in March we faced this problem in our Debates. I ventured to appeal to the Government to go a little further than the Prime Minister went, and to give a pledge that in conjunction with France and other Powers they would guarantee the security of Czechoslovakia while the Sudeten-Deutsch question was being examined either by a League of Nations Commission or some other impartial body, and I still believe that if that course had been followed events would not have fallen into this disastrous state. I agree very much with my right hon. Friend the Member for Sparkbrook (Mr. Amery) when he said on that occasion—I cannot remember his actual words—" Do one thing or the other; either say you will disinterest yourself in the matter altogether or take the step of giving a guarantee which will have the greatest chance of securing protection for that country."

France and Great Britain together, especially if they had maintained a close contact with Russia, which certainly was not done, would have been able in those days in the summer, when they had the prestige, to influence many of the smaller States of Europe, and I believe they could have determined the attitude of Poland. Such a combination, prepared at a time when the German dictator was not deeply and irrevocably committed to his new adventure, would, I believe, have given strength to all those forces in Germany which resisted this departure, this new design. They were varying forces, those of a military character which declared that Germany was not ready to undertake a world war, and all that mass of moderate opinion and popular opinion which dreaded war, and some elements of which still have some influence upon the German Government. Such action would have given strength to all that intense desire for peace which the helpless German masses share with their British and French fellow men, and which, as we have been reminded, found a passionate and rarely permitted vent in the joyous manifestations with which the Prime Minister was acclaimed in Munich.

All these forces, added to the other deterrents which combinations of Powers, great and small, ready to stand firm upon the front of law and for the ordered remedy of grievances, would have formed, might well have been effective. Of course you cannot say for certain that they would. (Interruption.) I try to argue fairly with the House. At the same time I do not think it is fair to charge those who wished to see this course followed, and followed consistently and resolutely, with having wishes for an immediate war. Between submission and immediate war there was this third alternative, which gave a hope not only of peace but of justice. It is quite true that such a policy in order to succeed demanded that Britain should declare straight out and a long time beforehand that she would, with others, join to defend Czechoslovakia against an unprovoked aggression. His Majesty's Government refused to give that guarantee when it would have saved the situation, yet in the end they gave it when it was too late, and now, for the future,

357

they renew it when they have not the slightest power to make it good.

All is over. Silent, mournful, abandoned, broken, Czechoslovakia recedes into the darkness. She has suffered in every respect by her association with the Western democracies and with the League of Nations, of which she has always been an obedient servant. . . .

I venture to think that in future the Czechoslovak State cannot be maintained as an independent entity. You will find that in a period of time which may be measured by years, but may be measured only by months, Czechoslovakia will be engulfed in the Nazi regime. Perhaps they may join it in despair or in revenge. At any rate, that story is over and told. But we cannot consider the abandonment and ruin of Czechoslovakia in the light only of what happened only last month. It is the most grievous consequence which we have yet experienced of what we have done and of what we have left undone in the last five years— five years of futile good intention, five years of eager search for the line of least resistance, five years of uninterrupted retreat of British power, five years of neglect of our air defences. Those are the features which I stand here to declare and which marked an improvident stewardship for which Great Britain and France have dearly to pay. We have been reduced in those five years from a position of security so overwhelming and so unchallengeable that we never cared to think about it. We have been reduced from a position where the very word " war " was considered one which would be used only by persons qualifying for a lunatic asylum. We have been reduced from a position of safety and power—power to do good, power to be generous to a beaten foe, power to make terms with

Germany, power to give her proper redress for her grievances, power to take any step in strength or mercy or justice which we thought right—reduced in five years from a position safe and unchallenged to where we stand now.

When I think of the fair hopes of a long peace which still lay before Europe at the beginning of 1933 when Herr Hitler first obtained power, and of all the opportunities of arresting the growth of the Nazi power which have been thrown away, when I think of the immense combinations and resources which have been neglected or squandered, I cannot believe that a parallel exists in the whole course of history. So far as this country is concerned the responsibility must rest with those who have the undisputed control of our political affairs. They neither prevented Germany from rearming, nor did they re-arm ourselves in time. They quarrelled with Italy without saving Ethiopia. They exploited and discredited the vast institution of the League of Nations and they neglected to make alliances and combinations which might have repaired previous errors, and thus they left us in the hour of trial without adequate national defence or effective international security.

In my holiday I thought it was a chance to study the reign of King Ethelred the Unready. The House will remember that that was a period of great misfortune, in which, from the strong position which we had gained under the descendants of King Alfred, we fell swiftly into chaos. It was the period of Danegeld and of foreign pressure. I must say that the rugged words of the Anglo-Saxon Chronicle, written 1,000 years ago, seem to me apposite, at least as apposite as those quotations from Shakespeare with which we have been regaled by the last speaker from the Opposition Bench. Here is what the Anglo-Saxon Chronicle said, and I think the words apply very much to our treatment of Germany and our relations with her:

> "All these calamities fell upon us because of evil counsel, because tribute was not offered to them at the right time nor yet were they resisted; but when they had done the most evil, then was peace made with them."

That is the wisdom of the past, for all wisdom is not new wisdom.

I have ventured to express those views in justifying myself for not being able to support the Motion which is moved to-night, but I recognize that this great matter of Czechoslovakia, and of British and French duty there, has passed into history. New developments may come along, but we are not here to decide whether any of those steps should be taken or not. They have been taken. They have been taken by those who had a right to take them because they bore the highest executive responsibility under the Crown. Whatever we may think of it, we must regard those steps as belonging to the category of affairs which are settled beyond recall. The past is no more, and one can only draw comfort if one feels that one has done one's best to advise rightly and wisely and in good time. I, therefore, turn to the future, and to our situation as it is to-day. Here, again, I am sure I shall have to say something which will not be at all welcome.

We are in the presence of a disaster of the first magnitude which has befallen Great Britain and France. Do not let us blind ourselves to that. It must now be accepted that all the countries of Central and

Eastern Europe will make the best terms they can with the triumphant Nazi Power. The system of alliances in Central Europe upon which France has relied for her safety has now been swept away, and I can see no means by which it can be reconstituted. The road down the Danube Valley to the Black Sea, the resources of corn and oil, the road which leads as far as Turkey, has been opened. In fact, if not in form, it seems to me that all those countries of Middle Europe, all those Danubian countries, will one after another, be drawn into this vast system of power politics—not only power military politics but power economic politics—radiating from Berlin, and I believe this can be achieved quite smoothly and swiftly and will not necessarily entail the firing of a single shot. If you wish to survey the havoc of the foreign policy of Britain and France, look at what is happening and is recorded each day in the columns of *The Times*. Why, I read this morning about Yugoslavia—and I know something about the details of that country—

" The effects of the crisis for Yugoslavia can immediately be traced. Since the elections of 1935, which followed soon after the murder of King Alexander, the Serb and Croat Opposition to the Government of Dr. Stoyadinovitch have been conducting their entire campaign for the next elections under the slogan: ' Back to France, England and the Little *Entente*; back to democracy.' The events of the past fortnight have so triumphantly vindicated Dr. Stoyadinovitch's policy. . . ."

—his is a policy of close association with Germany—

" that the Opposition has collapsed practically overnight; the new elections, the date of which was in doubt, are now likely to be held very soon and can result only in an overwhelming victory for Dr. Stoyadinovitch's Government."

Here was a country which, three months ago, would have stood in the line with other countries to arrest what has occurred.

Again, what happened in Warsaw? The British and French Ambassadors visited Colonel Beck, or sought to visit him, the Foreign Minister, in order to ask for some mitigation in the harsh measures being pursued against Czechoslovakia about Teschen. The door was shut in their faces. The French Ambassador was not even granted an audience and the British Ambassador was given a most curt reply by a political director. The whole matter is described in the Polish Press as a political indiscretion committed by those two Powers, and we are to-day reading of the success of Colonel Beck's blow. I am not forgetting, I must say, that it is less than 20 years ago since British and French bayonets rescued Poland from the bondage of a century and a half. I think it is indeed a sorry episode in the history of that country, for whose freedom and rights so many of us have had warm and long sympathy.

Those illustrations are typical. You will see, day after day, week after week, entire alienation of those regions. Many of those countries, in fear of the rise of the Nazi Power, have already got politicians, Ministers, Governments, who were pro-German, but there was always an enormous popular movement in Poland, Roumania, Bulgaria and Yugoslavia which looked to the Western democracies and loathed the idea of having this arbitrary rule of the totalitarian system thrust upon them, and hoped that a stand would be made. All that has gone by the board. We are talking about countries which are a long way off and of which, as the Prime Minister might say, we know nothing.

(Interruption.) The noble Lady says that that very harmless allusion is—

VISCOUNTESS ASTOR: Rude.

MR. CHURCHILL: She must very recently have been receiving her finishing course in manners. What will be the position, I want to know, of France and England this year and the year afterwards? What will be the position of that Western front of which we are in full authority the guarantors? The German army at the present time is more numerous than that of France, though not nearly so matured or perfected. Next year it will grow much larger, and its maturity will be more complete. Relieved from all anxiety in the East, and having secured resources which will greatly diminish, if not entirely remove, the deterrent of a naval blockade, the rulers of Nazi Germany will have a free choice open to them in what direction they will turn their eyes. If the Nazi dictator should choose to look westward, as he may, bitterly will France and England regret the loss of that fine army of ancient Bohemia which was estimated last week to require not fewer then 30 German divisions for its destruction.

Can we blind ourselves to the great change which has taken place in the military situation, and to the dangers we have to meet? We are in process, I believe, of adding, in four years, four battalions to the British Army. No fewer than two have already been completed. Here at least 30 divisions which [*sic*] must now be taken into consideration upon the French front, besides the 12 that were captured when Austria was engulfed. Many people, no doubt, honestly believe that they are only giving away the interests of Czechoslovakia, whereas I fear we shall find that we have deeply compromised, and perhaps fatally endangered, the safety and even the independence of Great Britain and France. This is not merely a question of giving up the German colonies, as I am sure we shall be asked to do. Nor is it a question only of losing influence in Europe. It goes far deeper than that. You have to consider the character of the Nazi movement and the rule which it implies. The Prime Minister desires to see cordial relations between this country and Germany. There is no difficulty at all in having cordial relations with the German people. Our hearts go out to them. But they have no power. You must have diplomatic and correct relations, but there can never be friendship between the British democracy and the Nazi Power, that Power which spurns Christian ethics, which cheers its onward course by a barbarous paganism, which vaunts the spirit of aggression and conquest, which derives strength and perverted pleasure from persecution, and uses, as we have seen, with pitiless brutality the threat of murderous force. That Power cannot ever be the trusted friend of the British democracy.

What I find unendurable is the sense of our country falling into the power, into the orbit and influence of Nazi Germany, and of our existence becoming dependent upon their good will or pleasure. It is to prevent that that I have tried my best to urge the maintenance of every bulwark of defence—first the timely creation of an Air Force superior to anything within striking distance of our shores; secondly, the gathering together of the collective strength of many nations; and thirdly, the making of alliances and military conventions, all within the Covenant, in order to gather together forces at any rate to restrain the onward movement of this Power. It has all been in vain. Every position has been successively undermined and abandoned on specious and plausible excuses. We do not want to be led upon the high road to becoming a satellite of the German Nazi system of European domination. In a very few years, perhaps in a very few months, we shall be confronted with demands with which we shall no doubt be invited to comply. Those demands may affect the surrender of territory or the surrender of liberty. I foresee and foretell that the policy of submission will carry with it restrictions upon the freedom of speech and debate in Parliament, on public platforms, and discussions in the Press, for it will be said—indeed, I hear it said sometimes now—that we cannot allow the Nazi system of dictatorship to be criticized by ordinary, common English politicians. Then, with a Press under control, in part direct but more potently indirect, with every organ of public opinion doped and chloroformed into acquiescence, we shall be conducted along further stages of our journey. . . .

I do not grudge our loyal, brave people, who were ready to do their duty no matter what the cost, who never flinched under the strain of last week—I do not grudge them the natural, spontaneous outburst of joy and relief when they learned that the hard ordeal would no longer be required of them at the moment; but they should know the truth. They should know that we have sustained a defeat without a war, the consequences of which will travel far with us along our road; they should know that we have passed an awful milestone in our history, when the whole equilibrium of Europe has been deranged, and that the terrible words have for the time being been pronounced against the Western democracies:

"Thou art weighed in the balance and found wanting."

And do not suppose that this is the end. This is only the beginning of the reckoning. This is only the first sip, the first foretaste of a bitter cup which will be proffered to us year by year unless by a supreme recovery of moral health and martial vigour, we arise again and take our stand for freedom as in the olden time.

Hansard, Fifth Series, Vol. CCCXXXIX, pp. 29–38, 41–42, 45, 47–50, 360–1, 362–4, 365–71, 373

65: NEVILLE CHAMBERLAIN: Extracts from Speeches in the House of Commons, August–September 1939

In the spring of 1939, the policy of appeasement was abandoned after the absorption, in March, of the rest of Czechoslovakia by Germany. British guarantees were given to Roumania and Greece, and to Poland; it was in pursuance of the latter, when German claims to Danzig led to an attack on Poland, that war started on September 3rd 1939. The statements in Parliament and elsewhere during the last weeks merely reiterate principles already familiar, but it is worth noting that the opposition to war was very small compared with that in 1793 or even in 1914. This was admitted by George Lansbury, leader of the pacifist section of the Labour Party in the House of Commons on August 24th: " I do not claim that . . . I represent more than a tiny majority in the country." The mood of the majority is expressed by the following extracts from speeches of the Prime Minister.

24 AUGUST: The Foreign Secretary, in a speech made on 29th June to the Royal Institute of International Affairs, set out the fundamental bases of British foreign policy. His observations on that subject were, I believe, received with general approval. The first basis is our determination to resist methods of force. The second basis is our recognition of the world desire to pursue the constructive work of building peace. If we were once satisfied, my noble Friend said, that the intentions of others were the same as our own, and if we were satisfied that all wanted peaceful solutions, then, indeed, we could discuss problems which are to-day causing the world so much anxiety. That

definition of the basic fundamental ground of British policy still stands. We want to see established an international order based upon mutual understanding and mutual confidence, and we cannot build such an order unless it conforms to certain principles which are essential to the establishment of confidence and trust. Those principles must include observance of international undertakings when they have once been entered into, and the renunciation of force in the settlement of differences. It is because those principles, to which we attach such vital importance, seem to us to be in jeopardy that we have undertaken these tremendous and unprecedented responsibilities.

If, despite all our efforts to find the way of peace—and God knows I have tried my best—if in spite of all that, we find ourselves forced to embark upon a struggle which is bound to be fraught with suffering and misery for all mankind and the end of which no man can foresee, if that should happen, we shall not be fighting for the political future of a far away city in a foreign land; we shall be fighting for the preservation of those principles of which I have spoken, the destruction of which would involve the destruction of all possibility of peace and security for the peoples of the world. . . .

Hansard, 5th Series, Vol. CCCLI, pp. 9–10.

1 SEPTEMBER: It now only remains for us to set our teeth and to enter upon this struggle which we ourselves earnestly endeavoured to avoid, with determination to see it through to the end. We shall enter with a clear conscience, with the support of the Dominions and the British Empire and the moral approval

of the greater part of the world. We have no quarrel with the German people, except that they allow themselves to be governed by a Nazi Government. As long as that government exists and pursues the methods it has so persistently followed during the last two years, there will be no peace in Europe. We shall merely pass from one crisis to another, and see one country after another attacked by methods which have now become familiar to us in their sickening technique. We are resolved that these methods must come to an end. If out of the struggle we again re-establish in the world the rules of good faith and the renunciation of force, why then, even the sacrifices that will be entailed upon us will find their fullest justification.

Ibid., pp. 132–3.

3 SEPTEMBER. This is a sad day for all of us, and to none is it sadder than to me. Everything that I have worked for, everything that I have hoped for, everything that I have believed in during my public life, has crashed into ruins. There is only one thing left for me to do; that is to devote what strength and powers I have to forwarding the victory of the cause for which we have to sacrifice so much. I cannot tell what part I may be allowed to play myself; I trust I may live to see the day when Hitlerism has been destroyed and a liberated Europe has been re-established.

Ibid., p. 292.

PART X

EPILOGUE 1940

THE summer of 1940 saw England fighting alone after the French surrender on June 14th. Mr. Churchill had become Prime Minister on May 10th " at the outset of this mighty battle."

66: WINSTON CHURCHILL. Speech in House of Commons

4 June 1940

... The British Empire and the French Republic, linked together in their cause and in their need, will defend to the death their native soil, aiding each other to the utmost of their strength. Even though large tracts of Europe and many old and famous States have fallen or may fall into the grip of the Gestapo and all the odious apparatus of Nazi rule, we shall not flag or fail. We shall go on to the end. We shall fight in France, we shall fight on the seas and oceans, we shall fight on the beaches, we shall fight on the landing grounds, we shall fight in the fields and in the streets, we shall fight in the hills; we shall never surrender, and even if, which I do not for a moment believe, this island or a large part of it were subjugated and starving, then our Empire beyond the seas, armed and guarded by the British Fleet, would carry on the struggle, until, in God's good time, the new world, with all its power and might, steps forth to the rescue and liberation of the old.

Hansard, Fifth Series, Vol. CCCLXI, pp. 745–6.

67: WINSTON CHURCHILL. Speech in House of Commons

20 August 1940

. . . A good many people have written to me to ask me to make on this occasion a fuller statement of our war aims, and of the kind of peace we wish to make after the war, than is contained in the very considerable declaration which was made early in the Autumn. Since then we have made common cause with Norway, Holland and Belgium. We have recognized the Czech Government of Dr. Beneš, and we have told General de Gaulle that our success will carry with it the restoration of France. I do not think it would be wise at this moment while the battle rages and the war is still perhaps only in its earlier stage, to embark upon elaborate speculations about the future shape which should be given to Europe or the new securities which must be arranged to spare mankind the miseries of a third World War. The ground is not new, it has been frequently traversed and explored, and many ideas are held about it in common by all good men, and all free men. But before we can undertake the task of rebuilding we have not only to be convinced ourselves, but we have to convince all other countries that the Nazi tyranny is going to be finally broken. The right to guide the course of world history is the noblest prize of victory. We are still toiling up the hill; we have not yet reached the crest-line of it; we cannot survey the landscape or even imagine what its condition will be when that longed-for morning comes. The task which lies before us immediately is at once more practical, more simple and more stern. I hope—indeed I pray— that we shall not be found unworthy of our victory if after toil and tribulation it is granted to us. For the rest, we have to gain the victory. That is our task.

There is, however, one direction in which we can see a little more clearly ahead. We have to think not only for ourselves but for the lasting security of the cause and principles for which we are fighting and of the long future of the British Commonwealth of Nations. Some months ago we came to the conclusion that the interests of the United States and of the British Empire both required that the United States should have facilities for the naval and air defence of the Western hemisphere against the attack of a Nazi power which might have acquired temporary but lengthy control of a large part of Western Europe and its formidable resources. We had therefore decided spontaneously, and without being asked or offered any inducement, to inform the Government of the United States that we would be glad to place such defence facilities at their disposal by leasing suitable sites in our Transatlantic possessions for their greater security against the unmeasured dangers of the future. The principle of association of interest for common purposes between Great Britain and the United States had developed even before the war. Various agreements had been reached about certain small islands in the Pacific Ocean which had become important as air fuelling points. In all this line of thought we found ourselves in very close harmony with the Government of Canada.

Presently we learned that anxiety was also felt in the United States about the air and naval defence of their Atlantic seaboard, and President Roosevelt has recently made it clear that he would like to discuss with us, and with the Dominion of Canada and with Newfoundland, the development of American naval and air facilities in Newfoundland and in the West Indies. There is, of course, no question of any transference of sovereignty—that has never been suggested—or of any action being taken, without the consent or against the wishes of the various Colonies concerned, but for our part, His Majesty's Government are entirely willing to to accord defence facilities to the United States on a 99 years' leasehold basis, and we feel sure that our interests no less than theirs, and the interests of the Colonies themselves and of Canada and Newfoundland will be served thereby. These are important steps. Undoubtedly this process means that these two great organizations of the English-speaking democracies, the British Empire and the United States, will have to be somewhat mixed up together in some of their affairs for mutual and general advantage. For my own part, looking out upon the future, I do not view the process with any misgivings. I could not stop it if I wished; no one can stop it. Like the Missisippi, it just keeps rolling along. Let it roll. Let it roll on full flood, inexorable, irresistible, benignant, to broader lands and better days.

Hansard, Fifth Series, Vol. CCCLXIV, pp. 1169–71.

68: WINSTON CHURCHILL. Broadcast Address

11 September 1940

WHEN I said in the House of Commons the other day that I thought it improbable that the enemy's air attack in September could be more than three times as great as it was in August, I was not, of course, referring to barbarous attacks upon the civil population, but to the great air battle which is being fought out between our fighters and the German Air Force.

You will understand that whenever the weather is favourable, waves of German bombers, protected by fighters, often three or four hundred at a time, surge over this island, especially the promontory of Kent, in the hope of attacking military and other objectives by daylight. However, they are met by our fighter squadrons and nearly always broken up; and their losses average three to one in machines and six to one in pilots.

This effort of the Germans to secure daylight mastery of the air over England is, of course, the crux of the whole war. So far it has failed conspicuously. It has cost them very dear, and we have felt stronger, and actually are relatively a good deal stronger, than when the hard fighting began in July. There is no doubt that Herr Hitler is using up his fighter force at a very high rate, and that if he goes on for many more weeks he will wear down and ruin this vital part of his Air Force. That will give us a very great advantage.

On the other hand, for him to try to invade this country without having secured mastery in the air would be a very hazardous undertaking. Nevertheless, all his preparations for invasion on a great scale are steadily going forward. Several hundreds of self-propelled barges are moving down the coasts of Europe, from the German and Dutch harbours to the ports of Northern France; from Dunkirk to Brest; and beyond Brest to the French harbours in the Bay of Biscay.

Besides this, convoys of merchant ships in tens of dozens are being moved through the Straits of Dover into the Channel, dodging along from port to port under the protection of the new batteries which the Germans have built on the French shore. There are now considerable gatherings of shipping in the German, Dutch, Belgian and French harbours—all the way from Hamburg to Brest. Finally, there are some preparations made of ships to carry an invading force from the Norwegian harbours.

Behind these clusters of ships or barges, there stand very large numbers of German troops, awaiting the order to go on board and set out on their very dangerous and uncertain voyage across the seas. We cannot tell when they will try to come; we cannot be sure that in fact they will try at all; but no one should blind himself to the fact that a heavy, full-scale invasion of this island is being prepared with all the usual German thoroughness and method, and that it may be launched now—upon England, upon Scotland, or upon Ireland, or upon all three.

If this invasion is going to be tried at all, it does not

seem that it can be long delayed. The weather may break at any time. Besides this, it is difficult for the enemy to keep these gatherings of ships waiting about indefinitely, while they are bombed every night by our bombers, and very often shelled by our warships which are waiting for them outside.

Therefore, we must regard the next week or so as a very important period in our history. It ranks with the days when the Spanish Armada was approaching the Channel, and Drake was finishing his game of bowls; or when Nelson stood between us and Napoleon's Grand Army at Boulogne. We have read all about this in the history books; but what is happening now is on a far greater scale and of far more consequence to the life and future of the world and its civilization than these brave old days of the past.

Every man and woman will therefore prepare himself to do his duty, whatever it may be, with special pride and care. Our fleets and flotillas are very powerful and numerous; our Air Force is at the highest strength it has ever reached, and it is conscious of its proved superiority, not indeed in numbers, but in men and machines. Our shores are well fortified and strongly manned, and behind them, ready to attack the invaders, we have a far larger and better equipped mobile Army than we have ever had before.

Besides this, we have more than a million and a half men of the Home Guard, who are just as much soldiers of the Regular Army as the Grenadier Guards, and who are determined to fight for every inch of the ground in every village and in every street.

It is with devout but sure confidence that I say: Let God defend the Right.

These cruel, wanton, indiscriminate bombings of

London are, of course, a part of Hitler's invasion plans. He hopes, by killing large numbers of civilians, and women and children, that he will terrorize and cow the people of this mighty imperial city, and make them a burden and an anxiety to the Government and thus distract our attention unduly from the ferocious onslaught he is preparing. Little does he know the spirit of the British nation, or the tough fibre of the Londoners, whose forebears played a leading part in the establishment of Parliamentary institutions and who have been bred to value freedom far above their lives. This wicked man, the repository and embodiment of many forms of soul-destroying hatred, this monstrous product of former wrongs and shame, has now resolved to try to break our famous island race by a process of indiscriminate slaughter and destruction. What he has done is to kindle a fire in British hearts, here and all over the world, which will glow long after all traces of the conflagration he has caused in London have been removed. He has lighted a fire which will burn with a steady and consuming flame until the last vestiges of Nazi tyranny have been burnt out of Europe, and until the Old World—and the New—can join hands to rebuild the temples of man's freedom and man's honour, upon foundations which will not soon or easily be overthrown.

Printed in Randolph Churchill, *Into Battle—Speeches by the Right Hon. Winston S. Churchill*, *P.C.*, *M.P.* (London 1941), pp. 272–4.

INDEX OF NAMES

[Extracts are given in italic type, other references in roman type. Mere incidental references are not indexed.]

379

INDEX OF NAMES